D1546335

essentials

Securities
Regulation

ASPEN PUBLISHERS

essentials

Securities Regulation

Stephen J. Choi
Murray and Kathleen Bring Professor of Law
New York University School of Law

A.C. Pritchard
Professor of Law
University of Michigan Law School

Wolters Kluwer
Law & Business

AUSTIN   BOSTON   CHICAGO   NEW YORK   THE NETHERLANDS

To contact Customer Care, e-mail customer.care@aspenpublishers.com, call 1-800-234-1660, fax 1-800-901-9075, or mail correspondence to:

Aspen Publishers
Attn: Order Department
PO Box 990
Frederick, MD 21705

Printed in the United States of America.

1 2 3 4 5 6 7 8 9 0

ISBN 978-0-7355-6551-7

Library of Congress Cataloging-in-Publication Data

Choi, Stephen Jung, 1996-
    Securities regulation: the essentials / Stephen J. Choi, A.C. Pritchard.
        p. cm
    Includes index.
    ISBN 978-0-7355-6551-7
    1. Securities — United States. I. Pritchard, Adam C. II. Title.

    KF1439 .C53
    346.73'0922 — dc22   2008001422

About Wolters Kluwer Law & Business

Wolters Kluwer Law & Business is a leading provider of research information and workflow solutions in key specialty areas. The strengths of the individual brands of Aspen Publishers, CCH, Kluwer Law International and Loislaw are aligned within Wolters Kluwer Law & Business to provide comprehensive, in-depth solutions and expert-authored content for the legal, professional and education markets.

CCH was founded in 1913 and has served more than four generations of business professionals and their clients. The CCH products in the Wolters Kluwer Law & Business group are highly regarded electronic and print resources for legal, securities, antitrust and trade regulation, government contracting, banking, pension, payroll, employment and labor, and healthcare reimbursement and compliance professionals.

Aspen Publishers is a leading information provider for attorneys, business professionals and law students. Written by preeminent authorities, Aspen products offer analytical and practical information in a range of specialty practice areas from securities law and intellectual property to mergers and acquisitions and pension/benefits. Aspen's trusted legal education resources provide professors and students with high-quality, up-to-date and effective resources for successful instruction and study in all areas of the law.

Kluwer Law International supplies the global business community with comprehensive English-language international legal information. Legal practitioners, corporate counsel and business executives around the world rely on the Kluwer Law International journals, loose-leafs, books and electronic products for authoritative information in many areas of international legal practice.

Loislaw is a premier provider of digitized legal content to small law firm practitioners of various specializations. Loislaw provides attorneys with the ability to quickly and efficiently find the necessary legal information they need, when and where they need it, by facilitating access to primary law as well as state-specific law, records, forms and treatises.

Wolters Kluwer Law & Business, a unit of Wolters Kluwer, is headquartered in New York and Riverwoods, Illinois. Wolters Kluwer is a leading multinational publisher and information services company.

For my wife Un Kyung, who always supports me.

Steve

For my parents, who only expected my best.

Adam

Summary of Contents

Table of Contents

CHAPTER 6

Insider Trading   149

CHAPTER 7

Public Offerings   183

CHAPTER 8

Civil Liability Under the Securities Act

CHAPTER 9

Exempt Offerings   297

CHAPTER 10

Resale Transactions   337

Preface

S ecurities regulation is hard. Studying the subject enmeshes the student in a spider's web of statutes, regulations, cases, interpretations, and conventional wisdom that interrelate in unexpected and non-intuitive ways. We can still remember (vaguely) the bewildered feeling that we experienced when we tackled the subject as law students. We also remember (distinctly) the overwhelmed feeling that we experienced when we taught the subject for the first time as law professors. The goal of this book is to share some of what we have learned about securities regulation over the years.

We try to present the big picture of securities regulation in an accessible fashion. When studying securities regulation, it is all too easy to get bogged down in the endless succession of rules. We try to teach securities law in an understandable way in our classes, and this book is our effort to convey those lessons as clearly and concisely as possible. We do this by setting forth the underlying business problem and discussing the relevant regulations as a solution to this problem. At certain points, we also provide questions and answers to the more technical rules covered in a typical securities regulation class.

It helps in understanding the securities laws to understand the securities markets and the policy options that regulators have for controlling abuses in those markets. A company issues securities to raise capital. Additional capital allows the issuer to invest in new business projects. Investors hope to share in the rewards of those projects. What can go wrong in this business relationship? Investors value their rights to cash flows in the issuer, but because securities are intangible, investors need information to value securities. You can't kick the tires of a stock or bond. An issuer can tell the investor that the issuer's common stock is worth $100 per share, but optimism and greed may taint that representation. Some investors facing an information deficit may invest anyhow, optimistically hoping for the best. These investors may do poorly in the securities markets. Other investors will respond more rationally to this information disadvantage by demanding a large discount of all issuers. The byproduct of this discounting, however, is an increased cost of capital for even honest issuers. If securities regulation can ameliorate this information problem, it can benefit issuers, investors, and ultimately the economy in general.

The lifeblood of the securities markets, and the primary tool of regulators, is information. For us, the unifying theme of securities regulation is information and its use. Accordingly, the principal focus of this book is the role that information plays in the operation of the securities markets and the disclosure requirements that the law imposes in an effort to get information into the hands of investors.

This focus on the role of information gives us a framework for evaluating the solution the law currently provides as well as assessing possible alternatives. Our aim with this book is to: (1) give students a better understanding for why we have securities regulation, and (2) enable students to start thinking critically about the regime. Along the way, we draw out certain common themes in securities regulation, including: (1) what assumption is made about the rationality of investors; (2) what role should third party intermediaries (underwriters, attorneys, auditors) play in protecting investors; (3) should the securities regulation regime be mandatory?

We hope that you find the book useful, and perhaps even enjoyable. Please let us know if there are things we can do better.

Stephen J. Choi
A.C. Pritchard
January 2008

essentials

Securities Regulation

⤝ 1 ⤞

Investors and Information

In a market economy, people face many choices about how best to use their money. Some use their hard-earned cash to purchase the coffee flavor of the day. Others prefer to put their consumption off to a later date, investing their earnings instead in the hope of seeing the money grow with the passage of time. Generally, in a market economy, people are left to their own devices when deciding how to allocate their funds. If you want to use your money to buy a vacation or a fancy new car, the legal system will not stand in your way. You will enjoy certain legal protections, such as common-law fraud and consumer-protection laws, but no dedicated federal agency enforces a regulatory regime to protect you in your consumption decisions. For securities, however, a dedicated federal regulatory agency, the Securities and Exchange Commission or SEC, enforces a broad array of federal statutes and regulations. Do the differences between fancy cars and securities justify the expansive regulatory regime for the latter in the United States? That is one of the questions this book will help you to think through.

When you purchase a car, you may literally kick the tires; you will certainly take the car out for a test drive. If the car is used, you would be prudent to have a mechanic check it out as well. The car represents a tangible asset. Imagine, however, that instead of a car, you are contemplating the purchase of common stock from Microsoft, a publicly traded company listed on the Nasdaq. How can you kick Microsoft's tires? Even if you use Microsoft's products, knowledge of its computer operating system and software will be of limited help in predicting the future returns for the company's common stock. A company's securities provide value to stockholders by conferring intangible rights to company cash flows. In the case of common stock, these cash flows can take the form of dividends over time or of assets, if the corporation is eventually liquidated. You cannot kick the tires of an intangible right, and this puts you at an informational disadvantage when determining how much to pay for a security investment.

Securities purchases differ in another significant way. Purchasers' preferences regarding securities are generally more similar than those for goods or services. Many consumers want to purchase cars, vacations, or ice cream cones. But as individuals, they vary considerably in what they desire from each product. Some may want a car of a particular style; others seek good gas mileage; still others look for the ability to accelerate from 0 to 60 in under 5 seconds. In contrast, investors valuing securities generally share a common goal: returns. Few investors purchase Disney shares because they feel an affinity for Mickey Mouse; rather, they expect to receive more money later from that investment. Although investors may differ in how much risk they are willing to bear, their main focus is return. This means that all investors want relatively homogeneous information: What return, and at what level of risk, can they expect from a given security?

Even though investors need and want essentially the same information, as a practical matter, they may find it very difficult to get. Assume that a thousand investors own the stock of a publicly traded company, say Disney, and that they all want the same information about the company's past financial results and current business plans. *All* Disney investors would benefit from having the information, but no single investor, owning only a fraction of Disney's shares, would receive the full benefit of that information. In addition, no single investor would perform the level of research and diligence in obtaining information that the group of investors might achieve by coordinating their efforts. Such collaboration would, of course, be difficult, if not impossible, to achieve. The necessary collective action can only be achieved if companies are induced to provide investors with the information they need. Mandating disclosure by public companies, as we will see, forms one of the chief foundations of the U.S. securities regulation regime.

These regulations may serve another purpose as well. Just as consumers may sometimes purchase vacations and cars on impulse, investors in the capital markets may also act irrationally at times. The consequences of irrational investment decisions, however, are often more severe than the consequences of impulse purchases of consumer goods. Few would expend their life savings on a car or a vacation, but stories of investors losing their life savings on bad securities investments are all too familiar. Securities have great potential for leading consumers astray. Investors who go into frenzies over the latest fad (think Internet stocks in the late 1990s) may be protected from themselves by a specialized regulatory regime.

Lastly, some markets are more central to the economy than others. Although vacations, cars, and candy bars are certainly substantial sectors of the economy, the capital market arguably stands in a central position. One function of the capital market is to direct money to its highest-value use. Consider two entrepreneurs competing for capital to launch their businesses, both of which will market products to sunbathers in Malibu. One proposes to sell winter parkas, while the other proposes to sell lemonade. The winter parka entrepreneur, perhaps optimistically, expects a profit of $1 on a capital investment of $100,000 each year; the lemonade entrepreneur expects a profit of $20,000 on an investment of $100,000 each year. Thus, the lemonade entrepreneur can offer a much more generous return to investors. A smoothly functioning capital market will direct investor funds to the lemonade entrepreneur and leave the winter parka entrepreneur searching for another business idea. If money flows to the highest-valued uses, goods and services will get to the people who want them. Efficient capital allocation also fuels economic growth.

In sum, securities purchases differ from other uses for money in that they (a) pose large informational problems; (b) create collective-action problems in information gathering; (c) lead potential purchasers to act at times irrationally; and (d) affect the capital markets at the center of the economy. The remainder of this chapter explores the basics of investment decisions and the federal securities regime.

1 INVESTMENT DECISIONS

What information do investors want? To think about this question, consider why individuals might invest their money. Why put off buying that new plasma TV until next year when you can purchase it today? The reward for waiting is that an investment may yield a larger amount in the future, allowing for more consumption. If I don't get a new Toyota today, but rather wait patiently and let my investments grow, I may be able to get a Lexus in the future.

How much future money does it take to persuade an investor to forgo consumption today? If we offered to pay you $100 in ten years for an investment of $100 today, you would likely pass on the offer (representing a not very impressive zero percent return). But suppose instead that in return for an investment of $1 today, we offer to pay you $100 in ten years (with appropriate security to back our promise). Most investors would gladly take us up on this offer; indeed, most would be willing to spend a good deal more than $1 for such an investment.

Timing is critical in valuing an investment. Two time periods must be considered: first, the period when the investor must pay out money for the initial investment; second, the period when the investor receives the return. In the case of the $100 investment offer above, the initial investment occurs today, and the return occurs ten years from now. More complex return arrangements are also possible. In the case of a bond, for example, an investor making an initial investment today might receive an annual flow of payments (that is, interest) over several years before receiving a lump sum at the bond's maturity date.

In evaluating an investment and comparing it with other possible investments, an investor needs some way of translating future investment returns into today's dollars. How does $1 today compare with $1 in the future? Many investors use *present discount valuation* to convert future dollars into current dollars. This formula, in which r represents the discount rate and x the number of periods (years in the case of an annual discount rate), calculates present discount valuation:

$$\text{Today's Value} = \frac{\text{Future Value}}{(1+r)^x}$$

This example, assuming a discount rate of 10 percent annually, shows the value of $100 provided two years from now:

$$\$82.65 = \frac{\$100}{(1+0.1)^2}$$

Why do we discount the future returns? What is the appropriate discount rate? A dollar today is worth more than a dollar in the future for several reasons. First, people are impatient.

How much would you pay for the right to receive $100 in ten years? How about in one hundred years? One factor explaining this impatience is the simple truth that "you can't take it with you." Many investors care about their descendants, but most people's descendants are likely to be wealthier than they are, so why exacerbate the intergenerational wealth gap? Generalized across the entire economy, this impatience means that money today is more highly valued than the same amount in the future. Second, most currencies suffer from inflation. Today's $100 will buy more real goods and services than will the same amount in the future. Investors discount future money because inflation will erode its real purchasing power. Third, not all promises are kept. Contrast a promise made by the federal government to pay $100 in ten years with a similar promise made by an Internet start-up company. Equity investments in Internet start-ups may average a $100 return in ten years, but return from any particular start-up may vary considerably from the average. Depending on how the company fares, the return could be $1, $10, $100, or even $1,000. Most people are risk averse, meaning, in practical terms, they will value a certain payment of $100 more than a return averaging $100 but with considerable variation around the average.

Not all risks are the same. Some risks may offset other risks. Consider two companies: an airline requiring a lot of jet fuel and an oil company. When oil prices are high, the airline suffers due to its high fuel costs, but the oil company benefits. The converse, of course, is also true when oil prices head lower. Thus, an investor can reduce exposure to the variability of oil prices by investing in both companies: The collective return will depend much less on the price of oil. Finding such smooth-fitting hedges for an entire portfolio of investments is difficult, but the task can be made easier by adding more and more companies. In discounting securities for risks, therefore, investors take into account only systematic risks not diversifiable through a well-constructed portfolio.

So investors considering whether to part with their hard-earned money care about (a) the expected return from the investment; and (b) the discount applicable to this return, given normal investor impatience, potential inflation, and any non-diversifiable risks specific to the investment. What information is needed to assess these factors?

Obviously, predicting the future is always difficult, and the more information that can be applied to the process the better. Most investors would want to know at least something about the following aspects of any corporation in which they were considering investing:

- properties and lines of business
- expected growth rate in its businesses
- management plans for capital expenditures and other expenses
- past financial performance
- existing capital stock and investor base
- regulatory environment
- competitors and competitive environment
- management and directors
- executive compensation

Even with such information, investment valuation may be more of an art than a science. How can these pieces of information be used to model a corporation's expected future returns and the appropriate discount rate for those returns? For example, if executives receive stock options as compensation, does this mean they will work harder for the corporation or that they will take unjustified risks? How do the consequences of this type of compensation translate into projections of future growth in revenues? If revenues increase, will future dividends increase for shareholders, or will these returns be reinvested in the business? How does knowledge about the type of business factor into the risk discount applicable to expected returns? Business school lessons can help in answering this question, as can years of experience on Wall Street. To understand securities regulation, however, it is sufficient to appreciate the decisions that investors must make and the types of information they need to make those decisions.

2 TYPES OF SECURITIES

2.1 Common Stock

Even casual followers of the stock markets are familiar with the concept of common stock. Open the pages of the *Wall Street Journal* or look at a finance-related Web site, and you will find a wealth of information on the common stock of publicly traded companies such as Apple Computer. How does ownership of a share of Apple common stock provide a return? A corporation's board of directors may, in its discretion, declare a dividend to be distributed pro rata to shareholders based on their share ownership. Not all corporations pay dividends. Typically, dividends are paid by more mature companies with a stable profit. If a corporation's board of directors chooses not to make a dividend, how else may a shareholder earn a return? Shareholders may sell their shares. If the shares are sold at a price higher than the original purchase price, the shareholder earns capital appreciation when selling the shares. Sometimes the corporation itself will purchase a portion of its shares in a stock buyback. A corporation may also choose to merge with another corporation, requiring shareholders to exchange their shares in return for some consideration as part of the merger. (Typical consideration includes cash or notes or stock issued by the surviving corporation.) When the merger consideration is greater than investors' original purchase price, they again will have earned a capital return on their investment.

Why would anyone be willing to pay more for the shares than the investor originally paid? If you bought Apple shares at

$100, why would another investor later be willing to pay $120 for the same shares? One reason might be that the shares have become more valuable because Apple is earning higher corporate profits, and increased profits will allow Apple to declare a large dividend or stock buyback in the future. Ultimately, all the different ways of receiving a return from share ownership depend on the corporation continuing to earn profits. Importantly, the corporation earns profits only after it pays all other claimants, such as employees, suppliers, and banks. This is known as the *absolute priority* rule; the application of the rule means that common shareholders are often referred to as holding a claim to the corporation's *residual* cash flows.

Holders of common shares may also receive a return when a corporation liquidates. Under state corporate law, corporations typically have perpetual existence. Nonetheless, a corporation's board of directors, with the consent of a majority of its shareholders, may elect to terminate the corporation's existence and distribute its assets to various claimants. Once again, the absolute priority rule applies; liquidating follows a strict hierarchy of who gets paid first out of the liquidated assets: Holders of common shares come last. Although this strict priority is sometimes altered in bankruptcy, for our purposes we will refer to common shares as the residual claimant in liquidation.

Can a residual claim be substantial? Consider those who bought Microsoft shares in its initial public offering in the 1980s. The residual claim of those Microsoft shareholders is now worth hundreds of billions of dollars, many times what they initially invested. Most shareholders do not enjoy such financial success. Indeed, because the board of directors, not the shareholders, controls the corporation, shareholders must bear the risk that the directors and management may fail to maximize the value of the shareholders' residual claim. Although improving shareholder value can enhance a manager's own earnings prospects, management may choose instead to reward themselves more directly with higher salaries, use of a company jet, and other perks, all at shareholders' expense. To protect against such wayward activities (*agency costs*), state corporate law typically provides shareholders with the right to elect the board of directors as well as the authority to approve certain major corporate transactions (including mergers and sales of substantially all the assets of a corporation).

The purchase of a share of common stock therefore gives the investor a number of intangible rights, including the right to receive a corporation's residual cash flows as dividends (subject to the discretion of the board of directors), rights to the residual assets in liquidation after all other claimants are paid, and voting rights to elect directors and to approve certain major corporate events. Using these three categories, we can now explore other types of securities and their attraction for investors.

2.2 Bonds

Bonds are another security commonly issued by corporations raising capital. Why do investors pay money for bonds? Bonds provide their owners with a fixed and certain return in the form of periodic interest payments as well as a final principal payment when the bond matures. In the case of liquidation, bondholders typically receive the return of their principal (and any interest due) before other claimants of the corporation (including holders of common stock).

Because of the protection afforded by the absolute priority rule, bondholders have less to fear from managerial avarice or incompetence. Before bondholders suffer any loss, the value of common stockholders must be wiped out (at least in theory). As a consequence, bondholders typically do not enjoy the right to elect directors or to ratify extraordinary corporate transactions. Instead, bondholders are protected by contractual rights.

For example, one typical contractual protection requires the issuer to maintain specified equity-to-debt ratio, thus providing bondholders with a minimum equity cushion and reducing the risk of default on the bonds. Holders of public bonds are also protected by the provisions of the Trust Indenture Act of 1939, which establishes a regime for the enforcement of those contractual rights.

Compared with common stock, bonds have stronger claims, in the form of interest payments, to the corporation's cash flows and stronger rights to assets in liquidation, but no voting rights. Why do people purchase bonds rather than common stock? Different investors have varying preferences. Retirees seeking a consistent flow of money with minimal risk may prefer bonds, while a twenty-something right out of law school may prefer the typically greater upside earned on common stock.

2.3 Preferred Stock

No law limits a corporation to selling securities that precisely follow the rights of a typical share of common stock or a typical bond, as described above. Rather, the market determines what types of instruments corporations will issue as the corporations cater to investor preferences for different combinations of risk and return. One such combination, falling between common stock and bonds, is preferred stock. Preferred stock provides an intermediate right to the cash flows of a corporation. A share of preferred stock often accords the holder a right to a "fixed" dividend each quarter. The dividend, however, unlike the payment of interest on a bond, is not guaranteed. If the board decides not to declare the preferred dividend, the dividend typically will cumulate. When dividends cumulate, the holder of the preferred share typically has the right to obtain the full unpaid dividends from prior quarters before the board may declare a dividend to common stockholders. For example, a preferred stock may provide a dividend of $1.25 per quarter.

If the dividend is not paid for four quarters, the preferred stockholder will have a cumulated dividend amount of $5.00. The corporation must pay the $5.00 to the preferred shareholder before paying a dividend to common stockholders.

Preferred stock also provides an intermediate level of rights to assets in the event of liquidation. After debt is paid off, preferred stockholders typically receive their cumulated dividends and a predetermined liquidation value for their shares before common shareholders are paid. Finally, preferred stockholders also receive an intermediate level of voting rights. In general, preferred shareholders do not enjoy the right to vote. If the corporation has skipped a specified number of dividend payments, however, the preferred stock contract may provide the preferred shareholder with the right to vote for directors. Preferred shareholders will also typically have the right to vote if the terms of their preferred stock contract are to be changed.

2.4 Options

Options come in two principal varieties: *call options* and *put options*. Call options represent a contractual right to buy a security, typically common stock, at a certain price (the *exercise price*) for a specified period of time. A put option conveys the corresponding right to sell a security; they are sometime used by people holding the underlying security to hedge against the risk of a price decline. Suppose an investor has a call option for Disney common stock, with an exercise price of $50 per share. If Disney's common-stock price is equal to $60 per share, the investor may exercise the option and purchase the Disney shares for the exercise price of $50, giving the investor who sells the shares for the $60 market price a profit of $10 per share.

Options provide a relatively inexpensive way of speculating on the future direction of a security's price, as options prices closely track the value of the underlying security. If the market price for the underlying security exceeds the exercise price of the call option, the holder can exercise the option and then sell the security, pocketing the difference between the exercise price and the market price. (Some options are designated *cash settled*. They do not require the physical delivery of the stock, simply payment of the difference between the exercise price of the option and the market price of the underlying security.) In this situation, the options are said to be "in the money." If the exercise price is higher than the market price, investors will have no incentive to exercise the option. In this scenario, the option is said to be "out of the money"; the value of an out-of-the-money option lies in the hope that the stock will eventually rise above the exercise price. If the option continues to remain "out of the money" until its expiration date, it will terminate without having been exercised.

2.5 Securities Market Transactions

Although the title of this book begins with the phrase *securities regulation*, the law really focuses on securities *transactions*. Securities market transactions can be divided into two broad categories: primary and secondary. Primary market transactions are sales by a corporate issuer to investors (sometimes called an *offering*). Secondary market transactions involve sales by one investor to another. We explain these two categories below.

Primary Markets   In terms of dollar volume, primary market transactions are dwarfed by the total amount of secondary market transactions. Despite the relatively small size of the primary market, it is through primary market transactions that corporations raise capital to fund their operations and expansion, a matter of vital importance to the economy. Encouraging investors to purchase securities in primary offerings is one of the central goals of securities regulation.

Companies raising capital for the first time are said to be making an *initial public offering,* or IPO. An IPO is a coming-out party of sorts for a corporation. As we discuss later, for most companies, selling securities in an IPO marks the first time the company will be required to disclose details about its operations and performance to the public. That disclosure requirement is ongoing; after the IPO, companies face periodic disclosure requirements, including annual Form 10-K and quarterly Form 10-Q filings.

Primary transactions also pose the greatest amount of uncertainty and risk for investors. The more issuers can convince investors to pay for offered securities, the greater the proceeds to the issuers. Particularly when attracted to IPOs, the issues of which are typically companies unknown to the market, investors may fall prey to efforts to inflate the value of the securities.

Secondary Markets   Imagine that you own and want to sell 100 shares of Microsoft. You could stand on a street corner and offer them to whoever happens to come along. Attempting to sell shares in this haphazard manner, however, is unlikely to work well. If you need to sell your shares immediately, you will face the problem that most people walking along the street may not be considering a purchase of Microsoft shares as they take their stroll. To sell to someone not looking to buy shares of Microsoft at that time, you may have to offer quite a hefty discount. At the right price, however, most people would agree to buy your shares.

If, by chance, you do find someone willing to purchase your shares, you then face a second problem: How do you — or your prospective purchaser — know you are getting a good transaction price? You, as the seller, run the risk that other buyers for Microsoft shares may be willing to pay more than the price you can get for your shares on your particular street corner. Without access to those other buyers, you as the seller would simply be in the dark as to what they might pay. So, too, will your prospective purchaser be in the dark about the price other sellers are asking: Their shares may be going for much less.

An organized marketplace allows buyers and sellers to come together. By bringing large numbers of buyers and sellers together in one space (which may be physical or, as is more often the case these days, virtual), an organized securities market helps ensure that any particular buyer or seller can quickly locate a counterparty willing to exchange. This feature of securities markets is often referred to as *liquidity*. In addition to providing liquidity, securities markets also provide buyers and sellers with information on previous transaction prices and outstanding offers to buy and sell at particular prices. This feature, known as *price transparency,* assures buyers and sellers that they will transact their exchange at the best possible price.

Reducing the costs of buying or selling shares makes share ownership more attractive. Investors value the presence of a liquid market when they initially purchase their shares, and they are consequently willing to pay more for those shares. Consider two possible investments: shares of Glue, Inc., a company with no liquid secondary market, and shares of Microsoft, widely traded on the Nasdaq. Putting to one side the possibility of resale, you value the expected cash flows from each company at $100 per share. Once the eventual need to resell the shares is taken into account, however, you, like most investors, would require a discount of 10 to 15 percent to purchase the shares of Glue, Inc., relative to the Microsoft shares. For Glue, Inc., a 15 percent illiquidity discount would mean that any offering of its securities to the public would result in a price of only $85. Thus, corporations offering securities in the primary market also want to provide a liquid secondary market. Corporations making an initial public offering will frequently seek a listing on an organized securities market.

What are the organized securities markets in the United States? Most securities transactions take place on the national securities exchanges. The securities exchanges include the New York Stock Exchange (NYSE), the American Stock

Exchange (AMEX), and, as of early 2006, the Nasdaq. The NYSE is the largest market in the United States, with an average daily trading volume of 1.8 billion shares, representing $68.2 billion in 2006. To qualify for a NYSE listing, a company must meet certain minimum requirements concerning issues such as market capitalization, number of shareholders, and corporate governance structure. In 2006, the market capitalization of NYSE-listed companies totaled $22.5 trillion. Those interested in learning more about the NYSE will find current information at *www.nyse.com*.

The Nasdaq marketplace is the second largest market in the United States. In the first several months of 2007, Nasdaq handled an average daily trading volume of 2.1 billion shares, representing $52.7 billion. More information on Nasdaq market data is available at *www.nasdaqtrader.com*. Like the NYSE, the Nasdaq has certain minimum listing requirements. These requirements vary, however, according to the market tier for which a listing is sought. Nasdaq has three tiers, with increasingly stringent requirements: the Capital Market, the Global Market, and the Global Select Market.

Several smaller securities exchanges also qualify as national securities exchanges, among them the Pacific Stock Exchange, the Philadelphia Stock Exchange, and the Boston Stock Exchange. These markets tend to specialize in trading options and other derivatives.

The national securities exchanges, other than Nasdaq, follow a similar pattern for trades. On the New York Stock Exchange, for example, only brokers with a seat on the NYSE may conduct transactions there. Through these brokers, investors are able to post their orders for shares. A *bid* is an offer by an investor to buy a security at a specified bid price. An *ask* is an offer by an investor to sell a security at a specified ask price. There are two basic types of orders. A *market order* allows an investor to specify the number of securities the investor is willing to buy or sell. The price for the order is simply the best price prevailing in the market. A *limit order* allows an investor to specify both the number of securities the investor will buy or sell and the price at which the investor will do so. If no one is willing to trade at that price, the order expires unfilled.

On the NYSE, a specialist broker is assigned to each listed security. Other brokers interested in transacting in a particular security will often congregate around that specialist's post. The specialist sets the opening price for a stock when the market opens in the morning. The specialist then collects all bid and ask offers for a security and posts them to the marketplace. If bid and ask offers become imbalanced, the specialist also has a duty to purchase (or sell) shares from its own account to help maintain liquidity.

Nasdaq operates differently from the NYSE. Unlike the NYSE, Nasdaq does not have a physical trading floor where brokers may interact. Instead, Nasdaq consists of a network of interlinked computers connecting a multitude of securities dealers to one another. Securities dealers that hold themselves ready to both buy and sell securities of a particular company are known as market makers for those securities. How can a market maker make a profit by simultaneously buying and selling securities of the same company? The market maker will issue both a bid price at which it is willing to buy securities (say $100 per share for 100 shares) and an ask price at which it is willing to sell securities (say $100.25 per share for 100 shares). The difference between the bid and ask prices, known as the bid-ask spread, enables the market maker to make a profit even as it both buys and sells the same securities. The bid-ask spread also insulates the market maker, albeit imperfectly, from the chance that an investor (such as a company insider) may know more about the value of a security than the market maker does. This disparity of knowledge is known as *information asymmetry,* an important theme of this book. The wider the bid-ask spread, the more profit, as well as greater protection from information asymmetry, the market maker enjoys. For actively traded securities, the bid-ask spread is unlikely to be more than pennies per share. Unlike the NYSE specialists, each of which has sole responsibility for a given security, multiple Nasdaq market makers can quote a particular company's securities. Competition among market makers helps constrain the size of the bid-ask spread.

Since the 1990s, investors have shifted a growing volume of securities transactions away from the traditional stock exchanges and Nasdaq to so-called electronic communication networks (ECNs). Early ECNs included Instinet and Island. ECNs are alternative trading systems that allow investors to directly post buy or sell orders and to find a match, typically through a computer-executed protocol, to investors willing to trade. ECNs allow investors (predominantly institutions) to avoid paying commissions to a broker.

The success of ECNs has led the major securities exchanges to acquire many of them. The NYSE, for example, purchased Archipelago Exchange, one of the more prominent ECNs, in 2005. Renamed NYSE Arca, in 2006, NYSE Arca reported that it handled trading volume of over a billion shares in a single day, representing a dollar value of almost $40 billion.

3 THE REGULATORY APPARATUS

The federal securities regime consists of a number of statutes, most of which were initially enacted during the Great Depression of the 1930s. The impetus for these statutes came from the pervasive sense that the relatively unregulated markets of the 1920s had led to the stock market collapse of 1929 and the resulting tremendous loss of wealth. The impulse behind regulation may also have contained an element of retribution against Wall Street for having "caused" the Great Depression, a belief fueled by a congressional investigation, led by Ferdinand

Pecora, that highlighted a number of abuses in the securities industry and corporate America.

The Securities Act of 1933 and the Securities Exchange Act of 1934 are the two most important securities statutes. The Securities Act of 1933 (or simply the Securities Act or 33 Act) principally regulates primary market transactions. As we will see later in the book, the Securities Act imposes mandatory disclosure requirements, in the form of registration statements and statutory prospectuses, as well as heightened antifraud liability for issuers selling securities in public offerings. The Securities Act also imposes a rigid process (termed the "gun-jumping" rules) for issuers making public offerings of securities. As part of the gun-jumping process, prior to an offering, issuers go through a quiet period during which communications that might arouse the interest of investors are limited. The Securities Act also provides for a number of exemptions from the public offering requirements. Under the Securities Act, an issuer may sell securities through a private placement to sophisticated investors or through offshore transactions to investors outside the United States. The key questions we will face when discussing the Securities Act are these: (1) who is protected by the public offering requirements; and (2) why should certain transactions be exempted from these requirements?

The Securities Exchange Act of 1934 (the Exchange Act or 34 Act) is much broader in its scope. In general terms, the Exchange Act deals with the secondary market. The Exchange Act provides for the registration of certain companies that achieve public company status. Registration requires ongoing periodic disclosures in the form of an annual Form 10-K filing, quarterly Form 10-Q filings, and episodic Form 8-K filings. The Exchange Act also provides for the registration and regulation of a number of secondary market participants, including broker-dealers, market makers, and national securities exchanges. In addition, the Exchange Act prohibits certain types of market manipulation. As we will see later in the book,

Rule 10b-5 of the Exchange Act is a broad, catch-all securities antifraud provision prohibiting insider trading.

A number of other statutes round out the federal securities regime. The Investment Company Act of 1940 deals with the regulation of mutual companies and other investment vehicles. The Investment Advisors Act of 1940 regulates the activities of those in the business of giving investment advice. The Trust Indenture Act of 1939 regulates the relationship of public bondholders and bond issuers, providing an indenture agreement with certain mandatory provisions. These additional statutes, however, go beyond what can be covered in the typical basic securities regulation course and therefore are not covered in this book.

Securities laws are enforced by the Securities and Exchange Commission (the SEC), established by the Exchange Act. In addition to enforcement, the SEC fleshes out the contours of the securities laws through rulemaking. The SEC is headed by a five-member commission. Each commissioner is appointed by the President for a five-year (staggered) term. The President may appoint no more than three commissioners from one political party. The President designates one commissioner to serve as chair, a position that carries considerable power in setting the SEC's regulatory agenda.

The five commissioners are served by an extensive staff organized into four main divisions: Corporation Finance, Trading and Markets, Investment Management, and Enforcement. The Corporation Finance division is charged with overseeing securities offerings as well as the periodic disclosure filings made by public companies; Trading and Markets focuses on the regulation of securities market professionals and entities operating in the secondary market; Investment Management regulates investment companies and investment advisors; and Enforcement deals with civil enforcement, both in federal court and through its own administrative proceedings. (Criminal enforcement matters are referred to the Justice Department for prosecution.) In addition to these divisions, the SEC has a number of offices devoted to specific functions, including the Office of Economic Analysis and the Office of the Chief Accountant; the latter plays an important role in setting accounting standards for public companies.

In 2002, Congress created a new regulatory body, the Public Company Accounting Oversight Board (PCAOB) to oversee the accounting industry responsible for auditing the financial statements of public companies. The PCAOB was created by the Sarbanes-Oxley Act (SOX), the statutory response to the then recent Enron and WorldCom scandals. SOX also shifted the focus of securities regulation away from its traditional province of disclosure and toward corporate governance. The Act imposed requirements on boards of directors, including establishment of mandatory independent audit committees. SOX also touched on executive compensation, corporate codes of ethics, and attorneys' duties to report fraud within a corporate organization. Finally, the Act requires corporate managements to certify their companies' financial results and systems of internal controls.

Although this book focuses on the SEC and the federal securities laws, readers should keep in mind that other laws affect the capital markets. State corporate law, of which Delaware law is the most prominent, provides for the substantive allocation of power between management and shareholders within the corporate structure. Despite the recent intrusions of the Sarbanes-Oxley Act, intended to regulate firms' internal corporate governance, the primary source of rules relating to corporate governance remains state corporate law. Federal tax law has important consequences for different types of transactions in securities as well. For example, a merger in which shareholders receive stock in exchange for shares potentially has different tax consequences than would a merger for cash consideration.

The remainder of this book explores the securities regulatory regime from a critical perspective. Securities may differ in some respects from other types of goods and services, but that does not necessarily justify regulation. Regulators and Congress make mistakes, and the market may in fact offer better solutions to the problems facing investors and the capital markets. As you go through this book, keep in mind the justifications for a specialized regulatory regime covering the securities markets. Consider the degree to which Congress or the SEC rely on these justifications in promulgating the various aspects of the securities regime, and consider too how well that regime protects the integrity of the capital market.

Chapter 2 discusses materiality, a central threshold issue for many aspects of the securities laws. Chapter 3 explores what types of financial instruments qualify as securities for purposes of applying the securities laws. Chapter 4 sets out the concept of a public company and the obligations, primarily disclosure, that follow from public company status, including the requirements of the Sarbanes-Oxley Act. With disclosure comes the need to ensure the accuracy of the information disclosed. Chapter 5 covers antifraud liability under Rule 10b-5 of the Securities Exchange Act. Chapter 6 deals with insider trading. Chapter 7 deals with public offerings, and Chapter 8 addresses liability issues in public offerings. Chapter 9 focuses on exempt offerings. Finally, in Chapter 10 we cover resale transactions in the secondary market.

⁀ 2 ⁀

Information and
Materiality

*Rob and his family have long owned and operated Blue Crab,
Inc., a crab-harvesting company located in Maine. In need of
additional capital to expand into lobsters, Rob, the CEO of
Blue Crab, attempts to sell common shares in Blue Crab to a
group of local investors. As part of the offering, Rob sends an
offering circular describing Blue Crab in which he discloses
that Blue Crab made $100 million in revenue for the last fiscal
year. Rob, however, made a mistake in adding up the revenue
numbers; in fact, Blue Crab made only $99.9 million in revenue.*

The securities regulatory regime in the United States
focuses on disclosure. In an oft-quoted phrase, Justice
Louis Brandeis wrote, "Sunlight is the best disinfec-
tant; electric light the best policeman." This is the animating
philosophy behind the securities laws adopted in response to
the abuses documented by the Pecora hearings, held between
1932 and 1934. Disclosure also allows investors to analyze the
risks and returns of the investment and, equally important, to
compare the investment with other potential investments.
Disclosure thus promotes accurate pricing of securities and
efficient allocation of resources.

Who should provide this information to investors and
the market? One possibility is to allow investors to fend for

themselves. Some investors would simply do nothing and remain uninformed. Other, more motivated investors might expend resources and expertise to acquire information. But either way, this fend-for-themselves system has three weaknesses.

First, information is costly to produce. Moreover, costs may vary depending on who produces the information. It is much cheaper for an issuer to disclose its prior revenues than it would be for an outside investor to attempt to uncover such information. The issuer has the revenue information in its accounting records: Management and the board of directors need the information to make sensible business decisions. Reporting these figures to all investors can be done relatively cheaply. How would an outside investor uncover such information?

Second, in allocating resources to research, investors would naturally focus only on their own interests. Investors will not expend more resources than the minimum needed to assure their own individual trading profits, even if greater expenditures would benefit the group of all investors. Nor will investors freely distribute to others any information they might obtain, because doing so would reduce or eliminate their own potential trading profits. The benefits to others of more accurate securities prices will be ignored.

Third, investors who do pursue information may duplicate one another's research. Imagine that it costs $100 to gather particular information about Blue Crab, no matter who does it. If Blue Crab gathers the information and distributes it to all investors, the total cost will be $100. However, if investors individually engage in research, they will expend $100 each. Suppose we have 100 investors engaging in such duplicative research, each seeking trading profits by being the first to gain an information advantage over other interested investors. The aggregate research cost to the group of investors will then be $10,000. Although individual investors with information may be able to generate trading profits (if they obtain the information before the other investors do), from the standpoint of the group of investors, the profits are zero sum: One investor's gains are another investor's losses. The investors as a group will be better off if Blue Crab gathers the information once and shares it with the group, thus saving each individual investor from having to reinvent the wheel by researching the company to obtain a fleeting information advantage.

Even without any regulatory requirements, an issuer such as Blue Crab will have incentives to disclose information to investors voluntarily. A company issuing securities will have difficulty selling those securities if it refuses to disclose to investors. Would you be willing to invest in an unknown company if its only response to your questions was "No comment"? Investors will discount the price of issuers' securities if issuers fail to disclose the information investors need to ascertain the investment's risk and return. Blue Crab can minimize this discounting, and thereby maximize its offering proceeds, if it discloses.

The need to disclose does not stop with the initial sale of the securities. Investors eventually need to sell, so they also care about the information available to the secondary market. Suppose Blue Crab refuses to provide follow-up disclosures after it sells its securities. Without ongoing disclosure after the public offering, secondary market investors will not know whether Blue Crab has had a good year or a bad one. Investors purchasing Blue Crab shares in the secondary market from the investors who initially purchased from Blue Crab will discount the securities for the risk posed by this lack of information. Let's take this analysis back a step. Because of the risk that this secondary market discount will affect the profit they can expect when reselling their shares, the initial purchasers will, in anticipation, discount the amount they pay Blue Crab in the first place. Blue Crab, therefore, to increase its share price in the primary market, may choose to commit to ongoing disclosure to the secondary market.

Notwithstanding this incentive to disclose voluntarily, companies may not willingly disclose the information that investors as a group, or society in general, would prefer to have. The management of a company may favor its own interests when making disclosure decisions, rather than the interests of the company itself and of its shareholders. Although Rob, the CEO of Blue Crab, may want to maximize Blue Crab's proceeds from its offering, Rob may also care about his own welfare. Suppose Rob has been slacking off, going golfing every other afternoon, thereby hurting Blue Crab's profits. Rob may choose to avoid disclosing the decline in profits, despite the discount Blue Crab shares will suffer in the market from the failure to disclose.[1] Rob may be more concerned with outsiders learning about his shirking. Even if companies do disclose, they may not do so in a format that facilitates comparison across different companies. If one company discloses revenue for the past twelve months and another discloses revenue for the past sixteen months, investors may have difficulty comparing the two numbers.

These reasons counsel in favor of a mandatory disclosure securities regime. But that raises another question: mandatory disclosure of what? One could imagine a regime in which companies must disclose all information about their business. But do shareholders really need to know the brand of sardines that Rob likes to eat for lunch? Too much disclosure is costly both for a company and for its investors. To generate the information it will disclose, a company must not only adopt expensive internal control systems with which to track its financials, it must also track Rob's eating habits. Investors faced with a flood of disclosures may fail to notice the most relevant pieces of information buried among the extraneous matter. Investors will

---

1. Of course, disclosure of falling profits may also result in a decline in prices. Even if the decline in prices from disclosure is less than the discount due to non-disclosure, Rob may choose non-disclosure to protect his own reputation as a hard-working CEO.

need to expend more time and attention to sift through all the surplus information, an effort that may deter some investors from examining the disclosure in the first place.

Under federal securities laws, the concept of *materiality* distinguishes the relevant from the irrelevant. Materiality serves as an important threshold requirement to determine when certain aspects of the securities laws apply.

1 HOW DOES DISCLOSURE MATTER?

Do investors use information? Conscientious investors receiving new information would take the time to read and digest the meaning of that information for their potential investments. Moreover, they would have developed the requisite expertise to do so. Few investors, however, are this conscientious; fewer still have the requisite expertise. Given these limitations, how does disclosure help investors? If investors ignore disclosure, the materiality concept does no important work.

Even if investors lack the time or expertise to digest disclosure, they may nonetheless benefit from it indirectly. Many investors do not invest in the securities markets directly; rather, they invest through investment companies, more commonly known as mutual funds. By purchasing shares in a mutual fund, investors purchase as well the expertise of the fund's manager. If the fund's manager incorporates this new disclosure into the valuation of the stock, the mutual fund's investors will benefit indirectly because the fund manager will have made better choices. Other investors invest through brokers, relying on the advice of the brokers and the brokerage house analysts to find good investments, making analysts influential consumers of disclosure.

For companies whose securities trade in liquid capital markets, another mechanism provides investors with the benefits of disclosure. As long as some investors in the market learn of the information and incorporate it into their valuation of securities, the information will be reflected in the stock prices. Good news will cause a company's stock price to rise. Other investors may then revise their outlook for the company based on the new stock price.

The process by which information becomes incorporated into a company's stock price is described by the *efficient capital market hypothesis*, or ECMH, which takes three general forms. In its weakest form, ECMH sees stock market prices as incorporating information contained in all past stock prices. Thus, looking at past stock price patterns will not help investors predict the direction the stock price will take in the future; in this view, stock prices take a "random walk."

Under a semi-strong form of the ECMH, the stock market price of a company is seen as incorporating not only past stock prices but also all publicly available information concerning the company. How does publicly available information come to be incorporated in the stock market price? One possible mechanism is *arbitrage*. Suppose several hedge fund and mutual fund managers know that IBM is underpriced because the company has just announced that it has exceeded the consensus analyst forecast for its quarterly earnings. The hedge funds and mutual funds will race to buy the IBM shares while the shares remain underpriced. The surge in orders for IBM shares will not be matched by an increase in the supply of shares at the current price. The imbalance between supply and demand will send a signal that some investors in the market have significant, positive information on IBM and are willing to trade based on this information. These market makers will quickly raise the bid and ask prices for IBM shares until supply and demand return to equilibrium. As a result, IBM's strong earnings will be translated into an increase in IBM's share price.

Note that informational efficiency does not necessarily equate with fundamental efficiency. Some argue that securities prices can become unlinked from the underlying fundamental value of companies, leading to bubbles in securities prices. A popular belief is that securities prices for high technology and other companies were artificially elevated in the late 1990s, the so-called Internet bubble. Such bubbles may be fostered by the presence of unsophisticated investors, sometimes termed noise traders, who may hinder the efforts of arbitrageurs to profit from trades based on information.

The strong version of the ECMH holds that securities market prices incorporate all information, both public and private. If this were true, securities disclosure and insider trading laws would be unnecessary. Stock market prices would automatically incorporate all information relevant to a company's valuation, eliminating any trading advantage that an insider might enjoy and making disclosure unnecessary. The significant profits insiders systematically earn from trades (even in the United States, where insider trading on material informational advantages is illegal) undercut any evidence in support of the strong form of the ECMH. We thus start from the assumption that the *semi*-strong ECMH best describes how information affects securities prices, at least for companies whose stock trades in a liquid secondary market. As we examine materiality, consider how a semi-strong perspective on the ECMH affects the scope of the materiality doctrine.

2 MATERIALITY

Materiality serves as a threshold issue for many aspects of the securities laws, including antifraud liability. Misstatements are actionable only if they are material. Companies are not required, however, to disclose all material information to investors, but instead may remain silent absent a duty to disclose.

The SEC's mandatory disclosure regime (discussed in Chapter 4) imposes a duty on public companies to disclose information on various forms, including Forms S-1 and S-3 (registered public offerings), Forms 10-K and 10-Q (periodic disclosure filings), and Schedule 14A (proxy statement). The various mandatory disclosure forms all reference Regulation S-K. Regulation S-K provides detailed instructions on what to disclose, but many of the requirements are limited by materiality. Item 101(a) of Regulation S-K, for example, requires disclosure of information on a company's general development of the business for the past five years, as well as from earlier periods if material to the understanding of the general development of business. In addition, Rule 408 of the Securities Act and Rule 12b-20 of the Exchange Act stipulate that disclosures must add "such further material information, if any, as may be necessary to make the required statements, in the light of the circumstances under which they are made, not misleading." Thus, companies must ensure the accuracy not only of their material disclosures but also ensure that they have disclosed other material information needed to give investors the full picture.

The Supreme Court in *TSC Industries, Inc. v. Northway, Inc.* set forth the definition of materiality.[2] *TSC Industries* involved a proxy solicitation, but its holding has been extended to the context of other securities laws. The *TSC Industries* Court wrote that information is material if there exists "substantial likelihood that the disclosure of the omitted fact would have been viewed by the reasonable investor as having significantly altered the 'total mix' of information made available." In providing this definition of materiality, the Court rejected a bright-line rule for materiality, instead opting for a balancing approach. The approach weighs the competing concerns of (1) providing investors with information they desire, and (2) avoiding too broad a definition of materiality, which would bury investors under extraneous information and impose

---

2. 426 U.S. 438 (1976).

unnecessary costs on issuers. Given these concerns, we should consider whether the *TSC Industries* test strikes the right balance or whether other concerns should also be reflected in the materiality test.

Suppose that Blue Crab reports that its revenues for the prior fiscal year were $100 million. Suppose, in addition, that Blue Crab's accountants made an addition error and that the prior fiscal year revenues in fact equaled $99.9 million. Is this mistake material? To answer this question, we need to weigh whether (1) a reasonable investor (2) would consider there to be a substantial likelihood (3) that the information significantly alters the total mix of information.

3 THE REASONABLE INVESTOR

The materiality doctrine focuses squarely on the information that a reasonable investor would find significant. But who is the reasonable investor? The judge hearing the case may assume that she represents the reasonable investor. After all, from the judge's perspective, who is more reasonable than the judge herself! Such an approach, however, may not protect investors well if the judge is, in fact, not representative of investors in the marketplace.

Why focus on the reasonable investor? What about *unreasonable* investors in the marketplace? Indeed, unreasonable investors are the ones most in need of protection. Why might investors act irrationally? Among the more important biases and irrationalities that may affect investors are the following:

Hindsight bias. Investors systematically exaggerate the *ex ante* probability of events that have actually occurred; for example, immediately after the exposure of a major corporate fraud, investors will overstate the general probability of fraud.

Overconfidence and overoptimism. Investors systematically inflate their own investment expertise. When their investments do well, they attribute the good returns to expertise, not luck.

Availability bias. When judging probabilities, investors systematically focus too much on readily available information and recent events.

Endowment effects. Investors prefer to maintain the status quo. They value avoiding a loss more than they value an equal improvement. The endowment effect means that an investor who already owns a security may value the security more than an investor who is considering purchasing the same security.

Given these biases, it may seem reasonable to ask if any investors are, in fact, reasonable. Even institutional investors may suffer from their own irrationalities, such as loss aversion. Why then does the materiality doctrine focus on the needs of reasonable investors?

Despite the prevalence of biases and irrationalities among investors, a strong argument favors focusing on the information needs of an objective, rational investor. First, disclosure may not help the truly irrational. An overconfident investor will invest regardless of any warnings received. Second, the potential for irrationality is endless. Once regulators and courts begin the attempt to address each type of irrationality, they will find no natural stopping point. Suppose a particular investor likes to invest based on how much exercise the CEO gets. Should courts consider the amount of exercise the CEO gets to be material information? Doing so would force companies to track the exercise habits of their CEOs and to disclose this information to investors. Companies faced with a requirement to disclose all information may avoid reducing sensitive inside corporate information to paper (or hard drive). Moreover, the benefit to investors as a group from such an open-ended definition of materiality is unclear. Too much disclosure may harm investors just as much as too little disclosure might. Too much information may also frustrate investors attempting to find the truly important information. It's one thing to find a CEO's salary in a proxy statement of 200 pages, but consider the challenge if this information is buried in a document of 2,000 or 20,000 pages.

Indeed, some courts have employed a "buried facts" doctrine under which a disclosure may be deemed false and materially misleading if the material information is buried in a document. For example, a federal district court in *Kohn v. American Metal Climax Inc.*[3] applied the buried facts doctrine to key disclosures about an amalgamation between two mining companies that were placed nonprominently within explanatory materials. The court wrote, "These facts should have in some way been highlighted to insure that the shareholders were aware of them. We need not speculate as to how this should have been done. . . . These facts could have been placed on the cover page in bold-face type. Nevertheless, their present location is not justified by their importance, especially in view of the length and complexity of the explanatory materials."

Note that the buried facts doctrine depends on certain assumptions about reasonable investors. Certainly securities analysts covering the mining companies at issue in *Kohn* would have the time, incentive, and expertise to ferret out the key facts, even if they were buried within the explanatory materials for the transaction. Nonetheless, the *Kohn* court seems to have a different type of reasonable investor in mind, someone with less time and incentive than the typical securities analyst.

We are thus left with a somewhat open-ended puzzle. Materiality is meant to limit disclosure requirements; a standard

---

3. 322 F. Supp. 1331, 1362 (E.D. Pa. 1970).

that deems everything material is too costly for issuers and too confusing for investors. Moreover, a reasonable investor would not be afflicted by the broad range of investing irrationalities exhibited by actual investors. On the other hand, the term *reasonable investor* does not indicate only the sophisticated securities analyst. Rational but less sophisticated investors are contemplated in the notion of reasonable investor. But how much time and expertise do we expect from our reasonable investor?

4 SIGNIFICANCE AND RULES OF THUMB

Once we have a sense (if somewhat vague) of who is a reasonable investor, we also need to determine what types of information such investors will find significant. There are some relatively bright lines. A reasonable investor would likely not find the amount of exercise the CEO gets to be significant, but the CEO's compensation agreement would be. But some gray areas remain. Will investors consider it significant that Blue Crab reported $100 million of revenues while its true revenues were $99.9 million? Courts may attempt to determine significance through introspection. Would a judge, herself, consider the difference between $100 million and $99.9 million in revenue significant in the Maine shellfish industry? If the judge does not know much about crabs or lobsters, she may conclude that she does not know the answer, even after long contemplation.

One response to the difficulty of determining what information a reasonable investor would find significant is to rely on simple rules of thumb. Although the *TSC Industries* test for materiality may make theoretical sense, does it provide a concrete, practical answer for issuers who must make disclosure choices? Issuers, and even more acutely, their attorneys, value certainty. No one wants to withhold information they think immaterial only to be second-guessed later, particularly when the wrong choice can mean substantial liability and the possibility of an SEC enforcement action. Certainty allows issuers to plan their disclosure and to focus their resources on verifying disclosures that investors will be sure to deem material. The SEC, however, has long rebuffed efforts to bring more certainty to the materiality definition, worrying that clear rules may create a "road map" to fraud.

Consider, for example, the SEC's response to one rule of thumb commonly used to guide materiality determinations. SEC Staff Accounting Bulletin No. 99 noted, "One rule of thumb in particular suggests that the misstatement or omission of an item that falls under a 5% threshold is not material in the absence of particularly egregious circumstances, such as self-dealing or misappropriation by senior management." The 5 percent threshold can provide a useful starting point for the materiality analysis, but the SEC has cautioned against exclusive reliance on such rules of thumb. Its view is that the final materiality determination must include an assessment of how the magnitude of the event interacts with the "total mix" of information. According to the SEC, even small quantitative events may rise to the level of materiality on a *qualitative* basis. Among qualitative factors identified by the SEC are the following:

- whether the misstatement masks a change in earnings or other trends
- whether the misstatement hides a failure to meet analysts' consensus expectations for the enterprise
- whether the misstatement has the effect of increasing management's compensation (for example, by satisfying requirements for the award of bonuses or other forms of incentive compensation)
- whether the misstatement involves concealment of an unlawful transaction[4]

---

4. See SEC Staff Accounting Bulletin, No. 99 (1999).

An example of one court's response to the use of a materiality rule of thumb can be found in *Ganino v. Citizens Utilities Company*.[5] Citizens, a communications and public services company, had reported 50 consecutive years of increased revenues and earnings. In 1995, however, Citizens faced a potential revenue shortfall and was in danger of ending its 50-year streak. Rather than end the streak, Citizens entered into an agreement with Hungarian Telephone & Cable Corp. (HTCC) under which Citizens made or guaranteed loans to HTCC in return for fees. Citizens proceeded to earn fees from HTCC in 1995. Rather than book the fees in 1995, Citizens chose to shift the fee revenue to 1996 as new income (without disclosing the relationship between the new revenue and the HTCC arrangement). As a consequence of this shift, Citizens was able to report continued revenue and earnings growth in 1996. In a subsequent suit alleging antifraud liability under Rule 10b-5 of the Exchange Act, the defendants urged that the revenues from HTCC were not material because they were less than 3 percent of total revenues. The Second Circuit held that materiality does not turn on formulaic rules of thumb. Instead, it noted that the fee income from HTCC was large both in absolute terms and as a percentage of net income, even though it was only a small percentage of revenue. The Second Circuit, following the SEC, also noted that even a small misstatement may be material if it masks a change in earnings or other trends or hides a failure to meet analyst expectations. In the case of Citizens, the misstatement about the fee income allowed Citizens to continue its streak of revenue and earnings increases, thereby meeting analyst expectations.

One problem with relying on rules of thumb is that determining a percentage threshold, such as 5 percent, depends crucially on the baseline used for the percentage. Profits are typically a fraction of revenues. Blue Crab may have

---

5. 228 F.3d 154 (2d Cir. 2000).

$100 million of revenues for the prior fiscal year, but it also had $95 million of expenses; Blue Crab's net profits would equal $5 million. In these circumstances, an accounting misstatement of $1 million may represent only 1 percent of revenues but a whopping 20 percent of profits. Should the baseline used be revenues or profits? The rule of thumb provides no standard with which to choose the baseline for its application.

Another problem with a bright-line rule of thumb is that it may, as the SEC fears, provide a road map to fraud. If those seeking to commit fraud recognized that courts would treat any misstatement of less than 5 percent of a company's revenues as immaterial, they could intentionally overstate revenues by 4.9 percent, thus misleading investors without fear of liability under this particular materiality rule of thumb.

What about the opposite rule of thumb: Large magnitude items are presumptively material? We could imagine, for example, a rule of thumb that any amount that represents more than 20 percent of a company's revenues is presumptively material. This rule would enhance certainty for issuers attempting to comply with their disclosure duties and avoid potential antifraud liability. On the other hand, even with large magnitude amounts, qualitative arguments may exist that diminish the importance of this information to investors. Some relatively large events (such as a one-time write-down of assets) may not indicate much about the company's future if they are nonrecurring.

5 SIGNIFICANCE AND THE MARKET RESPONSE (EVENT STUDIES)

An alternative approach to materiality, available only for publicly traded companies, is to look at the market reaction to the eventual public release of information. A significant response in the stock-market price to the release of the information can be seen as evidence that the market considered the information material; that is, investors adjusted their valuation of the company based on the information. Typically, reactions in stock-market prices are measured through a tool of financial economics known as the *event study*.

An event study involves a number of steps. First, the event window is identified, that is, the date (or dates) on which the information was first made public. Second, a baseline for the company's stock market returns is constructed. To create this baseline, the relation between the company's stock returns and the overall market return is assessed for a specified time period before the event window. Some stocks, for example, march in step with the overall market, while others are either less or more volatile. A company's sensitivity to the overall market is known as its *beta*. Using this beta, the expected return for the company's stock is derived from the market returns during the event window. Third, the expected returns are subtracted from the actual returns for the company's stock during the event window. The difference is the stock's excess or abnormal return for the stock. Finally, based on the volatility of the company's past stock price returns, the probability is calculated that the abnormal return is not just a random fluctuation, but instead reflects a significant departure from the expected stock return. If the departure is significant, courts may conclude that the information was material.

Event studies substitute the market's assessment, that is, the aggregate assessment of actual investors, for the court's own inexpert determination of materiality. Event studies, however, have their own problems. Selecting a proper event window is critical. It does no good to assess the stock market reaction on October 1 if the information was first released to the market on August 1. Although in this example the error seems clear, in many cases the first date on which information is revealed (or fully revealed) to the market may not be so obvious. The release around the same time of confounding information concerning the company can also undermine the validity of an event study. If a company simultaneously discloses both it just won a new contract and that its CEO is leaving, how do we know whether the resulting stock market reaction is due to the contract or to the CEO's departure? Finally, event studies depend crucially on a quick and accurate market-price reaction to the new information. The response of illiquid markets, for example, may lack the necessary efficiency on which to base a reliable event study.

Market assessments of information reappear in other areas of securities law. When we discuss reliance and loss causation in Chapter 5, we will see that the market response to information plays a central role in establishing these two elements of the antifraud cause of action. The analysis for those two elements overlaps considerably with this measure of materiality.

6 TOTAL MIX OF INFORMATION

Reasonable investors may consider a particular piece of information to be significant, but the information may not be material if it is already part of the total mix of information. Consider the price of oil. If oil refineries along the Gulf of Mexico are damaged by hurricanes, oil prices will rise. Blue Crab's fishing vessels depend on diesel fuel to operate; thus, damaged oil refineries will translate into significantly higher operating costs and correspondingly lower profits for the company. Nonetheless, this information is not specific to Blue Crab: News of damaged refineries is widely reported and commonly known. Courts would therefore treat information about the refineries, despite its importance to Blue Crab's investors, as part of the total mix of information and would not consider it a material disclosure to be made by the company.

Why does being part of the total mix render information immaterial? If investors already know a particular piece of information, having a company repeat the disclosure is a pointless distraction. This argument is clearest when information is generated by sources outside the company, such as news and other reports on damaged oil refineries. Not only is the information already in the public domain, the company has no particular insight into the information.

For firm-specific information, such as information about a particular company's operations, revenues, and business plans, the total mix of information argument is more difficult. For firm-specific information, the responsible issuer will typically be the lowest cost provider. Nonetheless, if the issuer or another source has already provided the market with similar information, courts may find further disclosure unnecessary. In applying the concept of total-mix information to firm-specific information, courts must wrestle with several questions. First, how similar was the prior disclosure? Suppose similar but not identical information was released in the past by another source, for example, a newspaper. Second, when has information made its way into the total mix? Suppose that information is disclosed to a college newspaper in Spokane. Is this enough to place the information in the total mix?

The Seventh Circuit in *Wielgos v. Commonwealth Edison Company*[6] provides one view on the incorporation of information into the total mix. Commonwealth Edison operated a number of nuclear reactors. Early in 1984, a unit of the Nuclear Regulatory Commission (NRC) denied an operating license for one of Commonwealth Edison's reactors then under construction, resulting in a dramatic drop in Commonwealth Edison's stock price. Wielgos then brought suit for material misstatements in the registration statement by which Commonwealth Edison had sold equity securities. Among other things, Wielgos alleged that Commonwealth Edison had understated the completion costs of the reactors in prior

---

6. 892 F.2d 509 (1989).

SEC filings incorporated by reference into the registration statement. The court accepted that the projected costs for completing the reactors were inaccurate at the time the securities were sold pursuant to the registration statement. Nonetheless, the court held that the inaccurate cost projections were not actionable. The court wrote:

> Securities laws require issuers to disclose *firm-specific* information; investors and analysts combine that information with knowledge about the competition, regulatory conditions, and the economy as a whole to produce a value for stock. . . . Just as a firm needn't disclose that 50% of all new products vanish from the market within a short time, so Commonwealth Edison needn't disclose the hazards of its business, hazards apparent to all serious observers and most casual ones.

The approach taken by the *Wielgos* court to materiality has become known as the "truth in the market" defense. Crucial to this defense is the assumption that information is rapidly incorporated into the stock price. Once incorporated into the stock price, the court wrote, "[k]nowledge abroad in the market moderated, likely eliminated, the potential of a dated projection to mislead. It therefore cannot be the basis of liability."

How precise does information already in the total mix need to be to invoke the truth on the market defense? The market did not know how far off the cost projections were, only that they were inaccurate. If the market knew the degree of error, of course, that would be the equivalent of knowing precisely the true cost projections. The court does not require this level of precision. The court instead implies that if Wielgos had alleged that Commonwealth Edison was markedly worse than the industry norm in making cost projections, this might be information not already part of the total mix. As long as the degree of inaccuracy does not deviate from the market's expected degree of inaccuracy, the truth in the market defense may hold.

Judge Easterbrook, in his decision in *Wielgos*, relies heavily on Commonwealth Edison's status as a seasoned issuer. Easterbrook assumes that, for a seasoned issuer, the market price will incorporate the accurate information, thereby correcting the inaccurate cost projections. The efficient capital market hypothesis assumes that public information is incorporated rapidly into the stock price of companies that trade in a (semi-strong) efficient market. For companies that trade in illiquid markets, however, or for information not made public, it is more difficult to conclude that corrective information will be included in the total mix.

The Fourth Circuit in *Longman v. Food Lion, Inc.*,[7] also addressed the issue of whether certain information counted as material given the total mix of information. Food Lion, a grocery chain, required its employees to meet certain goals. A union, in the middle of its effort to unionize Food Lion's workers, filed a complaint with the Department of Labor in September 1991, alleging that Food Lion's labor practice forced employees to work "off the clock" without pay to meet the work goals. Food Lion made a series of releases to the public denying the union's allegations. In November 1992, ABC's *PrimeTime* television program ran an episode on Food Lion stores, reporting on both Food Lion's off-the-clock work as well as unsanitary conditions. Shareholders of Food Lion brought a class action alleging securities fraud relating to the off-the-clock work practices, among other things, under Rule 10b-5 of the Exchange Act. The class period ran from May 1990 (from before the Union's complaint to the Department of Labor) to November 1992, when the *PrimeTime* episode aired. After the end of the class period, in August 1993, the Department of Labor announced that Food Lion had settled the labor practice complaints against it for $16.2 million.

---

7. 197 F.3d 675 (4th Cir. 1999).

The Fourth Circuit held that the information on the off-the-clock work practices at Food Lion was not material for purposes of securities antifraud liability. The court reasoned that the off-the-clock claims were "well known" to the market well before the end of the class period (in November 1992) due to the September 1991 complaint by the union to the Department of Labor. Once placed on notice about the complaint, the court wrote that "the market had a full opportunity to evaluate these claims and to reflect their risk in the market price for Food Lion stock." Moreover, the court looked to the size of the eventual $16.2 million settlement with the Department of Labor, split across two years, compared with Food Lion's earnings of over $200 million per year. Implicitly utilizing a rule-of-thumb analysis, the court held that the magnitude of the settlement was immaterial. Lastly, the court looked to the stock market response following the announcement of the Department of Labor settlement, noting that the lack of a drop in the stock market price was consistent with its materiality analysis.

One can wonder about the *Longman* court's application of the total mix of information analysis. How does the court know that the union's complaint to the Department of Labor in September 1991 made its way into the marketplace and thus into the total mix of information? Perhaps Food Lion's large size and liquid secondary market make the movement of information into the total mix likely. A more troubling question, however, is how does the court come to the conclusion that the information the market learned from the union's September 1991 complaint is the same information provided in the *PrimeTime* episode in November 1992? Even if the subject matter of the information is the same, investors may consider the messenger when determining the value of the information. Investors in the market may view information from a *PrimeTime* episode as more credible than information coming from a union locked in a battle to unionize Food Lion.

7 PUFFERY

Another tool for determining materiality is the doctrine of *puffery*. Statements deemed to be mere puffery are presumptively immaterial. *Eisenstadt v. Centel*[8] took up the issue of what constitutes puffery.

In *Eisenstadt*, Centel Corp., a telecommunications company, put itself up for sale. The auction efforts went poorly. Potential bidders announced that they would not bid. Despite these announcements, Centel issued a public statement that "the bidding process continues to go very well" and "very smoothly." Internally, Centel believed that it would get fewer bidders than it had expected. As the auction date approached, Centel's CEO stated to the public that there was "widespread interest." The auction occurred in April 1992 and produced few bids, none of which Centel accepted. Instead, Centel negotiated a sale to Sprint at a price of $33.50, fully $9 below the market price at the time.

In the subsequent lawsuit alleging that the company's representations concerning the auction were fraudulent, the Seventh Circuit held that Centel's general, nonspecific representations about the auction were not material. Judge Posner, writing for the court, stated, "We doubt that nonspecific representations that an auction process is going well or going smoothly could . . . influence a reasonable investor to pay more for a stock than he otherwise would. *Everybody* knows that someone trying to sell something is going to look and talk on the bright side. You don't sell a product by bad mouthing it. And everybody knows that auctions can be disappointing."

Posner's *Eisenstadt* opinion makes it clear that the puffery doctrine depends on the expectation of reasonable investors. Puffery assesses the preexisting mix of information and investors' expectations to determine the materiality of a statement.

---

8. 113 F.3d 738 (7th Cir. 1997).

If we assume that reasonable investors expect a certain degree of puffery and discount statements accordingly, no one is misled. The importance of the internalized expectations of reasonable investors highlights the limits of the puffery defense. If, even after discounting for possible puffery, a statement is still significantly misleading, a court may find even the general, nonspecific statement material.

Courts applying the puffery doctrine must still determine what information reasonable investors would discount as mere puffery. Perhaps some classes of information are so obviously puffery that such a determination is not difficult, even for a judge not well-versed in financial markets. When a company says that it has the "best deals" for its customers, an investor hearing this claim may not take "best deals" at face value, instead recognizing it as a sales tactic. But when a company putting itself on the auction block states that the auction will go "smoothly," would you find such a statement mere puffery to be ignored or a statement communicating new information?

8 FORWARD-LOOKING INFORMATION

Determining whether information is material is challenging, even for historic information such as revenues and profit numbers. But what about information relating to future, contingent events? Suppose Rob, the CEO of Blue Crab, issues a press release announcing that he expects Blue Crab's revenues to grow by 5 percent per year over the next five years. Or suppose Rob announces that Blue Crab is planning a merger with its competitor, the Softshell Company. At the time of these announcements, Blue Crab's future revenues and the possible merger are simply predictions of what might happen in the future. Is this information material?

One approach to establishing the materiality of projections about a company's future is to assume that investors take such information with a large grain of salt. Under this assumption, investors realize that information about the future is necessarily uncertain and discount it completely in valuing a company. This approach would treat all forward-looking disclosures as presumptively immaterial. This presumption would save companies from the headache of determining the materiality of a piece of forward-looking information. Such an approach also insulates companies from the specter of antifraud liability for future projections that do not pan out. Eliminating liability for forward-looking information may encourage companies to be more forthcoming with the marketplace.

Despite the uncertainty that attaches to forward-looking information, investors value company projections. The CEO of Blue Crab will know a lot more about Blue Crab's prospects than would outside investors or securities analysts. The assumption that investors give no weight to forward-looking information is contradicted by the available evidence. Sophisticated investors and analysts often put their greatest resources into analyzing forward-looking information, particularly projections of revenues and profits. This should come as no surprise; investors put money into a company because they want a share of its future, not its past, income streams. The company itself is the best source of information regarding future economic performance.

The Supreme Court took on the question of how to determine the materiality of forward-looking information in *Basic Inc. v. Levinson*.[9] Combustion Engineering entered into merger discussions with Basic Inc., but Basic publicly denied that it was negotiating. When Basic eventually announced its merger with Combustion, Basic's shares jumped from $28.25 per share to $44.375 per share. Basic shareholders who sold their shares at the lower price prior to the announcement

---

9. 485 U.S. 224 (1988).

argued that, had Basic told the truth about the possible merger, they would not have sold (or, alternatively, they would have sold at a higher price as the market incorporated information about the possibility of a merger into the stock price at an earlier date).

Writing for the Supreme Court, Justice Blackmun held that the materiality of a prospective merger requires balancing the probability of the event along with its anticipated magnitude. In determining the probability of a merger, Blackmun pointed to a nonexclusive list of factors including "board resolutions, instructions to investment banks, and actual negotiations." To determine magnitude, Blackmun pointed to the "size of the two corporate entities and . . . the potential premiums over market value."

Although this test might require disclosure earlier than the negotiation parties might like, Blackmun rejected the need for secrecy as unrelated to the issue of materiality. Some lower courts had argued that merger secrecy may help the shareholders of a potential target corporation such as Basic. Without secrecy, an acquirer may not wish even to enter into negotiations out of a fear that it will simply serve as a stalking-horse, used to attract other potential acquirers. Blackmun relegated this policy question to another legal doctrine: the duty to disclose. Here, because Basic engaged in affirmative falsehoods in its denials, the policy arguments dealing with the duty to disclose and secrecy did not apply. If you choose to speak, you *must* tell the truth. Blackmun also rejected the argument that investors may overreact to information relating to preliminary merger negotiations, stating that "[d]isclosure, and not paternalistic withholding of accurate information, is the policy chosen and expressed by Congress," and that it would be inappropriate to attribute to investors a "'child-like simplicity.'"

On one level, the lessons of *Basic* are straightforward. To determine the materiality of a forward-looking statement, determine the probability of an event and multiply by its magnitude. Consider these illustrations:

$$5\% \times \$100 \text{ million} = \$20 \text{ million}$$
$$10\% \times \$ \ 10 \text{ million} = \$ \ 1 \text{ million}$$
$$25\% \times \$ \ 20 \text{ million} = \$ \ 5 \text{ million}$$

Performing these calculations is simple. What is not so simple, however, is determining the probability of an event and its anticipated magnitude to plug into the formula. Are issuers, when planning their disclosures, and courts, when adjudicating materiality issues, likely to get these numbers right? Will they view them the same way? And what is the threshold above which a particular probability x magnitude is deemed material? If it is $10 million, only the first of the three examples above is material. But why $10 million rather than $3 million?

In sum, issuers disclosing forward-looking information must speculate on probability, magnitude, and the threshold of materiality. Making the wrong call stings: issuers face substantial legal liability if they guess wrong. Courts suffer from a hindsight bias when looking back at a disclosure decision. People systematically tend to place too much ex ante probability on events that actually occur. When most people see it is raining, they assume there was a much higher probability of rain for that day than there actually was. Similarly, courts, when they see that a merger has taken place, may exaggerate the ex ante probability that the merger would occur. To protect themselves against the combination of uncertainty and hindsight bias, nervous issuers may disclose in borderline cases, just to be safe.

Courts worried about the possibility of frivolous litigation have adopted the "bespeaks caution" doctrine, which allows them to dismiss such suits at an early stage. Under the bespeaks-caution doctrine, a forward-looking disclosure could be rendered immaterial if accompanied by meaningful cautionary language detailing factors that could cause actual results to differ. Critically, the lawsuit could be terminated at the motion to dismiss or summary judgment stages. The ability to dispose of litigation quickly means lower litigation costs, reducing defendants' incentive to settle frivolous litigation to avoid those costs. We will return to the bespeaks-caution doctrine in Chapter 5, along with the codification of that doctrine in the forward-looking safe harbor of the Private Securities Litigation Reform Act of 1995.

9 MANAGEMENT INTEGRITY

The SEC views information about a company's management team as a critical factor in investor evaluations. Without a good management team, even companies with great products and prospects may fall behind other better managed companies. The SEC, not surprisingly, mandates extensive disclosure about management in its various disclosure forms. These disclosure forms reference Regulation S-K, Subpart 400, which provides detailed requirements for disclosures relating to the directors and officers of a company. For example, Item 401 of Regulation S-K requires that companies disclose biographical information on directors and officers; Item 402 mandates disclosure of executive compensation, including compensation in the form of stock options; and Item 404 requires disclosures on related transactions between the issuer and certain parties, including directors or officers and their family members.

The SEC's regime does not mandate disclosure of all possible material information about a company's directors and officers. Directors need not, for example, list occupations going back beyond five years. Nonetheless, companies may need to disclose additional, non-mandated information about management if excluding that information would render materially misleading other information already disclosed. How much additional information is required? One possible counterweight is the interest of directors and officers in their own privacy. Suppose Rob, Blue Crab's CEO, has a serious heart condition. In describing the company's future prospects, would failure to disclose Rob's heart condition make other statements materially misleading?

The classic case on the materiality of disclosure relating to management is an SEC administrative decision, *In the Matter of Franchard Corporation*,[10] Franchard Corporation (previously named the Glickman Corporation) was controlled by Louis Glickman and served as a vehicle for Glickman's real estate business activities. Glickman had voting control over Franchard and served as its president and chairman of the board. In 1960 and 1961, Franchard registered its common stock for sale through a public offering. The prospectus for the public offerings highlighted Glickman's role with the company and his substantial success in real estate. The prospectus failed to mention, however, that Glickman had diverted substantial funds out of Franchard to his own benefit and that Glickman's shares were pledged as security for loans financing his personal real estate ventures.

The SEC found these omissions material and thus required to be disclosed under Rule 408 of the Securities Act. The SEC reasoned that disclosure about management integrity "is an essential ingredient of informed investment decision." In this case, Glickman was at the center of Franchard's business and the main reason why investors wanted to invest in Franchard. Indeed, Franchard had no operating history; investors were placing money in Franchard solely based on Glickman's personal reputation. Glickman's importance to the business magnified the relevance of his diversion of money and his pledge of shares. The undisclosed information reflected not only on Glickman's true business acumen but also on his integrity.

---

10. 42 S.E.C. 163 (1964).

Given the wide range of disclosures about management competency and integrity required by the line items in Regulation S-K, was the SEC right to require yet more disclosure about Glickman? Investors can already evaluate managers based on their prior biography, compensation, and conflicts of interests and on the firm's financial performance. These line-item disclosure requirements, in their predictability, provide clear advantages: They do not leave managers in legal limbo as they try to determine whether additional information is or is not material. On the other hand, financial performance may not always correlate with good or bad management. Occasionally, good managers will suffer from bad luck and poor managers will benefit from good. Despite the uncertainty it creates for managers, amorphous notions of additional material information may increase the benefits of disclosure to investors.

Was the SEC right to give so little weight to managers' privacy? Some information about CEOs, such as illness or a death in their family, has been shown to have a significant effect on their firms' performance. Nonetheless, shareholders might prefer to afford managers more privacy if it allowed companies to attract better managers. If managers truly dislike giving up their privacy, the best ones will either shift to managing private companies or will seek compensation through increased salaries. Disclosure is useful, but it has its costs.

↣ 3 ↢

What Is a Security?

At first glance, the question "What is a security?" seems deceptively simple. Typically, securities include a corporation's common stock and publicly traded bonds; indeed, in terms of dollar value, these stocks and bonds make up the vast majority of securities. Why, then, devote an entire chapter to the definition of a security under the federal securities laws? Promoters are constantly devising new investment scams, ranging from orange groves to pay phones; to keep on top of them, the definition of a security must sweep well beyond plain-vanilla stocks and bonds.

Underlying the doctrinal question of how to define a security is the policy question of whether the securities laws apply to a particular transaction. Only if a transaction involves a security do the securities laws apply. A policy-oriented approach to the question of what is a security must therefore consider the appropriate reach of securities regulation. An ancillary question is whether securities regulation should be mandatory or whether participants in the securities market should be allowed to decide if the regime applies. If securities are defined narrowly, entrepreneurs seeking to raise capital without the protection (and high cost) of the securities laws could do so simply by renaming their instruments.

The definition of a security involves a strategic interaction between policymakers and market participants. To prevent market participants from skirting the securities laws through creative investment devices, policymakers must adopt an expansive definition of *security*. Such a definition would ignore form and would instead focus on the *economic realities* of a security. From the other side of the equation, the financial markets are constantly developing new financial instruments. Financial intermediaries will often pool assets that are not securities (home mortgage loans, for example) and sell interests in the profits from this pool. This process, known as *securitization*, may transform assets that are not securities into securities. Assessing this transition from non-securities to securities again requires examining the substance of the instrument created to determine whether it has the substantive characteristics of a securities transaction.

How should we assess when an instrument qualifies as a security? One method is to start with the definitions under § 2(a)(1) of the Securities Act and § 3(a)(10) of the Exchange Act. These definitions contain an escape clause allowing the exclusion of instruments from the definition if "the context otherwise requires." The definitional sections then provide a laundry list of items commonly viewed as securities, including stocks and bonds. Beyond these obvious forms of securities, the definitions also include a catch-all category: *investment contract*. In this context, the Supreme Court has played a crucial role in shaping the definition of a security. In constructing the investment contract test, the Court has focused in particular on economic realities. Determining whether an instrument is a security will not always require a substantive examination of economic reality, however. On occasion, labels will be determinative, as in the case of a share of stock (at least if it has the traditional characteristics of stock). Economic reality is important in determining the scope of the securities laws, but the desire for certainty sometimes limits the influence of economic reality.

Against the doctrinal background, sales of instruments falling within the definition of a security will be subject to the elements of the securities regulatory regime, including (a) mandatory disclosure, (b) federal securities antifraud liability, and (c) specialized rules (the "gun-jumping" rules) for public offers. Moreover, the SEC may monitor trades in such instruments and bring its own enforcement actions relating to transactions in the instruments. When should we invoke these aspects of the securities regime? Application of the securities laws may be most justified when we have a number of investors all who desire common information through mandatory disclosure. Passive investors at an informational disadvantage relative to securities promoters may also require mandatory disclosure, antifraud liability, and application of the gun-jumping rules. On the other hand, limiting SEC enforcement resources may be desirable to protect investors making decisions related to the capital markets.

1 INVESTMENT CONTRACTS

The starting point for the definition of a security under the securities laws is the Supreme Court opinion in *SEC v. W.J. Howey Co.*[1] *Howey* involved the scope of the term *investment contract* in the definition of a security under § 2(a)(1) of the Securities Act. Although only one item on a laundry list of definitions of a security, the term *investment contract* does the lion's share of the work in the doctrine defining a security.

In *Howey*, W.J. Howey Co. made offers of land and service contracts to prospective investors, a number of whom purchased both. W.J. Howey Co. offered narrow strips of land in orange tree groves as well as service contracts (through its Howey-in-the-Hills affiliate) to service the land, collect the oranges, and sell the oranges at market. The service contracts provided that the oranges from all the strips of trees with a

---

1. 328 U.S. 293 (1946).

similar service agreement would be pooled. Profits from the pooled oranges then would be distributed pro rata (based on the number of trees purchased) to the various service contract holders. Under the service contract, Howey controlled the land and its cultivation; none of the investors was given access to the land. The investors were all from outside the state; they had been offered the land and service contract package while they were staying at a nearby resort owned and operated by Howey. Approximately 85 percent of those who purchased the strip of land also entered into a service contract with Howey-in-the-Hills.

The SEC brought an enforcement action against W.J. Howey Co. for violating the securities laws by making unregistered offers and sales of securities. Although some investors purchased only the land contract and not the service contract, the Supreme Court framed the issue as whether the *offers* of both orange grove and service contracts constituted offers of investment contracts and, hence, securities. The Court announced what is now known as the *Howey* test: "[A]n investment contract . . . means a contract, transaction or scheme whereby a person invests his money in a common enterprise and is led to expect profits solely from the efforts of the promoter or a third party." Along the way, the Court also held that the presence of "intrinsic" value in the orange grove land was irrelevant in determining whether the interests offered in *Howey* were offers of securities.

Howey raises several questions. First, what is an "investment of money"? Second, what constitutes a "common enterprise"? In *Howey*, the investors in the orange groves and service contracts received common returns. If the oranges sold well, they all did well. If the oranges sold poorly, they all did poorly. This form of commonality is referred to as horizontal commonality. Are other forms of commonality possible? Third, what type of profits count? Do profits include fixed returns, such as interest payments on a loan? Fourth, what if investors are not completely passive? Will this satisfy the "solely through the efforts of others" prong of the *Howey* test? Finally, how important are the economic realities — disregarding form in favor of substance — in determining whether an instrument qualifies as a security?

1.1 Investment of Money

Consider first the question of what constitutes an "investment of money." The polar cases are easy. When an investor parts with cash to purchase a share of common stock, that is an investment. When a consumer uses cash to purchase a ticket to an amusement ride, this is not an investment. But what about other types of consideration, in contexts other than an organized securities market, such as in an employment decision? Do these constitute an investment of money?

In *Int'l Brotherhood of Teamsters v. Daniel*,[2] the Supreme Court addressed the concept *investment of money*. Daniel was a long-time truck driver who had worked over twenty years for various trucking employers. Daniel's labor union, the International Brotherhood of Teamsters, had negotiated with several trucking employers to provide a pension plan for truckers. The pension plan was compulsory, but it did not require contribution from the employees. Instead, the plan was funded directly by the employers. A key provision of the pension plan provided that workers needed twenty continuous years of service to become eligible for plan benefits. For those that met the twenty-year threshold, benefits were paid regardless of the actual number of years of service. Unfortunately for Daniel, he was laid off for a brief period of time during his years as a trucker, leading to a break in his working years for pension purposes. When the plan administrator denied him a pension, Daniel filed a suit under the federal securities laws.

---

2. 439 U.S. 551 (1979).

The threshold question was whether Daniel's interest in the pension plan constituted a security. Justice Powell, writing for the Court, held that it was not. Noting that pension plans are not specifically delineated in the definition of a security under § 2(a)(1) of the Securities Act or § 3(a)(10) of the Exchange Act, Powell focused on whether the pension plan qualified as an investment contract. Turning to the first factor of the *Howey* test, the investment of money, Powell held that an *investment* may include the transfer of goods or services in return for a security investment; nonetheless, the Court held that Daniel's interest in the pension plan did not constitute an investment. The Court focused on the relatively insignificant portion of Daniel's entire compensation package represented by the pension plan. In Powell's view, the employee's "decision to accept and retain covered employment may have only an attenuated relationship, if any, to perceived investment possibilities of a future pension. Looking at the economic realities, it seems clear that an employee is selling his labor primarily to obtain a livelihood, not making an investment." Nor were the employers investing on behalf of Daniel and the other employees. Because the pension plan benefits did not correspond directly to the employees' time worked (other than meeting the twenty-year threshold), Powell ruled that the contributions could not be earmarked as on behalf of any specific employee.

What role does the investment of money prong of the *Howey* test serve? One concern with securities regulation is limiting its reach to situations implicating the capital markets. Although accurate prices are important in all areas of the economy, they are particularly important in the capital markets. These accurate prices ensure that resources in the economy move to their highest value use, improving the economic welfare generally of all participants in the economy. Focusing scarce enforcement resources on ensuring accuracy in this market is a defensible policy choice.

How should we determine whether transactions are sufficiently close to the capital markets? First, start by looking at the amount and type of consideration involved. Although Powell was explicit that consideration other than money could be an investment, the use of low-value, nonmonetary consideration may indicate that the transaction does not directly implicate the capital markets. Suppose we offer you the following business proposition: If you allow us to cut your grass and take away the clippings for conversion into Grass-ahol, a gasoline substitute, you will receive a pro rata share (along with your participating neighbors) of the profits from Grass-ahol sales. Is the contribution of your grass clippings an investment of money? The grass clippings have negligible value, and your "investment" in our venture scarcely seems to implicate the capital markets: You won't invest your grass clippings in stocks and bonds if you turn down our venture, you will simply be making your own compost. If the stock of Internet Inc. is overpriced, more resources than warranted will move into the Internet sector, disciplining other investments. If your grass clippings are wrongly priced, will that really appreciably affect the allocation of other resources in the economy?

Another approach to the question of the effect on the capital markets is to look at the decision-making process of the transacting parties. This is the approach taken in *Daniel*. The pension plan clearly has investment attributes. Nonetheless, it is not treated as an investment contract because Daniel's decision did not concern an investment, but rather, as the Court puts it, his "livelihood." When making his decision to work as a trucker, Daniel's alternatives did not include other capital market investments, but instead included other possible jobs (baker, fireman, teacher, and so on). Daniel's decision thus did not influence the capital markets in any important way. If Daniel were led astray due to a misrepresentation or omission, this would affect his choice about working as a baker, fireman, or teacher, but it would not implicate any choice among investment instruments. The common law of fraud and contracts would be sufficient to protect the integrity of his employment choice.

Moreover, today ERISA covers pension plans such as the one in which Daniel was enrolled. Even though ERISA did not exist at the time of Daniel's plan, ERISA, in Powell's view, demonstrates that Congress believed it was filling a "regulatory void" when it enacted ERISA. Moreover, the enactment of ERISA makes the extension of the Securities Act to cover pension plans one that would serve "no general purpose." The Court was worried that extending the reach of the securities laws too broadly would interfere with other regulatory schemes.

1.2 Common Enterprise

The federal circuit courts differ in their interpretation of the common enterprise prong of the *Howey* test. The most widely held view is that an investment scheme must have horizontal commonality to be an investment contract. Horizontal commonality requires the pooling of funds among multiple investors and an apportionment of profits from the enterprise to investors based on their pro rata investment in the pool. Although each investor may receive a different portion of profits based on their investment, their returns must correlate with their investment. If investor X put $100 in the pool and investor Y put $1,000 and the return is 10 percent, X would receive $10 and Y would receive $100. Conversely, if the enterprise does poorly and loses money, each investor suffers a negative return proportionate to their investment.

The minority view among the circuits is that commonality is satisfied by vertical commonality. Vertical commonality has two variants. Under both versions of vertical commonality, investors do not necessarily receive the same return relative to their investment. Investors are nonetheless connected in their dependence on a common promoter or manager. In *broad* vertical commonality, the common promoter or manager does not share in the returns of the investors. Put another way, the investor and promoter do not share risk; the promoter is compensated with a fixed fee. In *narrow* vertical commonality, the common promoter or manager does share returns with the investors and is exposed to the risk of the investment.

The First Circuit in *SEC v. SG Ltd.*[3] addressed the choice between horizontal and vertical commonality for the *Howey* test. SG Ltd. operated a virtual stock market game on the Internet. Investors were given the opportunity to invest in one of several virtual companies. SG represented to investors that it would set the price for the companies arbitrarily. For one of the companies, designated the "privileged company," SG promised investors that "[t]he share price of [the privileged company] is supported by the owners of SG, this is why its value constantly rises; on average at a rate of 10% monthly (this is approximately 215% annually)." Although SG disclosed that the share price of the privileged company could theoretically drop, it represented that the price was supported from several different revenue streams including (1) capital inflows from new participants; (2) profits from SG's commissions on each transaction; (3) the bid-ask spread for transactions in SG's shares; (4) manipulation of the market price for the nonprivileged shares; and (5) SG's ability to sell more shares. SG also provided investors with referral fees of up to 30 percent of the payments made by new participants brought into the virtual stock market game. When the scheme eventually collapsed, the First Circuit was called on to decide whether shares in the privileged company constituted investment contracts. As a preliminary matter, the First Circuit held that *Howey* required horizontal commonality, based on its view that that test best matches the facts of *Howey*, had been adopted by the

---

3. 265 F.3d 42 (1st Cir. 2001).

majority of the circuits, and was both ascertainable and predictable.

Applying the horizontal commonality test to the facts, the First Circuit noted that the investors' funds are pooled. The court then cited with approval two theories of horizontal commonality put forth by the SEC. First, because the nature of the SG game was in reality a Ponzi or pyramid scheme, the investors shared risks and profits to the extent that they all depended equally on "a continuous influx of new money to remain in operation." Second, SG's promise to support the privileged company's shares acted as a "bond" that tied together the collective fortunes of all the investors. Moreover, the court noted that SG promised the same 10 percent guaranteed return to all investors in the preferred shares. The referral fees paid for bringing in new participants undermined horizontal commonality; investors with the same number of shares who brought in different numbers of referrals would have varying returns. As the *SG* court wrote, "As long as the privileged company continued to receive net capital infusions, existing shareholders could dip into the well of funds to draw out their profits or collect their commissions. But all of them shared the risk that new participants would not emerge, cash flow would dry up, and the underlying pool would empty."

Is the *SG* court correct in focusing on the downside risk of investments in the privileged company's shares? Investors in *any* investment could be characterized as sharing the risk of insolvency. Upon insolvency, all participants potentially can receive the same −100 percent return. Yet this characterization means that all investments with multiple investors will meet the horizontal commonality requirement, since any investment may collapse and leave the investors with nothing. Perhaps what distinguishes the investment in *SG* from merely speculative investments is that *SG* was a Ponzi scheme. Ponzi schemes invariably fail when new money coming in can no longer support the returns promised to the ever-expanding group of existing investors.

The policy goals of the securities laws may support horizontal commonality. In *Wals v. Fox Hills Development Corp.*,[4] Wals entered into an agreement with Fox Hills to purchase a time-share interest in a condominium; Fox Hills also agreed to rent out the interest on Wals's behalf. Under the agreement, Fox Hills would attempt to rent out the weeklong interest in the time share, splitting the profits with Wals. Writing for the Seventh Circuit, Judge Posner held that the agreement with Fox Hills was not an investment contract (and therefore not a security) due to a lack of horizontal commonality. Because each person entering into an agreement with Fox Hills to rent out their time-share week could receive a different return based on the performance of their individual time-share interest, no horizontal commonality existed among the time-share owners. In concluding that horizontal commonality was required, Posner reasoned that the Securities Act "requires promoters and issuers to make *uniform* disclosure to all investors, and this requirement makes sense only if the investors are obtaining the same thing, namely an undivided share in the same pool of assets and profits."

Under horizontal commonality, each investor's return depends entirely on common factors (how well the pool does). Under vertical commonality, the returns of each investor are a function of both the common factors *and* individualized factors. When does vertical commonality merge with horizontal commonality? If an investor derives her investment return from 99 percent common factors and 1 percent individualized factors, are her informational needs sufficiently common with other investors to justify the imposition of uniform disclosure? What if the common factors account for

---

4. 24 F.3d 1016 (7th Cir. 1994).

80 percent of the return and the individualized factors account for 20 percent? Where should we draw the line?

One additional problem with vertical commonality is the possibility that an investment scheme may involve only one investor negotiating with a promoter or entrepreneur. Should a one-on-one negotiated transaction ever qualify as an investment contract? Recall that one of the rationales behind applying the securities laws is the need to overcome a collective action problem among multiple investors in negotiating for commonly desired information. Posner's opinion in *Fox Hills* implicitly endorses this view in focusing on the need for uniform disclosure. Unless offers are made (or potentially made) to multiple investors, a requirement of horizontal commonality, there is no collective action problem to worry about.

1.3 Expectation of Profits

The Supreme Court in *United Housing Foundation, Inc. v. Forman*[5] applies the expectation of profits prong of *Howey*. The United Housing Foundation (UHF) (and its subsidiary, Riverbay) initiated and sponsored the development of Co-Op City, a large housing cooperative in New York City. Prospective tenants in Co-Op City had to purchase shares in Riverbay at $25 per share. The number of shares required depended on the number of rooms in the desired apartment; tenants needed to purchase eighteen shares per room. Although labeled *stock*, the shares could only be sold back to Riverbay — at the same price of $25 per share — when the tenant terminated the lease. Tenants could not otherwise transfer, pledge, or encumber the shares. Although tenants voted on the cooperative's affairs, their votes were tied to the apartment (one vote per apartment) and not to the number of shares held.

---

5. 421 U.S. 837 (1975).

Were the shares of Riverbay stock securities? Focusing on the expectation of profits prong of the *Howey* test, Justice Powell, writing for the Court, noted that "[b]y profits, the Court has meant either capital appreciation resulting from the development of the initial investment . . . or a participation in earnings resulting from the use of investors' funds." In contrast, if the purchaser is motivated by the desire to consume the purchase, the securities laws do not apply. Here, Powell found, the motivation of the tenants was to acquire a place to live and not to make a profit.

Forman also offers guidance on the meaning of *stock*, which is included in the definition of a security in both the Securities Act and Exchange Act. The *Forman* plaintiffs argued that the shares they were required to buy to obtain an apartment were subject to the securities laws. Powell rejected the view that the Riverbay stock was stock for purposes of the definition of a security. He reasoned that the label *stock* was not dispositive. In Powell's view, Congress intended the securities laws to apply only if the economic realities called for the application of regulation. Powell also noted that the Riverbay shares lacked the traditional characteristics of stock. The shares did not carry the right to receive pro rata dividends contingent on the profitability of Riverbay; in addition, they were "not negotiable; they cannot be pledged or hypothecated; they confer no voting rights in proportion to the number of shares owned; and they cannot appreciate in value."

The expectation of profits prong of the *Howey* test distinguishes schemes in which people place money for investment from those involving consumption. One can imagine, for example, a group of people who pool their money together to purchase a ski lodge, along with a service contract from a company to care for the ski lodge. The group of people may all depend solely on the service company for the return they receive from ownership interests in the ski lodge. However, if the return expected is fun and relaxation, that is, consumption, putting money into the ski lodge will not meet the expectation of profits prong.

How does the expectation of profits prong differ from the investment of money prong of Howey? *Daniel* tells us that the investment of money prong also focuses on the motivation behind possible investors' decisions. If a person makes a decision that implicates the capital markets, the decision involves a security. If, on the other hand, a decision relates primarily to another market, such as determining how to earn a livelihood, as in *Daniel*, a relatively small investment component of that decision will not create an investment contract. Is it ever possible for investors to invest money without expecting profits? If not, the expectation of profits prong is superfluous.

Perhaps profits are defined more narrowly than is the investment of money. The Supreme Court in *Forman* defined profits in terms of capital appreciation and participation in earnings. Do financial instruments that provide only a fixed return (such as interest) qualify as expectation of profits? The Supreme Court answered this question in *SEC v. Edwards*.[6] The Court rejected any distinction between fixed and variable returns for purposes of determining the presence of profits. Promises of fixed, low-risk returns may prove particularly attractive for vulnerable, less sophisticated investors who may be most in need of the protections of the securities laws. According to the Court, "unscrupulous marketers of investments could evade the securities laws by picking a rate of return to promise."

Edwards limits further the separate importance of the expectation of profits prong. Perhaps it and the investment of money prong are really two sides of the same coin: The purchaser's decision in putting money into an instrument must be motivated by the promise of profit in the future, not by current consumption.

---

6. 540 U.S. 389 (2004).

1.4 Solely Through the Efforts of Others

Should the solely through the efforts of others prong of *Howey* be taken literally? Such an approach would drastically limit the applicability of the securities laws. Promoters are canny: They will respond to a plain language approach. One could expect unscrupulous promoters to avoid investment contract status under *Howey* by requiring that the investors each pick one orange per year as part of their agreement to invest.

The fact that an investor engages in minimal activities is irrelevant to the rationale for applying the securities laws to a particular transaction. If an investor depends primarily on a promoter, the promoter is likely to have a large informational advantage over the investor. Picking one orange does not give the investor insight into the marketing, cost structure, revenues, and future business plans of an orange harvesting company. On the other side of the transaction, investors will face a collective action problem in negotiating for and obtaining such information from the promoter, even if they are contributing a modicum of effort. To avoid this potential loophole produced by a literal reading of the word *solely*, no circuit court takes such an approach. Minimal effort on the part of investors will not exclude an investment scheme from the investment contract definition. Instead, the focus is whether the promoter or the investor provides essential managerial efforts.

Why the shift to essential managerial efforts? Even if investors contribute substantial effort to an enterprise, they may still be at an informational disadvantage as investors. Only if the investors are also helping to manage the business (and thus are not dependent on the managerial effort of others) will the investment be excluded from the investment contract definition. The focus on managerial efforts relates to the type of information that investors need to value an investment. Investors not involved in management are unlikely to have information relating to the business, its finances, and its future plans.

The focus on whether the investor relies on others to manage the business therefore acts as a proxy for the investor's access to information and thus for the investor's need for the protection of securities regulation.

How much managerial control must investors have to fall outside the range of efforts of others prong? What if investors have the power to control but do not exercise this power?

General partnership interests are ordinarily not investment contracts under the securities laws. Even if general partners do not actually exercise their power to control the partnership, the power (even if latent) to control is sufficient to find that the partners do not depend on the managerial efforts of others. Why focus on latent rather than actual control? There is an evidentiary problem in determining how much control individual partners exercised or could exercise. Particularly concerning the ability to exercise control, which might depend on the investor's sophistication, investors may downplay their actual sophistication in the context of litigation.

Another argument is that the power to control (and to obtain information) provides investors with a degree of protection. If a partnership's business suffers, the partners can protect themselves by removing the manager. The fact that the partners were in a position to negotiate for control may be significant for a couple of reasons. First, those who negotiate for control are typically in a position also to negotiate for disclosure, obviating the need to apply the securities laws to force mandatory disclosure. Second, those who negotiate for control of a particular investment are unlikely to consider the range of passive investments as alternatives, meaning that the transaction has fewer consequences for the capital markets. Under these circumstances, treating the investors' theoretical ability to control as removing the general partnership interest from the investment contract definition may make sense.

General partners have strong incentives to be active in partnership. Because general partners face unlimited liability for the debts of the partnership, their own personal fortunes are on the line when they participate in such a venture. In contrast, those who invest as limited partners limit their liability exposure to the extent of their investment. Courts therefore typically presume that limited liability partnership interests are investment contracts.

Consider the application of the *Howey* test to the limited liability partnership in *Steinhardt Group, Inc. v. Citicorp*.[7] Citicorp owned a pool of delinquent residential mortgage loans and real estate acquired through foreclosed loans. In order to remove the nonperforming assets from its balance sheet and to generate cash, Citicorp engineered a securitization of the assets. Citigroup created a limited partnership, Bristol Oaks, LP, to hold the assets; Bristol Oaks would issue both nonrecourse notes and limited partnership interests to investors. Steinhardt Group then invested $42 million in Bristol Oaks limited partnership interests (giving it over 98 percent of the limited partnership interests).

The Third Circuit focused on the "solely from the efforts of others" element of the *Howey* test. Following other circuit courts, the Third Circuit noted that de minimis effort on the part of investors was not inconsistent with the efforts of others prong of *Howey*. The efforts of others must be "undeniably significant ones" and "essential managerial efforts which affect the failure or success of the enterprise." Under the Bristol Limited Partnership Agreement, the consent of a majority of the limited partnership interests was necessary for the Managing Partner to engage in a number of activities related to the business characterized by the court as "crucial to turning the mortgages . . . into profit." The court found that the agreement gave Steinhardt, the majority holder of limited partnership interests, "pervasive" control over Bristol. Given the pervasive control, the court found that Steinhardt's returns were not

---

7. 126 F.3d 144 (3d Cir. 1997).

through the efforts of others and thus that the limited partnership interests were not securities.

What if the return to an investment flows from neither the efforts of an investor nor the efforts of the promoter or manager? Sometimes the significant factor influencing the return of an investment is some third factor, such as chance. The D.C. Circuit considered the importance of a third factor in *SEC v. Life Partners, Inc.*[8] Life Partners, LP, sold fractional interests in the life insurance policies of the terminally ill (termed *viatical settlement contracts*) to a number of retail investors. Life Partners established a pool that would purchase the life insurance policies for cash; the pool members received the proceeds from the policies upon the death of the insured. While the insured remained alive, the pool paid the premiums on the policies. After the sale of fractional interests in the pool to retail investors, Life Partners had no continuing interest in the pool. A separate escrow agent performed postpurchase administrative services, such as ensuring premiums were paid and collecting and distributing death benefits.

The court held that the fractional interest in the pool of viatical settlement contracts did not constitute investment contracts. The court ruled that the scheme failed the efforts of others prong of *Howey*. The court reasoned that while the investors in the pool were passive, the return on the viatical settlement contracts did not depend significantly on the postpurchase services provided by Life Partners or its agent. The "near exclusive" determinant of how well the pool performed was simply how long the insured survives. The court also ruled that the prepurchase services of Life Partners in assembling the pool would not, standing alone, constitute efforts of others for purposes of the *Howey* test. The court reasoned, "[I]f the value of the promoter's efforts has already been impounded into the promoter's fees or into the purchase price of the

8. 87 F.3d 536 (1996).

investment, and if neither the promoter nor anyone else is expected to make further efforts that will affect the outcome of the investment, then the need for federal securities regulation is greatly diminished."

Why should it matter that the return depends not on the efforts of a promoter but on some third, unrelated factor? In either case, investors are passive. Perhaps if the promoter is not the important factor in determining returns, an informational disparity between the promoter and investors is unlikely: Both sides of the investment are uncertain how long the insureds will live. Investors using the initial information on the pool of the insured will be just as capable of calculating the actuarial life expectancies of the pool as would the promoter. Lacking an information disparity, the disclosure required by securities laws may not provide much added protection for the investors.

1.5 Alternative Regulatory Regimes

Both § 2(a)(1) of the Securities Act and § 3(a)(10) of the Exchange Act cabin the definition of a security with the phrase "unless the context otherwise requires." Typically, this clause justifies the exclusion of instruments that would otherwise qualify as securities because of the presence of an alternative regulatory regime to protect investors.

Recall from *Daniel* the Supreme Court's view that the application of the securities laws to noncontributory, compulsory pension plans would serve "no general purpose" because of the presence of ERISA. Another example is provided in *Marine Bank v. Weaver*.[9] The Court held that a certificate of deposit was not a security, reasoning that Marine Bank, as a federally regulated bank, faced various reserve, reporting, and inspection requirements pursuant to the federal banking laws. Federal Deposit Insurance Corporation (FDIC) insurance

---

9. 455 U.S. 551, 556 (1982).

also protected depositors from loss on their deposits, making the repayment of the CD "virtually guaranteed." If an alternative regulatory regime insures the investor's return (as in *Marine Bank*) or the same level of protection as the securities laws (as in *Daniel*), the application of the securities laws provides little added benefit to investors.

What types of alternative regulatory protections give such assurance? The rationale of *Marine Bank* and *Daniel* would suggest that investment schemes promising full insurance or an adequate substitute for securities regulatory protection would qualify. Only another federal regulatory regime, however, will suffice. Courts have not found the provision of private insurance or the application of a foreign securities regime to justify excluding an instrument from the definition of security. Perhaps courts simply lack the ability to assess when investors are adequately protected. At least with respect to an alternative federal regime, courts may look to Congress to make the appropriate allocation of regulatory responsibility.

2 STOCK

Should the economic realities govern every determination of whether an instrument qualifies as a security? After the Supreme Court's opinion in *Forman*, one might wonder whether the Court, despite the enumerated list of items that qualify as securities in § 2(a)(1) of the Securities Act and § 3(a)(10) of the Exchange Act, might simply collapse the definition of a security into the *Howey* test, with its focus on the economic realities. Such an approach would treat substance over form. Regardless of the label attached to a financial instrument, the four-prong *Howey* test would determine status as a security for all financial instruments.

What would the downsides be of a unified approach under *Howey*? Transactions in common stock take place rapidly and in great volume on the organized stock markets. If each investor had to apply the *Howey* test for every transaction to determine whether the securities laws applied, transactions would be subject to a great deal of uncertainty. Investors must consider whether any of the other investors were participating in company management, thereby obviating the efforts of another prong of *Howey*.

In a case decided ten years after Justice Powell wrote the opinion in *Forman*, the Supreme Court, in *Landreth Timber Company v. Landreth*,[10] recognized the difficulties of taking a case-by-case approach to determining whether the securities laws apply. Several circuit courts had — following *Forman* — used the economic realities to fashion what came to be known as the "sale of business" doctrine. Under the sale of business doctrine, the purchase of substantially all stock of a corporation was deemed not to involve a securities transaction. In a purchase of all stock of a corporation, the purchasers did not expect to profit from the efforts of another but rather from their own direct control over the corporation. In *Landreth*, Samuel Dennis assembled a syndicate with several other investors to purchase all the stock of Landreth Timber from the Landreth family. The investment turned out poorly; Dennis sued the Landreth family for various securities law violations.

Justice Powell, again writing for the Court, held that stocks bearing the traditional characteristics of stock are presumptively securities. These characteristics include "(i) the right to receive dividends contingent upon an apportionment of profits; (ii) negotiability; (iii) the ability to be pledged or hypothecated; (iv) the conferring of voting rights in proportion to the number of shares owned; and (v) the capacity to appreciate in value." Powell noted that the stock in *Landreth*, unlike that in *Forman*, did possess the traditional characteristics of stock. Moreover, the sale of stock in a corporation is a context

---

10. 471 U.S. 681 (1985).

in which investors would reasonably expect the securities laws to apply.

In reaching his holding, Powell rejected the application of economic realities to the determination of whether stock is a security. Powell reasoned that the *Howey* test applied primarily to "unusual instruments" and not to common-place instruments such as "stock." The definitions of a security under § 2(a)(1) of the Securities Act and § 3(a)(10) of the Exchange Act enumerate a number of other items as securities, including stock. *Howey* was limited to determining whether an instrument is an investment contract, not the exclusive test for what is a security.

Powell also noted two additional problems with the sale of business doctrine. The securities laws anticipate large block transactions in stock that result in a transfer of control. The Williams Act, for example, covers tender offers for shares. There were also difficulties in the test's application: "The sale of business doctrine would also have to be applied to cases in which less than 100% of a company's stock was sold. This inevitably would lead to difficult questions of line-drawing."

Landreth halted the move toward unifying the definition of a security doctrine under *Howey* and the economic realities. The move in *Landreth* toward separately treating each of the enumerated items in the definition of a security was reinforced subsequently by the Court's approach to notes in *Reves*, discussed below.

3 NOTE

Section 2(a)(1) of the Securities Act provides that a security includes "any note, stock, treasury stock, security future, bond, debenture, evidence of indebtedness" and so on. Section 3(a)(10) of the Exchange Act provides a similar formulation.

Landreth demonstrated the Supreme Court's desire to provide certainty to the capital markets by treating stock — so long as it has the common characteristics of stock — as a security. Can we take a similar approach to notes, bonds, and debentures? Should financial instruments with the traditional characteristics of debt — a fixed maturity date, a fixed and certain interest payment, repayment of principal at the end of the maturity date — be presumptively treated as securities? After all, *stock* and *notes* are specifically delineated in the definition of a security in both the Securities Act and the Exchange Act. The statutory language gives no hint that notes should be treated differently than stock.

To treat notes and other instruments in this manner, however, would be an economic disaster. Consider the problems that would arise if courts did treat as securities any note, bond, or debenture that bore out the standard characteristics of debt. Suppose an individual decides to purchase a home using a bank loan to help finance the purchase. The resulting mortgage represents a debt agreement between the individual and the bank. If the home loan were a security, the bank would be the investor and the individual would be the issuer of the debt. Banks hardly need the protection of the federal securities laws from individual homeowners. Many species of consumer loans also fall into this category.

The Supreme Court in *Reves v. Ernst & Young*[11] addressed the issue of how broadly to define the scope of notes and other debt instruments for purposes of the definition of a security. In *Reves*, the Farmers Cooperative of Arkansas and Oklahoma used a broad-based marketing scheme to issue promissory notes payable on demand. Among other things, the Cooperative used ads claiming that the notes were "Safe . . . Secure . . . and available when you need it." After issuing the notes, the Cooperative filed for bankruptcy, leaving over a thousand

---

11. 494 U.S. 56 (1990).

holders of notes worth a total of $10 million feeling less than safe and secure. Understandably unhappy, the holders of the notes filed a class-action suit against the auditors of the Cooperative.

The Court held that the notes were securities. In reaching its holding, the Court stressed that antifraud liability under the securities laws was not meant to combat all fraud; moreover, the scope of the definition of a security was "not bound by legal formalisms." Mindful of the *Landreth Timber Company* decision, the Court then held that "notes" do not require the same special treatment as "stock." Despite the phrase "any note" in § 3(a)(10) of the Exchange Act, the Court explicitly rejected the view that "any note" constitutes a security. The Court also rejected the use of the *Howey* test to determine whether an instrument qualifies as a note, noting that *Howey* serves as the test for "investment contracts," not notes.

Instead, the Court adopted a version of the Second Circuit's family resemblance approach to determine which notes are securities. The family resemblance test begins with a rebuttable presumption that every note is a security. The test then provides a laundry list of notes that have been held to fall outside of the definition of a security. Among these non-securities are notes related to consumer financing, securing home mortgages, and certain short-term business loans relating to the working capital or current operations of a business. Notes bearing a family resemblance to these non-security notes can rebut the presumption that they are a security. The *Reves* Court provided factors to help determine whether a note resembled one of the excluded laundry list of notes. The factors included the following:

(1) the motivations of the reasonable seller and buyer of the note, in particular whether the seller (the borrower) desires capital to fund consumption or a commercial purpose (in which case the instrument is not a security) or the purpose

      is to fund substantial investments or for general business purposes (a security);

(2) the plan of distribution to determine whether there will be "common trading for speculation or investment";

(3) reasonable expectations of the investing public;

(4) other factors that reduce the risk of the investment (such as another regulatory regime).

Applying the reformulated family resemblance test to the Cooperative notes, the *Reves* Court noted that the Co-Op sold the notes to fund general business operations and that the purchasers of the notes sought to make a profit in the form of interest. The plan of distribution was broad based (offered to over 23,000 members and nonmembers of the Co-Op), and more than 1,600 people held the notes prior to the Co-Op's bankruptcy. Despite the lack of a trading market, the fact that the notes were offered and sold to a substantial number of people was sufficient to demonstrate "common trading" in the notes. As to the public's reasonable expectations, the Court pointed out that the notes were advertised as "investments," bolstering the impression in the mind of the public that the notes were securities. The Court also found an absence of any risk-reducing factor, such as an alternative federal regulatory regime. Moreover, the notes were uncollateralized and uninsured. Although holders of the notes could demand their money back at any time, the Court found that this demand feature did not sufficiently reduce the risk of holding the notes. The Court wrote, "just as with publicly traded stock, the liquidity of the instrument does not eliminate risk altogether."

The Court also addressed the exclusion in § 3(a)(10) from the definition of a security for "any note . . . which has a maturity at the time of issuance of not exceeding nine months." Although in theory the holders of the Co-Op's demand notes could get their money back immediately, the Court reasoned that holders of demand notes might not make the demand for many years. Because demand notes might not necessarily have a short term, the Court held that the nine-month exclusion under § 3(a)(10) did not apply to the Co-Op's notes.

Reves provides a framework for excluding consumer-related financing arrangements from the definition of a security. It makes little sense to force consumers (the issuers in a consumer financing arrangement) to comply with the mandatory disclosure, antifraud, and other aspects of the securities laws in the name of protecting lenders (the investors). But what about commercial loans? Why does the Court make a distinction between business loans made for commercial as opposed to general business purposes? Most commercial loans are either relatively small in amount or short-term in duration. Commercial loans include loans to cover working capital needs. A store selling goods, for example, may need cash on hand to pay its suppliers before it receives payments from customers. The relatively small amount of the loans combined with their short duration reduces the risk for the lenders. In addition, many commercial loans are negotiated in one-on-one transactions between a business and a bank, a situation posing few investor protection concerns.

How much does the *Howey* test differ from the *Reves* test? The *Reves* test is a multifactor balancing test; the *Howey* test, in contrast, requires that all four of its prongs be met. *Reves* also focuses on the motivation of the borrower (the issuer) in a way the *Howey* test does not; recall that *Howey* focused only on the investment motivation of the investor (the lender in the case of a debt instrument). Borrowers may want money for investment purposes; as discussed above, borrowers may also want money for consumption or commercial purposes. Although *Howey* does look at the presence of a common enterprise, this potentially differs from *Reves'* focus on the presence (or possibility) of a common trading market. Recall that the *Howey* common enterprise requirement looked at whether the investors received a common return (in case of horizontal common enterprise). Does the possibility of common trading for an instrument suggest that horizontal commonality is satisfied? Common trading implies that the instruments traded are identical in the returns they offer, making them fungible and thereby facilitating common trading. If so, they would satisfy the horizontal commonality requirement of *Howey*. On the other hand, it is possible for a financial instrument to exhibit horizontal commonality (for example, all investors receive the same return) without facilitating common trading, perhaps because the number of investors and the amount of the instrument sold is relatively small.

Does it matter that the *Reves* test and the *Howey* test are not identical? The *Reves* Court explicitly stated that a financial instrument may qualify as a security under *Reves* even if the *Howey* test does not apply. But what about the converse? Suppose a note fails the *Reves* test. Can a note that is not a security under *Reves* nonetheless qualify as an investment contract? Or does placing the label "note" on a financial instrument mean that the *Reves* test will be the exclusive measure of whether the instrument is a security? Does it matter whether it has the common characteristics of a note? The *Reves* Court's emphasis that the "enumeration of many types of instruments" in the definition of security not be made "superfluous," suggests that an instrument that is not a security under *Reves* may still be considered a security under the *Howey* test.

Suppose a potential homeowner puts together a syndicate of banks to finance the purchase of a (very big) home. The homeowner signs loan agreements, secured by a series of mortgages, with ten banks. Each agreement provides for the same interest rate, say 6 percent per year. And assume that the mortgages have equal priority in the event of default. In this case, the loan would likely fail the *Reves* test, given the consumption purpose of the homeowner. *Howey*, however, ignores the purposes of the issuer (the homeowner-borrower in this example). Consider the application of the *Howey* factors:

(1) investment of money: yes;

(2) expectation of profits: yes, interest payments;

(3) common enterprise: yes, each bank stands in horizontal commonality with the other banks;

(4) solely through the efforts of another: yes, the banks depend on the homeowner to pay interest.

Should *Reves* provide the exclusive test for determining whether an instrument with the traditional characteristics of debt is a security?

4 OTHER FINANCIAL INSTRUMENTS

The question of what is a security is important for at least two reasons. First, the definition of a security determines when the securities laws apply. Congress did not intend the securities laws to apply to all transactions. As we discussed in Chapter 1, the securities laws make sense for transactions bearing certain characteristics, that is, (1) transactions related to the capital markets; (2) in which participants face a collective action problem in obtaining commonly desired information; and (3) the intangible nature of the investment may pose large information problems for investors. The *Howey* test perhaps best captures these intuitions. The focus on investments of money with an expectation of profits limits the application of *Howey* to investment contexts related to the capital markets. The *Howey* requirement that the investment provide horizontal commonality in its returns implies that investors need common information and face a collective action problem in obtaining this common information. *Howey*'s focus on the efforts of another acts as a proxy for situations in which investors are not directly involved in the investment and therefore are at an informational disadvantage relative to the issuer.

The second reason why the question of what is a security is important is to help determine when newly created financial instruments should be regulated under the securities laws. The capital markets are not static. Although common stock and bonds are widely traded in the capital markets, Wall Street investment banks constantly invent new types of instruments. The constant evolutionary process within the markets requires a flexible approach to the definition of a security.

Great Lakes Chemical Corp. v. Monsanto Co.[12] applies *Howey* to interests in limited liability companies (LLCs). First, a bit of background. LLCs are hybrid vehicles combining aspects of a partnership and a corporation. Those who invest in a LLC, termed members, are taxed as if they had invested in a partnership (and thus receive only a single level of taxation, as opposed to corporate shareholders who face a double tax). Like corporate shareholders, LLC members enjoy limited liability.

Great Lakes purchased all of the interests in NSC Technologies Company, LLC — a manufacturer of a key ingredient for NutraSweet — from Monsanto and STI, Inc. (a wholly owned subsidiary of Monsanto). The membership interests in the LLC were determined by each LLC member's capital contribution. Prior to the sale to Great Lakes, Monsanto had an 81.5 percent interest and STI an 18.5 percent interest in the LLC. The LLC membership agreement provided that any net cash flows (essentially profits minus losses) were to be allocated first to pay back capital contributions pro rata and second to distribute any remaining profits pro rata according to membership interests. The membership agreement also gave the Board of Managers of the LLC control over the business and affairs of the LLC and the ability to determine the net cash flow amount. Individual members, in contrast, were given

---

12. 96 F.Supp. 2d 376 (2000).

no authority to bind the LLC or otherwise manage or control the business of the LLC. The LLC members did, however, have the power to remove the Board of Managers without cause.

Subsequent to the purchase, Great Lakes brought a Rule 10b-5 antifraud suit against Monsanto. The court faced the issue of whether the LLC interests were investment contracts under *Howey*. The court held that they were not. The court held that Great Lakes, because it bought 100 percent of the interests of the NSC LLC, did not have horizontal commonality because of the lack of pooling with other investors. In determining whether the return to members was through the efforts of others, the court distinguished general partnerships (presumed not to be securities) in which each partner typically enjoys equal rights to management of the partnership and, because of the specter of unlimited liability, have strong incentives to actively monitor the business. Members in a LLC enjoy limited liability and thus have more of an incentive to remain passive. Whether LLC members rely on the efforts of others therefore turns on the terms of the specific LLC agreement. Because the members could remove the managers without cause, which Great Lakes in fact did after purchasing all the interests, the court found that the return to Great Lakes from the specific LLC interests in NSC Technologies Company was not through the efforts of others. The ingenuity of the capital markets means that courts will be called on to make similarly detailed assessments of the economic characteristics of new financial instruments.

～ 4 ～

Public Companies and Disclosure

Ariel is the CEO of Triton Yachts, Inc., a builder of sailing vessels for the wealthy. Triton was founded twenty years ago, and it has grown to the point where it now has over $50 million in assets with only incidental liabilities. Since its founding, Triton has sold shares periodically to Ariel and her friends and family through private placements to raise capital for expansion. Some of those shares have been resold in the over-the-counter market, and the number of Triton's shareholders has grown, recently reaching 500. Eric, the CFO of Triton, is also in charge of the company's investor relations. Eric believes that Triton will soon need to do an initial public offering to raise the capital necessary to continue its growth, and he wants the company to be ready for that event. Ursula, a venture capitalist and yachting enthusiast, serves as a Triton outside director. She is also the chair of the board's audit committee.

We covered in the last chapter the principal threshold issue for the federal securities laws: the definition of a security. We begin this chapter by discussing a second critical dividing line for the federal securities laws: the demarcation between a public and a private company. Although some of the provisions of the securities laws, such as the Rule 10b-5 antifraud provision, apply generally to transactions in securities, the most intrusive and far-reaching regulations under the federal securities laws are reserved for larger companies with substantial numbers of shareholders.

The rationale for dividing companies based on the size of the company and the number of shareholders is that such "public" companies raise the greatest investor protection concerns. The large number of outside investors makes it more likely that at least some of the investors will be individual investors, with less sophistication and information than institutional investors. The large number of investors also exacerbates collective action problems among investors. Although each investor may want similar information on the company, its finances, and its prospects, no single investor internalizes the full benefit to the investors as a group from obtaining this information.

Companies making the transition from private to public encounter a host of regulatory obligations geared toward providing investors with complete and accurate information about the company. (The SEC sometimes refers to public companies as "Exchange Act reporting companies" or just "reporting companies." We use these terms interchangeably.) These regulatory obligations imposed on public companies are the main focus of this chapter.

The Securities Exchange Act of 1934, along with the rules adopted by the SEC pursuant to the Exchange Act, also determines what information public companies must disclose, how often they must disclose it, and in what manner. Moreover, these disclosure obligations are backed up by a raft of rules intended to ensure that Exchange Act reporting companies disclose only accurate information. Obligations are imposed on a variety of persons associated with the company — officers, directors, auditors, and lawyers — to promote the goal of accurate disclosure. In sum, public company status carries with it a complex and costly web of regulations.

1 WHICH COMPANIES ARE "PUBLIC"?

The Exchange Act has three trigger points that render a company "public" and thereby subject to the Act's provisions: (1) § 12(a), for companies with securities listed on a national securities exchange; (2) § 12(g) (as modified by Rule 12g-1), for companies with both $10 million in total assets and 500 shareholders of record for a class of equity securities (often referred to as the securities subject to § 12(g) registration); and (3) § 15(d), for companies that register to make a public offering. We discuss the registration process for a public offering in Chapter 7.

Triton, for example, has recently reached the 500 shareholder level, so the Exchange Act obliges Triton to register pursuant to § 12(g), unless Triton can reduce the number of its shareholders to below 500 before the end of its fiscal year. Companies typically do this through targeted share repurchases or self tender offers. Either strategy may put a strain on a company's balance sheet, forcing the company to reduce its available cash or take on additional debt.

What follows from public company status? One consequence from crossing any one of the three trigger points is that public companies must comply with the Exchange Act periodic disclosure requirements examined in more depth below. Section 13(a) of the Exchange Act requires that companies registered under either § 12(a) or (g) make periodic disclosures as required by the SEC. Section 15(d) applies the same § 13 periodic disclosure requirements directly to companies that fall within its scope. Similarly, the various provisions of the Sarbanes-Oxley Act and Regulation FD, discussed later in this chapter and Chapter 6, respectively, also apply to public companies regardless of the specific trigger that led to public company status. The fact that Triton has neither made a public offering nor listed on an exchange is irrelevant to its

status as a public company for Exchange Act reporting purposes; the application of § 12(g) alone is sufficient to make
Triton a public company.

Other consequences also follow from public company status. Here the path to public status matters. Companies that
trigger either §§ 12(a) or 12(g) must comply with the tender
offer and proxy rules in the Exchange Act.[1] Insiders of such
companies are also subject to the stock transaction reporting
requirements and short-swing profits rule of § 16 (discussed in
Chapter 6). Section 15(d) differs from the other two triggers in
that it does not subject companies to either the tender offer or
the proxy rules; similarly, insiders are not subject to the stock
transaction reporting requirements and short-swing profits rule
of Exchange Act § 16.

Obviously, these three categories will frequently overlap.
A company undertaking its initial public offering will need
to register that offering, the shares will likely be listed for trading on an exchange in connection with the offering, and the
offering is likely to be sold to more than 500 investors and to
leave the company with more than $10 million in total assets.
The listing standards of exchanges typically require a minimum
number of shareholders and assets. If a company is subject to
§ 12(a) or § 12(g) status, its § 15(d) obligations are irrelevant.
These overlapping requirements may also prompt companies
to do an initial public offering. A pre-IPO company may sell
sufficient securities to employees and others through private
placements to reach more than 500 shareholders of record. If
the pre-IPO company also has more than $10 million in total
assets, public company status is inevitable under § 12(g). One
of the principal costs of a public offering—public company
status—is no longer relevant. If the company is subject to
§ 12(g) regardless of whether it goes public, § 15(d) imposes

---

1. Due to space considerations, these topics are not covered in this book.

no marginal cost when the company does eventually sell securities in a registered initial public offering.

2 ESCAPING PUBLIC COMPANY STATUS

Once a company is subject to reporting status, can it escape that status? The obligations (and attendant costs) of being a public company include periodic filing obligations, auditing costs, internal controls, corporate governance standards, scrutiny from shareholders and analysts, and the tender offer and proxy rules. Moreover, many of these costs have a heavy fixed component. Many smaller issuers, for example, have complained about the high fixed cost of complying with the requirement that an outside auditor must attest to the adequacy of the issuers' internal controls under § 404 of the Sarbanes-Oxley Act. These obligations impose a particular burden on smaller companies, which do not enjoy economies of scale in compliance. Some companies will decide that these costs outweigh the benefits and choose to "go dark," that is, to terminate their public status.

Since each trigger alone leads to public company obligations under the Exchange Act, escaping from public company status depends on avoiding all three triggers. Consider companies subject to public company status pursuant § 12(a) because they are listed on a national securities exchange. Terminating public company status under § 12(a) is straightforward: The issuer must delist from the exchange, which may hurt the issuer's liquidity and send a negative signal about its future prospects. Even after delisting, however, the company must still avoid the § 12(g) trigger.

Now consider companies subject to public company status as a result of crossing the total asset and number of shareholder thresholds provided under § 12(g) and Rule 12g-1 of the Exchange Act. Section 12(g) focuses on equity securities, so a company can terminate its reporting obligations if its shareholders of record for the subject class of equity securities drop to fewer than 300 or if it has fewer than 500 shareholders and its total assets have been less than $10 million for three fiscal years. (Rule 12g-4, Exchange Act.) Reaching a level of assets below $10 million is unlikely to work as a practical matter for many businesses. In any event, that exit strategy entails a three-year delay. Can a company manage its number of shareholders to escape public company status? The answer is yes, but the effort to reduce the number must be bona fide. Once Triton has reached the end of its fiscal year with 500 shareholders, it can only escape public company status by buying out over 200 shareholders immediately.

Now consider companies subject to the public company status under § 15(d) because they have made a registered public offering. If fewer than 300 shareholders own securities previously registered in a company's public offering, the company can suspend its public company status under § 15(d) after one fiscal year has elapsed from the time of the offering (§ 15(d)). If the securities are held by more than 300, but fewer than 500 shareholders, the company can suspend under § 15(d) only if its total assets have been less than $10 million on the last day of each of the last *three* fiscal years. (Rule 12h-3, Exchange Act.) The assets threshold is sufficiently low that the company is unlikely to attain it short of bankruptcy.

The prospect of suspension under § 15(d) is not all that comforting for companies. A company may achieve suspension from § 15(d) in one year only to find itself once again subject to public company status once the number of its shareholders exceeds 300 (or 500 if the company also has had less than $10 million in assets for the prior three fiscal years).[2] Responding in part to concerns of foreign issuers eager to exit the U.S. market after the enactment of Sarbanes-Oxley, the SEC

---

2. See Rule 12h-3(b)(2).

provides for termination of public company status under § 15(d) through the operation of Rule 12h-6.

The following diagram summarizes the three triggers for public company status.

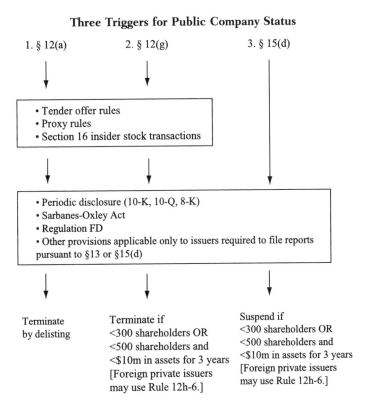

Three Triggers for Public Company Status

1. § 12(a)   2. § 12(g)   3. § 15(d)

- Tender offer rules
- Proxy rules
- Section 16 insider stock transactions

- Periodic disclosure (10-K, 10-Q, 8-K)
- Sarbanes-Oxley Act
- Regulation FD
- Other provisions applicable only to issuers required to file reports pursuant to §13 or §15(d)

Terminate by delisting

Terminate if <300 shareholders OR <500 shareholders and <$10m in assets for 3 years [Foreign private issuers may use Rule 12h-6.]

Suspend if <300 shareholders OR <500 shareholders and <$10m in assets for 3 years [Foreign private issuers may use Rule 12h-6.]

3 PERIODIC DISCLOSURE REQUIREMENTS

Whatever their path to public company status, public issuers face the same periodic disclosure requirements under the Exchange Act. Section 13(a) authorizes the SEC to specify the information that public companies must disclose and the form of that disclosure. The SEC has implemented this authority by requiring three principal forms to be filed by public companies: the 10-K, the 10-Q, and the 8-K.

The 10-K, filed annually, is the most comprehensive of the three forms. The 10-K can be combined with the annual report to shareholders required by the proxy rules under § 14. The 10-K is intended to give a complete picture of the company's business, with narrative items drawn from the SEC's Regulation S-K. Those items include a discussion of the company's business, the properties it holds, legal proceedings against it, the market for its common stock, biographies of its officers and directors, disclosure relating to the compensation of those officers and directors and the securities they hold, related party transactions, and accounting fees. Perhaps of greatest interest to analysts and investors is Item 303 of Regulation S-K, the section titled Management Discussion and Analysis of Financial Discussion and Results of Operations, commonly known as the MD&A. The MD&A section supplements the financial disclosures in the 10-K specified by Regulation S-X, and it provides management's explanation of the company's performance in the past year. Management is also required to share its expectations regarding "trends or uncertainties" that management "reasonably expects" will influence the company's results in the future.

The financial statements filed with the 10-K must be audited by an independent public accountant. This is the principal difference between the 10-K and the less extensive 10-Q, which is filed quarterly (for the three quarters other than the one for which the 10-K covers the quarter's results), updating the results from the firm's prior 10-K. Both the 10-K and 10-Q must be certified by the company's CEO and CFO, who must attest that:

- They have reviewed the report;
- To the best of their knowledge, it does not contain any misstatements or omissions;

- The financial statements "fairly present in all material respects" the issuer's results and financial condition; and
- They have reviewed the financial controls of the issuer and disclosed to the company's auditors and audit committee any weaknesses in those controls.

This certification requirement, adopted pursuant to the Sarbanes-Oxley Act, puts corporate officers firmly on the hook for inaccuracies in filings with the SEC. Understandably nervous, CEOs and CFOs at many public companies have adopted a process of internal certification. Lower level managers and division heads are required by their bosses to certify the accuracy of the results they provide to management. This process gives some comfort to the CEOs and CFOs who must put their own names (and fortunes!) on the line by certifying the 10-K and 10-Qs. Ariel, the CEO of Triton, will not be happy if some mid-level sales manager tries to pump up his year-end bonus by inflating the number of signed contracts for delivery of yachts. Such a deception would put Ariel at considerable risk of liability.

The periodic 10-K and 10-Q reports are supplemented by Form 8-K, which must be filed within four business days following certain specified events. Although the list has recently been expanded, events requiring relatively prompt disclosure through Form 8-K have generally been big-ticket items, such as bankruptcy or receivership, purchase or sale of assets representing more than 10 percent of the company's total assets, delisting, change in the company's auditor (and the reason for the change), restatement or intention to make a restatement, change in control, or change in directors or principal officers. The company may, at its option, use the 8-K to disclose anything else about which the issuer would like to inform its security holders.

Why not require companies to disclose *all* material information as it becomes available to them? Wouldn't that improve the informational efficiency of the securities markets (our central topic in Chapter 2)? Other countries, such as Canada, require companies to disclose material information as it becomes available to the company (with certain limits and exceptions). Congress, when it adopted the Sarbanes-Oxley Act in 2002, authorized the SEC to require real-time disclosure, but the SEC has not yet adopted such a requirement. Substantial hurdles block such a proposal. Most conspicuously, speed may come at the expense of accuracy. If haste makes the information sufficiently unreliable, real-time disclosure could potentially make securities markets less informationally efficient, not more. Moreover, real-time disclosure would require a substantial increase in the resources devoted to periodic reporting. Requiring companies to disclose as they happen all events material to their business puts a lot of stress on the mechanisms for delivering the company's internal flow of information. Of course, companies have procedures in place to bring information to the attention of the relevant internal decision-maker. If mistakes occur in transmitting information internally, the consequences may be a poor capital allocation decision or the launch of a new product for which customer demand is insufficient. If erroneous information is sent forth into the securities markets, however, the company risks a securities fraud class action. These concerns have kept the SEC from demanding more prompt disclosure beyond the specific items enumerated by the Form 8-K.

4 WHAT MECHANISMS PROMOTE ACCURATE DISCLOSURE?

Willful fraud in connection with a reporting company's security is a criminal offense. (18 U.S.C. § 1348.) But company disclosures can be rendered inaccurate by more subtle defects. Even if management prepares the company's disclosures in perfectly good faith, those disclosures will only be as accurate as the information available to management when the disclosures are being drafted. To paraphrase the old saying, "garbage in, garbage out": inaccurate information in, inaccurate disclosure out. To be sure, managers value accurate information about their business's operation because it helps them make intelligent decisions. If Triton's CFO, Eric, is not providing Ariel, the CEO, with accurate information about Triton's financial situation, Ariel will be hobbled in charting the company's future. Ursula, the outside director, will demand accurate information about the company's performance so she can fairly evaluate how well Ariel is doing her job.

The federal securities laws reinforce this internal incentive for accurate information flows. Private antifraud liability under Rule 10b-5 of the Exchange Act provides one source of incentives for a corporation to disclose only accurate material information. Chapter 5 examines Rule 10b-5 liability. The federal securities laws also impose a number of other non-antifraud requirements on reporting companies — and individuals connected to those companies — intended to encourage accurate disclosure. Although a detailed discussion of these other mechanisms is beyond the scope of this book, we briefly canvass several of these requirements.

4.1 Accurate Books and Records; Internal Controls

Section 13(b) was added to the Exchange Act in the 1970s in response to large-scale corporate bribery scandals. U.S. corporations were caught paying bribes to foreign officials from largely undocumented slush funds.[3] (Clear paper trails of bribery can be so embarrassing!) The reach of § 13(b), however,

---

3. Bribery of foreign officials was also subsequently made illegal by the Foreign Corrupt Practices Act. 15 U.S.C. § 78dd-2.

is much broader than mere bribes. All of a company's transactions must be accurately recorded, regardless of whether they reach the threshold of materiality to investors. Note, too, that the provision imposes strict liability: Purely inadvertent errors are just as actionable as are fraud and looting. Specifically, public companies are required to maintain books and records that "accurately and fairly reflect the transactions and dispositions of the assets of the issuer" "in reasonable detail." (Section 13(b)(2)(A), Exchange Act.) If Ariel, Triton's CEO, has a discretionary account she uses for entertaining potential purchasers of Triton yachts, reasonably detailed records must be kept of her spending from that account. A $3.00 cup of coffee probably need not be independently documented; a $500 dinner tab, however, should likely be seen as a different story. The standard is "such level of detail . . . as would satisfy prudent officials in the conduct of their own affairs." (Section 13(b)(7), Exchange Act.)

Not only must companies have accurate books and records, they must also have procedures in place to produce that laudable outcome. Section 13(b)(2)(B) of the Exchange Act adds considerable teeth to the quest for accurate books and records. It is also the wellspring of the "internal controls" requirements that have inundated U.S. corporations in recent years. That provision requires internal accounting controls sufficient to offer "reasonable assurances" that:

   i. transactions are executed in accordance with management's general or specific authorization;
   ii. transactions are recorded as necessary (I) to permit preparation of financials statements [in conformity with GAAP], and (II) to maintain accountability for assets;
   iii. access to assets is permitted only in accordance with management's general or specific authorization; and
   iv. the recorded accountability for assets is compared with the existing assets at reasonable intervals and appropriate action is taken with respect to any differences.

The bottom line of this provision is that all public companies are required to have internal accounting procedures of reasonably high quality. This is a goal that most directors would likely insist on as a matter of sound management, but it is backed up by the threat of legal sanctions with a strict liability standard.

The strict liability sting of § 13(b) is lessened somewhat by two factors: (a) § 13(b)(2) does not give rise to a private cause of action, so shareholders cannot sue for inaccurate books and records (although inaccurate books and records may give rise to a Rule 10b-5 cause of action if the other elements of that provision are satisfied); and (b) no criminal liability attaches for violations of § 13(b)(2). (Section 13(b)(4), Exchange Act.) Criminal liability is reserved for persons who "knowingly circumvent or knowingly fail to implement a system of internal accounting controls or knowingly falsify" a required book or record. (Section 13(b)(5), Exchange Act.)

Despite these legal requirements for accurate books and records imposed in the 1970s, corporate fraud continued. When the size of corporate fraud became sufficiently salient (that is, events at Enron and WorldCom in the early 2000s), Congress acted again to bolster the internal accounting controls requirements imposed by § 13(b). Three provisions of the Sarbanes-Oxley Act sharpen companies' focus on their internal controls. The first is § 302 of Sarbanes-Oxley (as implemented by Rule 13a-14 of the Exchange Act), which requires CEOs and CFOs to certify, in connection with the company's periodic filings, that they have recently reviewed and evaluated the company's internal controls. (Rule 13a-15, Exchange Act. There is a parallel certification provision backed up by criminal sanctions: 18 U.S.C. § 1350.)

The review process for internal controls takes on special urgency for CEOs and CFOs in light of § 304 of the Sarbanes-Oxley Act, which requires those officers to return bonus and other incentive compensation to the company for any period for which company is required to restate its financial results as a result of misconduct. Critically, misconduct is not limited to wrongdoing by the CEO or CFO; they are on the hook for misbehavior by their subordinates, as well, if the misconduct leads to a restatement for the company.

Although §§ 302 and 304 of the Sarbanes-Oxley Act have heightened the importance of internal controls, the cost of internal controls has ramped up sharply in response to another Sarbanes-Oxley provision: § 404. That section requires the company's external auditors to attest to management's assessment of the company's internal controls. The auditor now certifies not only its belief that the company's financial statements were prepared in accordance with GAAP, but also that it has independently reviewed the company's accounting controls. This review by the auditors of the company's internal controls does not come cheap; audit fees have spiked since the implementation of § 404.

4.2 Auditor Independence

The Sarbanes-Oxley Act also sharpened the definition of *independence* as applied to independent auditors. The accounting firms that perform a public company's annual audits have always been independent in the sense that they are not employees of the firm. The uncomfortable fact remains, however, that the company pays the audit firm's fees and has the power to terminate the relationship. That threat could potentially compromise the auditor's independence of judgment when it comes to accounting determinations susceptible, as many are, to more than one interpretation. Termination may be a salient threat for the audit partner in charge of that client because a large public corporation may be one of his or her few audit clients (sometimes the only one). Moreover, the partner may have the possibility of future employment with the client in the back of his mind. Finally, that partner's compensation may be related to the fees paid by that client. Until recently, this relation allowed for more subtle pressure than the threat of termination. Accounting firms were heavily involved in cross-selling their audit clients more lucrative services, such as financial consulting and tax advice. The threat to take that business away from the auditing firm gave the auditor's client considerable — and less conspicuous — leverage when the auditor and the client disagreed on the appropriate resolution of an accounting issue.

The Sarbanes-Oxley Act includes a number of provisions intended to bolster auditor independence. Most directly, it limits the other services that auditing firms can provide to their clients. For example, the external auditor cannot provide consulting advice to its client on the internal audit function. (Section 10A(g), Exchange Act.) The independence of the audit firms' individual partners is strengthened by the required rotation at least once every five years of partners in charge of an account. (Section 10A(j), Exchange Act.) Finally, the revolving door problem is addressed by prohibiting accounting firms from auditing a company if the company's CEO, controller, CFO, or chief accounting officer was employed by the accounting firm during the past year and participated in the company's audit. (Section 10A(*l*), Exchange Act.) If the partner in charge of the audit moves into direct employment by the client, the client will be forced to find a new auditor.

The securities laws also encourage auditor independence by regulating arrangements made within the client companies. Officers and directors of the client company are prohibited from misleading the auditor. (Rule 13b2-2, Exchange Act.) Moreover, it is now a criminal offense to destroy corporate audit records. (18 U.S.C. § 1520.) The audit committee, rather than the company's managers, is put in charge of retention, compensation, and oversight of the company's external auditors. (Section 10A(m)(2), Exchange Act.) The logic here is that management's accounting decisions are being scrutinized by the auditors; management should not have the power to terminate the auditors if they do not like the scrutiny. To ensure that the audit committee remains independent of management, only outside directors may serve on that committee. (Section 10A(m)(3), Exchange Act.) This means that Ursula, an outside director and the chair of Triton's audit committee, is forbidden from having any business relations with Triton other than her role as director.

The audit committee must not only be independent, it must also be informed. The auditors must report to the audit committee any "critical accounting policies and practices," any alternative accounting treatments discussed with management, and any other material written communications between the auditor and management. (Section 10A(k), Exchange Act.) To promote relevant expertise among audit committee members, the SEC requires companies to disclose whether any member of the audit committee qualifies as a "financial expert." (Item 309, Regulation S-K.) A financial expert must have either experience as an accountant or accounting officer or experience supervising an accounting officer or overseeing public accountants. This disclosure requirement is bolstered by listing requirements of the NYSE and Nasdaq, which require all audit committee members to have at least financial literacy.

4.3 Whistle-blowing

In addition to mandating accuracy and adequate internal controls and bolstering auditor independence, the Exchange Act also encourages the reporting of disclosure inaccuracies. The Exchange Act imposes whistle-blowing obligations on both auditors and attorneys. Auditors are required to have procedures in place to detect illegal acts that would materially affect financial statements. (Section 10A(a)(1), Exchange Act.) If the auditor detects an illegal act, it must report it to management and to either the audit committee or the board of directors.

(Section 10A(b), Exchange Act.) The board must then notify the SEC; if it fails to do so, the responsibility for notifying the agency falls to the audit firm. A similar obligation — minus the requirement to notify the SEC — is imposed on lawyers. (SEC Rules of Practice 205.3.) Lawyers *may* disclose to the SEC, however, to "prevent the issuer from committing a material violation that is likely to cause substantial injury to the financial interest or property of the issuer or investors" or to rectify the consequences of such violation.

The audit committee is charged with setting up procedures for dealing with complaints relating to accounting and internal controls. Whistle blowers are protected from retaliation by both civil and criminal provisions. The law does nothing, however, to promote the future job prospects of whistle blowers; having *corporate whistle blower* on one's resume is typically a nonstarter for future employment. Potential whistle blowers are therefore likely to think long and hard before revealing their employer's fraud.

↗ 5 ↖

Rule 10b-5

The Professors Pension Plan ("ProfPlan") has a multibillion dollar portfolio of securities invested on behalf of the professors who are beneficiaries of the plan. ProfPlan has recently been amassing a substantial holding in the stock of Logistique Solutions, Inc. Logistique is in the business of producing customized logistics software that helps companies make sure that their products are delivered where they need to be, on time and in the right quantities. Logistique's stock, which is traded on the Nasdaq, has been seeing substantial gains as more and more companies seek technology that will allow just-in-time delivery. Investors have also been encouraged by repeated assurances from Dax, Logistique's CEO and a substantial shareholder, that the company is developing technology that will allow its customers to use GPS technology to pinpoint instantly the location of all of their goods in transit. ProfPlan and Logistique's other shareholders were very disappointed, however, when Logistique disclosed its earnings for the last quarter, which showed a substantial slowing in revenue growth. Worse yet, Dax simultaneously disclosed that the GPS project has been substantially delayed because of difficulties in getting the system to run at an acceptable cost. In response to this bad news, Logistique's stock price plummeted by more than 20 percent on the day of the announcement.

1 SECURITIES FRAUD AND PRIVATE RIGHTS OF ACTION

Investors face a number of risks when they buy securities: recession, increases in interest rates, emergence of new competitors, technological obsolescence of a company's principal product, and so on. Generally speaking, investors are not entitled to compensation if any of these types of risk occur, even if their investment suffers a substantial reduction in value as a result. The reason for this general policy of noncompensation is straightforward. As we discussed in Chapter 1, investors receive a return on their investment in exchange for bearing risk; if they faced no risks, their investment returns would be much lower. Moreover, investors may reduce, or indeed eliminate, risks that are specific to a given firm by diversifying their portfolio of securities holdings.

For one risk, however, our legal system does promise compensation to investors: fraud. Why is fraud different? For face-to-face transactions, the answer to this question is relatively simple. Suppose Dax sells some of his Logistique shares directly to ProfPlan, but Dax lies about Logistique's past revenues. Lying imposes social costs in at least two forms: (1) investors spending real resources attempting to verify representations made to them (sometimes referred to as "precaution" costs), and (2) investors demanding a discount, or avoiding transactions altogether, if there is a sufficiently high probability of being defrauded. This second cost affects companies as well as investors. Not all firms commit fraud, but if investors cannot distinguish honest firms from fraudulent ones, they will discount securities issued by all firms. Honest firms will then face an increased cost of capital because investors will demand a discount to compensate them for the risk of fraud. Some truthful firms may then be tempted to lie themselves. This is the "lemons" problem: investors will demand an even greater discount as the proportion of fraudulent firms rises in the overall marketplace. This discount will affect all firms raising capital.

Damages serve two functions. By providing compensation, the legal system encourages potential investors to rely on representations. By requiring those who commit fraud to pay damages to investors, the legal system discourages fraud. Deterrence also encourages reliance on representations. With perfect deterrence, there would be no fraud; investors would rely on representations without discounting securities.

How much should those who commit fraud pay to ensure adequate deterrence? In a face-to-face transaction, a starting point would be to look at the harm imposed on investors. The harm to ProfPlan from the fraudulent sale of Logistique securities by Dax — the amount by which the price of the stock is inflated — is likely to correspond closely to the benefit to Dax from having committed the fraud. Dax is playing a zero-sum game at ProfPlan's expense; for every dollar Dax is able to get ProfPlan to pay over the true value of Logistique's securities, Dax profits by a dollar. We need to deprive Dax of his entire gain from the fraud in order to discourage him and others from committing fraud in the future. Indeed, because Dax may avoid detection and sanction, we may need to punish Dax *more* than the amount he gained from the fraud. Otherwise, Dax will still have an incentive to take the chance and commit fraud. Someone who keeps $100 of ill-gotten profits 10 percent of the time expects to make an average of $10 from fraud.

The question becomes more complicated when we shift from face-to-face transactions to secondary market transactions that may have been affected by fraud. Because investors will pay attention to what Dax has to say about Logistique and its prospects, Dax has the power to affect thousands of transactions to which neither Dax nor Logistique is a party. Investors who have been purchasing shares of Logistique in the secondary market are unquestionably harmed if Dax has made misstatements about Logistique. Dax, however, does not receive the corresponding benefit from the fraud in this scenario. The actual beneficiaries are the sellers of the securities, who receive a higher price for their shares due to Dax's fraud. Those sellers, however, are likely to be as ignorant of the fraud as are the victims and thus beyond the reach of antifraud prohibitions.

This mismatch between the perpetrator and the beneficiary of the fraud has two important implications. The first is that the role compensation plays becomes less clear. If investors are sometimes on the losing end of secondary market fraud and sometimes on the winning end, their *expected* loss from fraud is somewhere around zero. To be sure, for some investors the losses will not actually net out against the gains (and vice versa), but the expectation is what matters in assessing the effect of fraud on investor behavior. If expected losses are zero, investors are unlikely to take significant precautions against the risk of fraud, and they are unlikely to be discouraged from participating in the stock market. On the other hand, some investors may profit from researching a company's credibility, which may allow them to earn trading profits by selling a company short.

Compensation in the case of secondary market fraud is problematic for another reason. To the extent the perpetrator of the fraud is the corporation (through the statements of its agents), the corporation will pay the compensation to its investors. However, the corporation's residual claimants are its shareholders. If the corporation is not issuing securities, the corporation's shareholders will often be the principal investors harmed by the fraud. Thus, the economic effect of requiring the corporation to pay compensation may be simply to move money from investors' one pocket to their other. Such a transfer is largely pointless, but, worse yet, it is expensive. Plaintiffs' attorneys will take a cut of this transfer, ranging from 20 to 33 percent of the award. Defense attorneys working for the corporation may receive even more.

The second implication goes to deterrence. If the damages that Dax and Logistique must pay do not correspond to the benefit they derive from the fraud, there is a risk of overdeterrence, particularly if sanctions are not precisely administered. Given the volume of secondary market transactions for most public companies, the potential damages in a class action lawsuit are enormous, reaching hundreds of millions, in some cases even billions, of dollars. The prospect of such a punitive sanction could produce overdeterrence in one of two forms. Logistique could invest too many resources into ensuring the accuracy of its disclosures, hiring extra lawyers, accountants, and the like. Few investors would be willing to pay for perfect accuracy in disclosure. Alternatively, Logistique could reduce its voluntary disclosures. Public companies such as Logistique have the option of limiting their disclosures to those mandated by the SEC, such as the 10-K, 10-Q, and 8-K discussed in Chapter 4. In most cases, as we shall see, silence is golden under Rule 10b-5. If you don't say anything, you usually cannot be held liable for fraud. Unfortunately for investors, less disclosure also means diminished share price accuracy, because share prices reflect less information.

The enormous potential damages in securities fraud class actions under Rule 10b-5 have another important implication: Plaintiffs' attorneys may be willing to file a lawsuit even if they anticipate a relatively low probability of recovery. Putting to one side the costs of bringing suit, a lawsuit that alleges $500 million in damages to the class members may well be worth bringing, even if the lawyer assesses his likelihood of recovery as only 10 percent. The expected value of the suit is $50 million, and under these circumstances the defendant company is likely to see the logic of settling the case for some nontrivial sum.

Even when damages are less substantial, several factors may lead companies and other potential securities fraud defendants to settle litigation with only a negligible probability of success at trial. First, defending a securities fraud suit is often a very public event, leading to embarrassment for the corporation and its officers and directors. The defense of a suit may cast a cloud of suspicion over the company, hurting the company's relations with customers and suppliers. Second, companies and other defendants bear the direct costs of defending a securities fraud suit even if they eventually win, including attorneys' fees. Moreover, the discovery process is not fun for directors and officers. (Would you enjoy getting grilled by a plaintiffs' attorney during a seven-hour deposition?) Settling early with the plaintiffs (or perhaps more accurately with the plaintiffs' attorney driving the litigation), may save the defendants this cost and annoyance, even if they would win eventually at trial.

This prospect of coercive settlements has persuaded both the Supreme Court and Congress to impose limits on securities fraud actions intended to discourage frivolous suits. Those limits will be a central theme of this chapter. Rule 10b-5 has been subject to a number of narrowing interpretations by the Supreme Court, with the Court usually invoking the threat of coercive settlements as a justification. The classic statement of the Court's skepticism toward securities class actions came in *Blue Chip Stamps, et al. v. Manor Drug Stores*.[1] We discuss the Court's holding below in our discussion of who has standing to bring a Rule 10b-5 private action. For now, note that the opinion's rhetoric says a good deal about the Court's attitude toward private class actions. The Court voiced general concerns "that litigation under Rule 10b-5 presents a danger of vexatiousness different in degree and in kind from that which accompanies litigation in general." The Court worried that

> even a complaint which by objective standards may have very little chance of success at trial has a settlement value to the plaintiff out of any proportion to its prospect of success at trial

---

1. 421 U.S. 723 (1975).

so long as he may prevent the suit from being resolved against him by dismissal or summary judgment. The very pendency of the lawsuit may frustrate or delay normal business activity of the defendant which is totally unrelated to the lawsuit.

The Court also worried that discovery could be open to abuse through the "extensive deposition of the defendant's officers and associates and the concomitant opportunity for extensive discovery of business documents," creating "an *in terrorem* increment of settlement value."

Concerns about the costs of frivolous litigation similar to those expressed by the Court in *Blue Chip* animated Congress twenty years later when it adopted the Private Securities Litigation Reform Act (PSLRA) over President Clinton's veto. The PSLRA erects a series of procedural barriers to securities class actions. We will discuss those barriers in the PSLRA as we discuss the elements of the plaintiffs' Rule 10b-5 claim that they most directly affect. We cover the 10b-5 elements in this order: (a) standing and class representation; (b) material misstatement; (c) scienter; (d) reliance; (e) loss causation; (f) secondary liability; and (g) damages.

2 STANDING AND REPRESENTATION

2.1 Standing

Securities fraud actions alleging violations of § 10(b) and Rule 10b-5 are commonplace, so it is somewhat surprising that neither provision mentions a private right of action. This silence is all the more surprising given the explicit provision of private rights of action under §§ 9 and 18 of the Exchange Act and under §§ 11 and 12 of the Securities Act (we cover these latter two sections in Chapter 8). Indeed, one might have inferred from this silence that Congress did not intend to provide a private cause of action at all under § 10(b) and that its enforcement was to be left in the hands of the SEC and the Justice Department. The courts, however, saw the matter differently, taking the position that a right to be free from fraud implied a remedy to make that right effective. It is now well established that Rule 10b-5 provides a private right of action to investors.

It is also well established that this implicit right is available even in cases where it may overlap with explicit causes of action. In *Herman & MacLean v. Huddleston et al.*, the Court held that the explicit cause of action for fraud in a public offering registration statement provided by § 11 did not displace the more general implied cause of action that courts had found in Rule 10b-5 and § 10(b).[2] The Court distinguished the two causes of action on the ground that § 11 "places a relatively minimal burden on the plaintiff" but that the cause of action was "limited in scope." The Rule 10b-5 cause of action, by contrast, was available to the purchaser or seller of " *'any* security' against *'any* person' who has used 'any manipulative or deceptive device or contrivance' in connection with the purchase or sale of security." The broad scope of the Rule 10b-5 cause of action, however, was balanced against the considerably more demanding requirements that it imposed on the plaintiff, most importantly, the requirement of scienter (a topic we discuss below). Moreover, the Court concluded that a "cumulative construction of the securities laws also furthers their broad remedial purposes."

Although the scope of Rule 10b-5 is broader than the explicit private causes of action afforded by the securities laws, it is not unlimited. The plaintiff in a private action must have been a "purchaser" or a "seller" of securities. This is commonly referred to as the *"Blue Chip"* rule, after the case in which the Supreme Court adopted the rule, *Blue Chip Stamps, et al. v. Manor Drug Stores.*[3] The Court adopted the

---

2. 459 U.S. 375 (1983).
3. 421 U.S. 723 (1975).

rule in the course of rejecting a claim brought by plaintiffs who claimed they had been deceived into *not* buying shares in Blue Chip. The Court's rationale was grounded largely in policy concerns: expanding the class of plaintiffs to whom the Rule 10b-5 cause of action was available would multiply the potential for abusive strike suits brought solely for the nuisance settlement value.[4]

In making the litigation process more manageable, the *Blue Chip* rule leaves "holders" of securities without a remedy, notwithstanding the harm that they unquestionably suffer when a company that they have invested in commits fraud. The revelation of fraud at a company can substantially depress its stock price, but only those who purchased the shares while the fraud was ongoing have standing to pursue a Rule 10b-5 action. The problem for holders goes deeper, however; the Court has also held that their state fraud remedies are preempted by the Securities Litigation Uniform Standards Act.[5]

Blue Chip tells us that the plaintiff must be a purchaser or seller, but what about the defendant? Must defendants have purchased or sold the affected security? The answer requires interpretation of the "in connection with the purchase or sale of securities" language of Rule 10b-5. Imagine that Dax lies to ProfPlan about the past revenues of Logistique. ProfPlan subsequently purchases shares of Logistique directly from Dax. Note three aspects of this transaction: (1) the defrauded party (ProfPlan) is in contractual privity with the fraudster (Dax); (2) the fraud goes directly to the underlying intrinsic value of the securities involved in the transaction; and (3) Dax's fraud is reasonably calculated to influence the investing public. For this fact pattern — involving privity, the intrinsic value of the traded security, and the foreseeable effect of the fraud on

---

4. This requirement obviously does not apply to the SEC or Justice Department. *SEC v. National Securities, Inc.*, 393 U.S. 453, 467 n. 9 (1969).

5. *Merrill Lynch, Pierce, Fenner & Smith, Inc. v. Dabit*, 547 U.S. 71 (2006).

investor decision-making — courts uniformly hold that the fraud is in connection with the purchase of securities.

Does the "in connection with" language encompass other types of fraud that may affect securities transactions? Dax, speaking on behalf of Logistique, may tell market analysts that Logistique's revenue numbers are "looking up," when in fact they are declining. Dax's statement will drive up the secondary market price of Logistique's common stock, leading those who purchase Logistique stock to suffer a later loss once the truth about Logistique's revenues is revealed. In this case, note that (1) the defrauded parties (the investors in the secondary market) are not in privity with the party committing the fraud (Dax and Logistique); (2) the fraud goes to the intrinsic value of traded securities; and (3) the fraud is reasonably calculated to influence the investing public. Courts are again united in holding that this scenario meets the in-connection-with requirement of Rule 10b-5, despite the lack of contractual privity. Indeed, it is this lack of a privity requirement that leads to the enormous damages facing defendants in secondary market Rule 10b-5 fraud cases that we discussed above in the introduction.

What about other possible situations? The Supreme Court has provided few guideposts, the most recent of which is *SEC v. Zandford*.[6] Zandford was a crooked broker who stole from his elderly client, Wood, cleaning out Wood's $400,000 account. Zandford defended against the SEC's enforcement action on the ground that his actions were simple theft, not securities fraud. (Don't worry. He was criminally convicted in a separate action.)

The Supreme Court was not sympathetic to Zandford's argument. Looking at the details of Zandford's fraudulent scheme, the Court concluded that Zandford's misappropriation was "in connection with the purchase or sale of securities."

---

6. 535 U.S. 813 (2002).

The mechanism that Zandford used to misappropriate Wood's funds is important to understanding the Court's conclusion. Zandford wrote himself a check from Wood's account, knowing that securities would have to be sold to cover the check. Because Zandford did not disclose to Wood that he intended to misappropriate Wood's assets, each check that Zandford wrote involved a fraudulent non-disclosure. By not disclosing his intention to misappropriate Wood's money, Zandford breached a fiduciary duty he owed Wood (as Wood's broker). Because the sale of securities in Wood's account was a necessary step in Zandford's scheme to steal from Wood, his fraudulent misappropriation of Wood's assets coincided with a sale of securities.

Note the lack of transactional privity between the perpetrator of the fraud (Zandford) and the party selling the securities (Wood). Wood was in privity with the investors in the secondary market who purchased the securities from his account but not with Zandford, the broker. Moreover, Zandford's fraud does not go to the intrinsic value of any of the securities in Wood's account; instead, Zandford's fraudulent non-disclosure goes to Zandford's intentions with respect to his handling of Wood's account. Despite the lack of privity and no connection to intrinsic value, the *Zandford* Court required only that a securities transaction be a necessary step in the completion of a fraudulent scheme. If Zandford had simply stolen cash sitting in Wood's account without the necessary sale of securities, the theft would not satisfy the in-connection-with requirement.

Other challenging questions exist with respect to the in-connection-with requirement involve misstatements by public companies and their officers and foreseeability. What if a company's statements have an effect on the securities of another company? If Dax's statements about Logistique's GPS project affected the stock price of Novatec, Inc., a principal competitor, should Novatec shareholders who sold their stock have a cause of action against Dax and Logistique? If Logistique's union makes materially false statements about the company in an effort to extract contract concessions, should Logistique shareholders be able to sue the union? Are the effects on the stock prices in either situation foreseeable? Should this matter? The lower courts are divided on where the outer reaches of the in-connection-with requirement lie.

2.2 Class Action Representation

As noted above, the PSLRA adopted a series of provisions intended to make it more difficult to bring securities fraud actions generally. The PSLRA adopted another provision, a rebuttable lead plaintiff presumption, focused solely on representation in securities fraud *class* actions. Congress intended the lead plaintiff provision to align more closely the interests of plaintiffs' lawyers with the interests of their clients. Prior to the PSLRA, plaintiffs' lawyers typically recruited small shareholders as plaintiffs to bring claims. Courts would commonly award the lead counsel provision to the first lawyer to file a claim, which created a "race to the courthouse" after a company revealed bad news. Because the shareholders' claims were small, the shareholders typically gave the lawyer who brought the suit free rein to conduct the litigation and negotiate a settlement. (Lawyers would also sometimes pay kickbacks to the lead plaintiff in return for being selected as class counsel.) After a settlement was reached, the attorney would submit a fee request to the court for a fraction of the class's recovery, typically a third. Defendants ordinarily agreed not to oppose the fee award request, and courts routinely rubber-stamped the fee award. Critics charged that these circumstances led to over-payment of the class action bar. They also charged that plaintiffs' lawyers frequently settled too early to avoid the risk of having no recovery from which they could be paid.

The PSLRA's lead plaintiff provision substantially reforms the selection process for representing the class in a securities fraud class action. It creates a rebuttable presumption that the shareholder (or group of shareholders) with the largest financial interest among those that move to become lead plaintiff in a class action litigation should take on the role. (Section 21D(a)(3)(B), Exchange Act.) Congress hoped that enlisting a plaintiff with a substantial financial interest in the litigation would provide a more effective monitor for class counsel. Congress also hoped that the lead plaintiff would be an effective negotiator for the members of the class.

First, a brief summary of how the lead plaintiff provision works. Suppose that ProfPlan files a class action naming Logistique and Dax as defendants. The PSLRA requires ProfPlan to issue a public notice summarizing the main allegations of the complaint and informing the prospective members of the class that they can file a motion to serve as lead plaintiff for the class. (Section 21D(a)(3)(A), Exchange Act.) Any class member, in this example, purchasers of Logistique, can then come forward to file a motion to serve as lead plaintiff. The court will then select from among the class members who have come forward, following a presumption that the class member with the largest financial interest in the class recovery (that is, the class member who suffered the largest losses) should be the lead plaintiff. The court must also determine that the prospective lead plaintiff otherwise satisfies the requirements of Rule 23 of the Federal Rules of Civil Procedure, namely, the plaintiff's claims are typical of the class and the plaintiff can adequately represent the class. The PSLRA allows groups of shareholders to band together to act as the lead plaintiff, aggregating their losses for purposes of establishing the lead plaintiff presumption. (Section 21D(a)(3)(B), Exchange Act.)

This contest for the role of lead plaintiff also decides who will be the lead counsel for the class. The lead plaintiff is authorized, subject to the court's approval, to select the counsel for the class and to negotiate the terms of the lawyer's compensation. (See Section 21D(a)(3)(B)(v), Exchange Act.) In the *In re Cendant Corp. Litigation,*[7] the Third Circuit faced the issue of whether the district court abused its discretion by holding an auction to select the lead counsel. The Third Circuit overturned the district court's use of an auction, stating "there is no need to 'simulate' the market in cases where a properly-selected lead plaintiff conducts a good-faith counsel selection process because in such cases — at least under the theory supporting the PSLRA — the fee agreed to by the lead plaintiff is the market fee." If the PSLRA's selection procedure results in the selection of a lead plaintiff who is an adequate class representative, *Cendant* assumes that the lead plaintiff is best placed to select lead counsel and should not be displaced by the judge or an auction procedure.

The lead plaintiff provision and the lead plaintiff's role in selecting lead counsel have substantially reshaped securities class action practice. The impact of the lead plaintiff provision was initially muted, as plaintiffs' lawyers jockeyed to attract large groups of small shareholders. Although one large institutional investor may act as an effective monitor of class counsel, it is less clear that a group of individual investors cobbled together as a group lead plaintiff has the same effectiveness. The lead plaintiff group essentially recreated the prior regime's agency cost problems that had motivated Congress to adopt the law. These efforts to cobble together unrelated groups of shareholders were rebuffed by the courts, however; now lead plaintiff groups are generally limited to a handful of substantial institutional investors, and most cases have only one lead plaintiff. As a result, class action attorneys now spend less time worrying about who can be the first to file a lawsuit and more time courting large institutional investors, sometimes well before any actual litigation is filed.

---

7. 264 F.3d 201 (3d Cir. 2001).

One lingering concern with the lead plaintiff provision is that the interest of institutional investors has been limited primarily to the largest cases with the highest profiles. In these cases, the potential recovery justifies the institution's time and effort spent monitoring the litigation. Practice in smaller cases appears to be little changed from the pre-PSLRA regime. Another concern is the type of institutional investor that has come forward to seek the lead plaintiff provision: government-sponsored and labor union pension funds. Mutual funds have not come forward, perhaps because they are skeptical of securities fraud class actions generally or, perhaps, because they are reluctant to alienate corporate customers for retirement management services by developing a reputation as a vigorous class action plaintiff willing to sue corporations.

3 MATERIAL MISSTATEMENT

In Chapter 2, we discussed what types of information investors consider material. Recall that materiality acts as a threshold issue for Rule 10b-5 liability, screening out less important information from the purview of the securities laws. Courts will look at whether reasonable investors view the information as significant, given the total mix of information available.

Plaintiffs must also demonstrate the presence of a misstatement or omission, because Rule 10b-5 requires not only materiality but also the presence of deception. This is the main holding of *Santa Fe Industries, Inc. et al. v. Green et al.*[8] In *Santa Fe*, the plaintiff claimed that Santa Fe had committed fraud by freezing out the minority shareholders of a subsidiary company by paying them an unfairly low price for their shares. Santa Fe disclosed that higher appraisals of the value of the

---

8. 430 U.S. 462 (1977).

subsidiary existed. The lower court of appeals had held that plaintiffs may bring a Rule 10b-5 claim for "breaches of fiduciary duty by a majority against minority shareholders without any charge of misrepresentation or lack of disclosure." Rejecting the lower court's position, the Supreme Court held that, absent some deception, the plaintiff had no actionable Rule 10b-5 claim. Put another way, abuse of shareholders is not actionable under Rule 10b-5 if you tell them that you are abusing them! The truth — even if ugly — is *always* golden for Rule 10b-5.

Another knotty question is whether opinions are actionable misstatements. If Dax, the Logistique CEO, says Logistique is a "superb" company with "top notch" growth prospects, is this something an investor would want to know? Should investors be allowed to sue if Dax is lying about his true beliefs? Should a material opinion count as a misstatement?

The Court addressed this issue in *Virginia Bankshares v. Sandberg.*[9] *Virginia Bankshares* involved a freeze-out merger between the First American Bank of Virginia (Bank) and a subsidiary of First American Bankshares, Inc. (FABI). FABI, through its subsidiary, held 85 percent of the common stock of the Bank, with the remaining 15 percent held by minority shareholders. FABI's investment bank gave an opinion that a fair price for the minority shareholders in the freeze-out merger was $42 per share. The directors of the Bank solicited a shareholder vote on the merger, telling the minority shareholders that the merger offered them "high" value and a "fair" price for their shares. A minority shareholder, however, alleged that the directors did not believe that the merger provided "high" value or a "fair" price for the minority shareholders, but instead were simply doing the bidding of FABI, the 85 percent shareholder of the Bank.

---

9. 501 U.S. 1083 (1991).

Were the directors' alleged misstatements actionable? The Court distinguished the issues of materiality and whether there was an actionable misstatement. The Court acknowledged that director opinions concerning a merger are likely material to investors: "Shareholders know that directors usually have knowledge and expertness far exceeding the normal investor's resources, and the directors' perceived superiority is magnified even further by the common knowledge that state law customarily obliges them to exercise their judgment in the shareholders' interest."

Turning to whether false statements of opinion could be actionable misstatements, the Court split opinions into two parts: "Attacks on the truth of directors' statements of reasons or belief . . . are factual in two senses: [1] as statements that the directors do act for the reasons given or hold the belief stated and [2] as statements about the subject matter of the reason or belief expressed." Allegations of mere disbelief alone would not qualify as an actionable statement: "To recognize liability on mere disbelief or undisclosed motive without any demonstration that the proxy statement was false or misleading about its subject would authorize § 14(a) litigation confined solely to . . . the 'impurities' of a director's 'unclean heart.'" Nonetheless, the Court also held that statements relating to reasons or beliefs are actionable if such reasons and beliefs are capable of being supported or attacked using "evidence of historical fact outside a plaintiff's control." In the case of the Bank merger, the Court noted that a court could look to the Bank's assets and operations to establish whether the $42 per share merger price was indeed "high" and "fair" for minority shareholders.

3.1 Omissions and the Duties to Correct and Update

Suppose Dax, Logistique's CEO, lies to securities analysts about Logistique's earnings. If the magnitude of the lie is sufficiently large, Dax will have made a material misstatement that deceives the securities analysts. That deception will be transmitted, through the analysts, to investors in the market-place. But suppose Dax had instead simply remained silent (making for a boring meeting with the analysts). When are omissions actionable under Rule 10b-5?

Neither Rule 10b-5 nor, for that matter, any other part of the federal securities laws impose a general obligation for parties to disclose *all* material information. Instead, Rule 10b-5 requires that for an omission, even if material, to satisfy the deception requirement, it must occur in a situation in which the defendant breaches a duty to disclose the omitted information. What circumstances give rise to a duty to disclose? Rule 10b-5 states that it is unlawful to "omit to state a material fact necessary in order to make the state-ments made, in the light of the circumstances under which they were made, not misleading." In other words, asserting an affirmative half-truth imposes a duty to disclose the full story. The periodic disclosure system — embodied in Forms 10-K, 10-Q, and 8-K — imposes a duty to disclose certain delin-eated items. Rule 12b-20 then imposes a duty to disclose additional material information necessary to make the required disclosure not misleading. A duty to disclose may also arise out of state corporate and agency law. State law fiduciary duty imposes a duty on insiders and others either to disclose any material, nonpublic information they may have or to abstain from trading. (This is insider trading, our topic in Chapter 6.)

Two additional duties to disclose are worth mentioning here: the duty to correct and the duty to update. The duty to correct involves a statement that was false when made but that the speaker did not know was false. Is there a duty to correct that statement when the speaker learns the truth? The lower courts agree that there is and that the failure to correct is actionable under Rule 10b-5 (once the speaker learns that his prior statement was incorrect, thus satisfying the scienter requirement discussed below).

The duty to update, however, is disputed. The duty to update involves statements of fact or intention that were correct when made but that have been rendered misleading by subsequent events.[10] According to some courts, such as the Seventh Circuit, companies are under no obligation to ensure that their public disclosures are kept continually up to date, outside the periodic disclosure events, such as the 10-Q or 8-K. Other courts have disagreed, however, finding a duty to update in fairly narrow circumstances. The Second Circuit has held "that when a corporation is pursuing a specific business goal and announces that goal as well as an intended approach for reaching it, it may come under an obligation to disclose other approaches to reaching the goal when those approaches are under active and serious consideration."[11] The status of the duty to update has not yet been resolved by the Supreme Court.

Is a duty to update more problematic than a duty to correct? Consider the scope of both duties. A duty to correct is limited to information that was incorrect when originally released. In comparison, a duty to update could involve any previously disclosed information. Companies under a duty to update regime would face an ongoing and indefinite obligation to assess the accuracy of their previously disclosed information and to update the information as needed. A duty to update moves companies much closer to a system of continuous disclosure, a move considered but not yet adopted by the SEC.

But why does the SEC allow corporations to remain silent when in the possession of material, nonpublic information? If mandatory disclosure is good, wouldn't continuous mandatory disclosure be better? The corporation typically is the least cost

---

10. *Gallagher v. Abbott Laboratories*, 269 F.3d 806 (7th Cir. 2001).
11. *In re Time Warner Inc. Sec. Litig.*, 9 F.3d 259 (2d Cir. 1993).

provider of material information about itself. Disclosure of such information will improve stock price accuracy and curtail the incentives of investors to waste resources attempting to uncover information already known to the corporation. Finally, imposing a system of continuous disclosure of material information would dramatically limit the ability of insiders to use their positions to profit through trades. So why not impose a duty on corporations to disclose immediately any and all material information?

A continuous disclosure requirement could be extremely costly for companies. Determining materiality is fraught with uncertainty. A system of continuous disclosure would force companies to make such determinations frequently and with little time for reflection, a recipe for legal liability under Rule 10b-5. Corporations also need some degree of secrecy to conduct their business. If companies must disclose to investors plans for new products or entry into new markets before implementation, they may be discouraged from those plans altogether because disclosure will also tip off competitors.

3.2 Forward-Looking Statements

Forward-looking statements by a company about its expectations for the future receive special treatment under Rule 10b-5. Congress was concerned that earnings projections and other forecasts exposed companies to strike suits. After a drop in a company's stock price, discrepancies between prior projections and actual outcomes allow plaintiffs' attorneys to file suit against the company for fraud. Although the projection or forecast may have been made in good faith, juries (or judges) may fall sway to the hindsight bias, placing undue weight on the actual outcome in assessing probabilities. This risk of liability in turn may discourage companies from making projections or forecasts in the first place, reducing the amount of information in the marketplace and share price accuracy.

To address these concerns, the PSLRA creates a safe harbor for forward-looking statements (codified in § 21E of the Exchange Act and § 27A of the Securities Act). The safe harbor defines forward-looking statements to include projections of revenues, income, or earnings; statements of plans and objectives of management for future operations; statements relating to future economic performance; and assumptions relating to any of these projections or statements. A statement about a company's past fiscal year revenues would not fit the definition. But what if the company issues a statement such as "We believe that the challenges unique to this period in our history are now behind us"? Is this a statement about "future economic performance"? In *Harris v. IVAX Corp.*,[12] a federal district court held that such a statement implies future good performance and thus qualifies as a forward-looking statement.

Whether the forward-looking safe harbor shields a projection from liability is typically determined at the motion to dismiss stage. The timing here is critical. Recall that defendants may settle even frivolous litigation to avoid various costs of defending against a lawsuit, including the distraction cost on management, the cloud affecting a company's reputation, and defense attorney fees. These costs all increase as litigation drags on. Dismissing a lawsuit early on cuts these costs sharply, thereby reducing the defendants' incentive to settle frivolous litigation.

The forward-looking statement safe harbor shields statements from liability under three circumstances:

(a) if the statements are immaterial;
(b) if the statements are made without actual knowledge of their falsity; or
(c) if the statements are "accompanied by meaningful cautionary statements identifying important factors that could cause actual results to differ materially from those in the forward-looking statement."

---

12. 998 F. Supp. 1449 (1998).

The first prong is a codification of the bespeaks caution doctrine under which courts hold that certain forward-looking misstatements can be deemed immaterial as a matter of law because they are accompanied by cautionary language discussing reasons why the projection may not be borne out.[13] This is an application of the total mix approach to materiality that we discussed in Chapter 2. By including this provision in the safe harbor, Congress simply confirmed the continued availability of this materiality defense. The second prong raises the scienter required for liability for a forward-looking statement from recklessness (discussed below) to actual knowledge of falsity. If plaintiffs can demonstrate only that defendants recklessly made materially misleading forward-looking statements, the safe harbor protects the defendants from Rule 10b-5 liability. Finally, even knowingly false statements may be protected from liability under the third prong, which expands the bespeaks caution doctrine. Under the third prong, forward-looking misstatements are protected from liability if they are accompanied by "meaningful cautionary statements." To gain this protection, the identification of risks must be "meaningful." Can cautionary statements ever be meaningful if the defendants knowingly made false projections or forecasts? Without openly admitting that their projections or forecasts are false, the defendants arguably are omitting one very important meaningful cautionary statement: the defendants' forward-looking statements are a lie! But the structure of the statute makes clear that even knowingly false statements are protected from liability.[14]

---

13. See, for example, *Kaufman v. Trump's Castle Funding*, 7 F.3d 357 (3d Cir. 1993).

14. Some district courts have disagreed with our conclusion that knowingly false statements can be afforded protection by "meaningfully cautionary" statements. We believe that their holdings cannot be squared with the structure of the statute.

What is required to meet the meaningful cautionary language prong of the forward-looking statement safe harbor? A case that has generated considerable controversy with respect to this question is *Asher v. Baxter International Inc.*[15] Beginning in November 2001, Baxter International made a number of projections about revenue and earnings growth and cash flow for 2002. Baxter reiterated these projections repeatedly, until finally announcing in July 2002 that second quarter earnings would not meet expectations, which sent Baxter's stock price plummeting. That stock price drop triggered a class action alleging violations of Rule 10b-5, which Baxter met with a motion to dismiss invoking the forward-looking safe harbor.

The court addressed a number of questions with respect to the safe harbor. Must meaningful cautionary statements identify all of "the important factors that could cause actual results to differ materially"? No: If the company had identified "all of those factors, it would not be possible to describe the forward-looking statement itself as materially misleading." Do the statements need to cover the actual risk that caused results to differ? Again, no: "As long as the firm reveals the principal risks, the fact that some other event caused problems cannot be dispositive. Indeed, an unexpected turn of events cannot demonstrate a securities problem at all, as there cannot be 'fraud by hindsight.'" Must the cautionary language accompany the forward-looking statement? Again, no: If the company's stock trades in an informationally efficient market, the information from the cautionary language will presumably already be incorporated in the stock price. (If the market is not informationally efficient, the forward-looking statement would at least need to reference where the cautionary language could be found. Such language is typically found in the company's 10-K in the "Risk Factors" section.) In this case, the plaintiffs

---

15. 377 F.3d 727 (7th Cir. 2004).

had alleged that the market was informationally efficient in an effort to invoke fraud on the market presumption of reliance (discussed below). Having made this allegation, they would not be heard to argue that it was not informationally efficient for purposes of the forward-looking safe harbor.

All of these questions were answered favorably for the defendants. But the last question proved to be the defendants' downfall. Must the warnings include those that the company deemed "important" at the time? Here the court answered yes, and Baxter could not show at the motion to dismiss stage that it had disclosed these risks. Baxter's failure was that its "cautionary language remained fixed even as the risks changed." The plaintiff alleged that during the period in which Baxter issued repeated forward-looking statements, Baxter had experienced a sterility failure at a plant and other reverses, but "the forecasts and cautions continued without amendment." Consequently, discovery was necessary to ascertain whether or not Baxter had disclosed the most important risks facing its business.

Certain readings of *Asher* suggest that it completely undermines the value of the safe harbor at the motion to dismiss stage. How can the defendant company show what the important factors were at the time before discovery reveals the company's internal thought processes? Making it more difficult to use the forward-looking statement safe harbor to eliminate lawsuits at the motion to dismiss stage also diminishes the value of the safe harbor as a weapon against frivolous litigation. Without the ability to rid themselves quickly of strike suits, defendants may simply settle such litigation. This reading, however, probably overstates the breadth of the *Asher* court's holding.

A more reasonable interpretation is that the plaintiffs in *Asher* succeeded in calling into doubt the risk factors disclosed by the company based on the plaintiffs' specific allegations of developments in the company's business that were not reflected in those risk factors. These allegations undermined the defendants' argument that the factors disclosed were the important ones under the specific facts of *Asher*. In the absence of these specific facts, defendants generally need not wait for discovery for a determination of the important risk factors.

Consider whether any Section 21E issues arise in the following series of hypotheticals:

1. Logistique releases its balance sheet as part of its most recent Form 10-K filing. The balance sheet includes gain-on-sale receivable assets that provide the present discounted valuation of future expected revenues from several contracts entered into by Logistique.

Answer: Section 21E does not apply. Section 21E(b)(2)(A) excludes information included in a financial statement prepared in accordance with generally accepted account principles (or GAAP). Balance sheets are part of the financial statements.

2. Logistique, Inc., was late in filing its most recent Form 10-K with the SEC. Despite the late Form 10-K filing, Logistique moves forward with a seasoned public offering of common stock. As part of the seasoned offering, Logistique issues a press release containing earnings projections and assumptions. Assume that the earnings projections and assumptions are materially misleading.

Answer: Section 21E (and its counterpart in the Securities Act, § 27A) shields the press release from private liability. First, this is a forward-looking statement because it is a projection of earnings with a statement of assumptions (Section 21E(i)(1)). Second, the issuer is covered under the safe harbor (Section 21E(a)) because it is subject to the reporting requirements of § 13(a). The fact that Logistique was late in its recent Form 10-K filing is irrelevant. Third, none of the exclusions in Section 21E(b) apply; this is a seasoned offering, not an initial public offering. Lastly, this is a written statement. We need to check whether the issuer identified the statement as a forward-looking statement and included meaningful cautionary language (or alternatively, whether the plaintiff failed to prove actual knowledge on the part of the approving executive officer of Logistique as to the false or misleading character of the projections) (Section 21E(c)(1)). Note that the SEC could still bring an enforcement action for a violation of Rule 10b-5. Section 21E shields only against private liability.

3. OnTime, Inc., is a privately held competitor of Logistique. OnTime is in the midst of preparations for its upcoming initial public offering. As part of its selling efforts, OnTime distributes a press release touting its earnings potential and provides detailed earnings projections for the next five years. **Answer:**   Section 21E does not apply. Section 21E(b)(2)(D) excludes communications made in connection with an initial public offering from the coverage of the safe harbor.

4 SCIENTER

We have seen that plaintiffs must allege that forward-looking statements were made with actual knowledge that they were false to state a claim under Rule 10b-5. What state of mind is required to state a claim for a false statement of historical fact? At one extreme is strict liability: A completely innocent mistake gives rise to liability. At the other is an actual intent to defraud: The defendant intended to deceive the person to whom the statement was directed. One intermediate position includes negligence: The defendant did not take reasonable care to ensure the truth of his statements. Another intermediate position is knowledge: The defendant knew that the statements were false at the time they were made.

The policy trade-off is straightforward. The lower the bar for the state of mind requirement, the easier it will be for plaintiffs to state a claim and the greater the litigation exposure for companies and their officers. Prospective defendants are likely to respond to a minimal state of mind requirement by (1) taking greater care to ensure the accuracy of their disclosures; and (2) reducing their disclosures to the minimum required by the SEC. The first precaution clearly helps investors by providing them with more accurate information, while the latter clearly hurts investors by reducing the amount of available information, with predictable effects on share price accuracy and capital formation generally. A higher standard for state of mind, such as intent to defraud, encourages companies to be more forthcoming with disclosure, but it may also encourage more fraud by allowing more subtle frauds to go unpunished.

An evidentiary issue lurks in the choice of a state of mind requirement. Suppose we were to require actual intent for the state of mind in a Rule 10b-5 action. How would a plaintiff demonstrate actual intent on the part of a defendant? Short of a "smoking gun" memorandum signed by the defendant admitting to an intention to commit fraud, plaintiffs would be hard pressed to show actual intent. Few defendants are likely to volunteer that they willfully defrauded investors. Expanding the state of mind requirement to include actual knowledge ameliorates this evidentiary problem. If the plaintiff can show that a particular defendant stated one thing but had actual knowledge that the statement was false at the time it was made, this discrepancy may be used as an evidentiary proxy for actual intent to defraud.

The Supreme Court has had two occasions to address the state of mind required by Rule 10b-5. The first case, *Ernst & Ernst v. Hochfelder*,[16] dealt with the substantive standard to be applied. The second case, *Tellabs v. Makor Issues & Rights*,

---

16. 425 U.S. 185 (1976).

Ltd.,[17] dealt with the pleading requirements for scienter. Taken together, the scienter standard of these two cases poses a substantial obstacle for plaintiffs making Rule 10b-5 claims.

Ernst & Ernst arose from the collapse of a brokerage firm, with the plaintiffs alleging that the firm's auditors were negligent in failing to discover fraud by the firm's president. The question for the Court was whether an allegation of negligence alone (with no allegation of actual intent or knowledge) would suffice for a Rule 10b-5 action. The Court held that it would not, relying on its understanding of the words "manipulative or deceptive" and "device or contrivance" in § 10(b). In the Court's view, that language suggested "intentional or willful conduct." Instead of negligence, the Court concluded that § 10(b) (and hence, Rule 10b-5), required scienter, which it defined as "a mental state embracing intent to deceive, manipulate, or defraud." Significantly, the Court did not decide whether recklessness would be sufficient to satisfy this definition.

In the thirty-plus years between *Ernst & Ernst* and *Tellabs*, every appellate court to address the question concluded that recklessness would satisfy the scienter requirement of Rule 10b-5. Most appellate courts have construed recklessness as follows:

> Highly unreasonable omissions or misrepresentations, involving not merely simple, or even inexcusable negligence, but an extreme departure from the standards of ordinary care, and that present a danger of misleading buyers or sellers which is either known to the defendant or is so obvious that the defendant must have been aware of it.[18]

---

17. 127 S. Ct. 2499 (2007).

18. *Sundstrand Corp. v. Sun Chemical Corp.*, 553 F.2d 1033 (7th Cir. 1977).

Recklessness expands further the evidentiary proxy for actual intent. Those who can be shown to be reckless with respect to the accuracy of their statements will frequently have an appreciation of the inaccuracy and an intent to deceive. Proving this intent, however, may be a challenge for the plaintiffs. Allowing plaintiffs to demonstrate recklessness, therefore, will include many of these wrongdoers within the scope of Rule 10b-5 liability. Despite the universal acceptance of recklessness at the appellate court level, the Supreme Court has yet to rule on recklessness as a method of demonstrating scienter for Rule 10b-5.

In the PSLRA, Congress required that plaintiffs' complaints plead with particularity the facts giving rise to a strong inference of scienter. (Section 21D(b)(2), Exchange Act.) *Tellabs* afforded the Court its first opportunity to interpret the PSLRA's pleading provision for scienter. The question decided in *Tellabs* was "What counts as a 'strong inference'?" The Court interpreted *strong* to mean "powerful or cogent" and outlined a process for assessing the strength of the inferences to be drawn from the allegations in the plaintiff's complaint (and the documents referenced there). Courts assessing Rule 10b-5 complaints must consider the nonculpable inferences that can be drawn from the facts alleged as well as the inference of fraudulent intent suggested by the plaintiff. The plaintiff's theory must be "at least as compelling as any opposing inference one could draw from the facts alleged." This was a small victory for the plaintiffs: the tie goes to them. Nonetheless, the pleading standard is a substantial obstacle to going forward with a securities fraud complaint.

How does the pleading with particularity requirement discourage frivolous litigation? In theory, if we can select a set of facts that correlate with defendants more likely to have committed fraud, requiring such facts in the pleadings will screen out ordinary, law-abiding companies and corporate officers. For example, one could imagine a complaint in which the plaintiffs plead that the corporate officers committed fraud to boost the overall profitability of their company. *All* corporate officers, however, would like to boost the profitability of their companies. Such pleadings do not help distinguish among companies. On the other hand, some sets of facts are not universal to all companies. Consider pleadings showing abnormal levels of insider trading by corporate officers during the period of an alleged fraud. Abnormal levels of insider trading may correlate with corporate executives who have a heightened motive to boost (or lower) a company's share price to increase the profits from sales (purchases) or the company's stock. This heightened motive would be specific to the particular company with the abnormal levels of insider trading and not general to all companies.

The combination of *Ernst & Ernst* and *Tellabs* erects a formidable barrier for Rule 10b-5 plaintiffs. Plaintiffs are required to plead facts "giving rise to a strong inference" of recklessness in their complaint before they have access to the defendant company's documents and internal records and before they have had a chance to depose the defendant company's officers. (As noted above, the required state of mind for forward-looking statements is knowledge under the § 21E safe harbor rather than the recklessness required for misstatements of historical fact.) In conjunction with its pleading requirement, the PSLRA also imposes a stay of discovery, requiring that "all discovery and other proceedings shall be stayed during the pendency of any motion to dismiss" (subject to narrow exceptions to preserve evidence). Defendants typically will move to dismiss arguing that the plaintiffs have failed to meet the pleading with particularity requirement. In the absence of discovery before the motion to dismiss, how can plaintiffs come up with the specific facts necessary to meet the pleading requirement? To plead that a company acted with fraudulent intent, plaintiffs generally must rely on the company's publicly available disclosures, although they may get some assistance from whistle blowers and disgruntled former employees.

5 RELIANCE

Rule 10b-5 carries over the common law's requirement that the plaintiff must show reliance on the materially misleading statement, that is, that the plaintiff entered into the allegedly fraudulent transaction because of the statement. The reliance requirement is straightforward in face-to-face transactions: If Dax tells a representative of ProfPlan about the development of the GPS system, and ProfPlan decides to buy Logistique stock because it believes the GPS system is promising, the reliance requirement is satisfied.

In the class action context, however, the reliance requirement as it was understood by the common law conflicts with the requirements of Rule 23 of the Federal Rules of Civil Procedure. Rule 23 requires that "questions of law or fact common to the members of the class predominate over any questions affecting only individual members." Proving reliance by the individual members of the class would quickly overwhelm the common questions of fact, making a class action uncertifiable. Moreover, many — perhaps most — class members will not have heard the misstatement before investing. The class of investors who have actually heard or read the misstatement before investing is likely to be limited to institutional investors who have professional money managers whose job it is to follow corporate disclosures. Ordinary retail investors generally have better things to do with their time than read 10-Ks and corporate press releases.

Given this tension between Rule 23 and the reliance requirement of Rule 10b-5, something had to give if Rule 10b-5 actions were to be brought on behalf of a class. What gave was Rule 10b-5's reliance requirement. After the two Supreme Court cases discussed below, the reliance requirement has largely been a formality for Rule 10b-5 class actions.

5.1 Reliance and Omissions

Affiliated Ute Citizens of Utah v. United States[19] involved a case of fraudulent *non*-disclosure. Ute Development Corporation was organized to manage the tribal assets of mixed-blood members of the Ute Indian Tribe. The corporation issued shares to the mixed-blood members and hired First Security Bank of Utah to serve as the stock transfer agent for those shares. The corporation's articles provided for a right of first refusal, requiring tribe members who wished to sell their shares to first offer them to other tribe members. Only if no member was interested could the shares be sold to nonmembers of the tribe. This arrangement effectively created two markets for the shares, with the share prices generally higher in the nontribal market. Gale and Haslem, assistant bank managers, acquired some of the shares from tribe members both for themselves and for other nontribe members. They did not disclose to the selling tribe members the higher prices that generally prevailed in the nontribal market.

The Court ruled that the bank and its managers, Gale and Haslem, owed a fiduciary duty of disclosure to the tribal members with whom they traded. Failing to disclose the higher prices in the nontribal market was the omission of a material fact that violated that duty. So the defendants committed fraud, but did the plaintiffs rely? Requiring the plaintiffs to prove that they relied on a fact that was hidden from them seems like an impossible task. Recognizing the difficulty, the Court essentially waived the requirement:

> Under the circumstances of this case, involving primarily a failure to disclose, positive proof of reliance is not a prerequisite to recovery. All that is necessary is that the facts withheld be material in the sense that a reasonable investor might have considered them important in the making of this decision.

---

19. 406 U.S. 128 (1972).

So for cases involving the breach of a duty to disclose, reliance will be presumed if the omitted fact is material.

One can wonder whether the waiver of the reliance requirement in the case of omissions is irrebuttable. Suppose that Stanley, one of the members of the Ute tribe, must sell his stock immediately to Gale and Haslem to raise money to pay back unrelated debts. The need for cash is immediate, and no other buyers are readily available. Stanley, in other words, would sell to Gale and Haslem even with full knowledge that a secondary market exists for the shares trading at a higher price than that offered by Gale and Haslem. In such a case, the omission did not affect Stanley's decision to sell. Nonetheless, should we still apply *Affiliate Ute*'s waiver of the reliance requirement?

5.2 Reliance and Affirmative Misstatements

Affiliated Ute resolves the tension between reliance and FRCP Rule 23 for fraudulent non-disclosure, but it does not solve the problem in the much more common case of affirmative misstatements. To solve this problem, the Court mixed a dollop of procedural innovation with a dash of modern financial economics. The financial economics ingredient was the efficient capital market hypothesis discussed in Chapter 1, which postulates that informationally efficient markets rapidly incorporate all publicly available information about the asset being traded (the semi-strong version of the ECMH). Note that the information need not be accurate to be incorporated in the stock price; garbage in, garbage out. Inaccurate information is likely to yield an inaccurate stock price.

That insight underlies the Court's procedural innovation in *Basic Inc. v. Levinson*.[20] The procedural innovation is the fraud

---

20. 485 U.S. 224 (1988). We saw this case earlier, in Chapter 2, where we discussed its materiality holding for forward-looking statements.

on the market presumption of reliance. The Court reasoned that individual proof of reliance was unnecessary in an informationally efficient market because the misstatement was transmitted to the investor "in the processed form of a market price." The Court concluded that "an investor who buys or sells stock at the price set by the market does so in reliance on the integrity of that price."

To invoke this presumption of reliance, the plaintiff was required to plead and prove four elements:

(1) a public misrepresentation;
(2) materiality;
(3) that the shares were traded on an efficient market; and
(4) the plaintiff traded the shares between the time of the misrepresentation.

The first, second, and fourth elements overlap with other elements of the plaintiffs' cause of action, so the critical element for the fraud on the market presumption is the efficient market. Courts look to the trading volume and analyst following in assessing this element. Stocks traded on the NYSE and Nasdaq typically qualify for the presumption; stocks traded in the over the counter market and debt securities typically do not. (This may change as the debt market becomes more transparent.) This division creates the oddity that the stocks most prone to fraud — thinly-traded shares of small companies — are those which face the least exposure to class action suits.

The fraud on the market presumption is rebuttable. According to the Court, "Any showing that severs the link between the alleged misrepresentation and either the price received (or paid) by the plaintiff, or his decision to trade at a fair market price, will be sufficient to rebut the presumption of reliance." The Court provided the example of the truth on the market defense, that is, market participants were aware of the falsehood, so it did not affect the market price. Note the overlap of this defense with the question of materiality and, for that matter, with loss causation and damages (covered below). If the truth is already part of the total mix of information, the falsehood is unlikely to affect the market price, so it is not material, there is no loss causation, and the plaintiff has not suffered damage.

The presumption can also be rebutted if the defendants can show that the plaintiff bought or sold for reasons other than reliance on the market price, such as "antitrust concerns or political pressures." This rebuttal option has limited practical significance because it is not feasible to make this showing for every member of the class, but it does play a role at the class certification stage if the defendant can show that the lead plaintiff is subject to defenses not typical of the class. This argument is sometimes invoked against short sellers, that is, investors who have borrowed stock to sell in the expectation that the stock price will go down before they are required to cover their borrowing.

Basic's fraud on the market presumption revolutionized securities litigation practice, opening the floodgates for a deluge of securities fraud class actions in the early 1990s. This swell in the number of securities class actions undoubtedly fueled the angst over class actions that led Congress to adopt the PSLRA procedural devices intended to screen out frivolous suits. Congress did not, however, limit the use of the fraud on the market presumption.

6 LOSS CAUSATION

If a fraud falls in the woods and nobody hears it, is it really a fraud? That is the question posed by the loss causation element of Rule 10b-5. The idea behind this element is that the fraud must have actually affected the plaintiffs before they will be allowed to recover. Note the difference between loss causation and reliance (sometimes referred to as *transaction causation*).

Investors may listen to fraudulent information and change their investment decisions as a result (reliance), but loss causation would still be missing if the fraud was never revealed. In contrast, investors may be forced to purchase securities, due to a prior contractual commitment, for example, in which case the fraudulent information would not have been relied on in making the purchase. The investors may nonetheless suffer loss causation when the fraud is made public and the securities purchased plummet in value. A plaintiff must satisfy both elements.

How can an investor demonstrate loss causation? Suppose that Dax has made misrepresentations about the development of the GPS system. Before it is revealed that the GPS system has run into development problems, however, Logistique's software becomes the victim of hackers, whose attack cripples the logistics systems of Logistique's customers. The resulting bad press about Logistique's poor security protocols sends the company into insolvency, wiping out Logistique's stock price. Can ProfPlan recover its damages incurred because it paid too much for its Logistique stock even if the misrepresentations about the GPS system development were never disclosed to the marketplace and therefore did not lead to the stock price drop?

The answer is no. In *Dura Pharmaceuticals, Inc. v. Broudo*,[21] the Supreme Court addressed loss causation. Congress had previously acted in this area, requiring as part of the PSLRA that plaintiffs prove that the defendant's fraud was the cause of their loss.[22] As the Court recognized, the PSLRA largely settled the issue of who bore the burden of proof at trial on this element but that Congress had not resolved the question of whether plaintiffs needed to plead loss causation in their complaints.

---

21. 544 U.S. 336 (2005).
22. Exchange Act § 21D(b)(4).

In February 1998, Dura Pharmaceuticals revealed that its revenues and earnings per share were both lower than expected due to weaknesses in the sales of one of its existing drugs; a large drop in Dura's stock price (from $39 per share to $21) followed the announcement. Plaintiffs' attorneys responded with a securities fraud class action against Dura, with a class period that ran from April 15, 1997, to February 24, 1998. In addition to allegations based on Dura's revenues and earnings per share announcement, the class action complaint included allegations related to the regulatory approval process for a new asthmatic spray device that Dura had developed. Although the class period ended on February 24, 1998, it was not until eight months later, in November 1998, that Dura announced that the FDA would not approve the asthmatic spray device. Dura's stock responded to the FDA announcement with a slight drop the next day, but the price recovered almost fully within a week.

The Court focused on whether the plaintiffs met their burden of proof to demonstrate loss causation with respect to the regulatory approval process for the asthmatic spray device. If the market had responded with a large stock price drop immediately following the first public revelation of the FDA's denial of approval for the spray device, the plaintiffs could easily have demonstrated loss causation (due to the loss in their share value following the stock price drop). Dura's stock price decline posed a more difficult scenario for the plaintiffs: Note the mismatch between the stock price drop (in February 1998) and the allegation of fraud with respect to the asthmatic spray device (failure to gain FDA approval became known to the market in November 1998). Despite the lack of a significant stock price drop in November 1998, the plaintiffs argued that the mere purchase of stock at an inflated price resulted in harm to investors and therefore met the loss causation requirement of Rule 10b-5. The Ninth Circuit court accepted the plaintiffs' loss causation argument and held that the plaintiffs were harmed when they purchased their Dura shares at an inflated price.

The Supreme Court rejected the Ninth Circuit's position, holding that the mere allegation of inflated prices due to a misrepresentation or omission is not sufficient to plead loss causation. The Court reasoned that the purchaser of such inflated shares might have sold at an equally inflated price before the revelation of the bad news. Moreover, if the purchaser sold at a lower price after the truth was revealed, "that lower price may reflect, not the earlier misrepresentation, but changed economic circumstances, changed investor expectations, new industry-specific or firm-specific facts, conditions, or other events, which taken separately or together account for some or all of that lower price." To ignore this possibility, the Court argued, would be to use a Rule 10b-5 fraud action "to provide investors with broad insurance against market losses," rather than to protect them "against those economic losses that misrepresentations actually cause." Allowing plaintiffs to proceed with claims that failed to allege the requisite causal link would be an invitation to strike suits filed solely for their settlement value.

Why don't we insure investors against market losses? One answer is provided by Judge Richard Posner in *Bastian v. Petren Resources Corporation*[23] on the need for a loss causation requirement: "No social purpose would be served by encouraging everyone who suffers an investment loss because of an unanticipated change in market conditions to pick through offering memoranda with a fine-tooth comb in the hope of uncovering a misrepresentation."

The Supreme Court is right that it makes little sense to compensate people who have not been harmed by the fraud, but that logic only works if compensation is the driving force for secondary market class actions. If deterrence is the main point

---

23. 892 F.2d 680 (7th Cir. 1990).

(as we suggested in the introduction to this chapter), perhaps sanctioning defendants for fraud should not turn on the probabilistic question of whether anyone was actually harmed by that fraud. Put another way, if someone commits a fraud, why not throw the book at them? Making those who commit fraud pay for a crushing amount of unrelated losses will surely deter even the most diehard among them from telling a lie.

This crush-out view of deterrence has problems. If we are certain that a defendant has committed fraud, then imposing extremely large damages will stop the fraud. But can we be certain? Judges and juries make mistakes. Given that scienter embodies not only actual intent but also reckless conduct, even those without any actual intent to commit fraud may face exorbitant damages in the absence of a loss causation requirement. Companies and individuals may respond by taking excessive precautions in ensuring the accuracy of every piece of information they release. Although some amount of precaution is valuable, perfect accuracy is not cost justified. Spending $1,000 to produce $100 worth of improved accuracy is a waste.

Loss causation also serves as an important backstop for materiality determinations. Recall that the materiality requirement screens out misstatements and omissions deemed too small to concern investors. Excluding immaterial information from the scope of Rule 10b-5 allows companies to focus on improving the accuracy of the information that investors care about without wasting resources on reporting trivial information accurately. Determining materiality is often not an easy task. Courts, as we discussed in Chapter 2, often turn to qualitative factors, such as management integrity, as well as to event studies that reveal market assessments of materiality through stock price reactions to fraud revelations. If courts did not rely on event studies, we might worry that error-prone judges could get the materiality assessment wrong. Requiring a securities price drop to demonstrate loss causation ensures that, regardless of how materiality is determined, the market must deem the fraud at issue to be important information before a Rule 10b-5 fraud suit can move forward.

7 SECONDARY LIABILITY

A question vital to both the deterrence and compensation functions of Rule 10b-5 is *who* can be liable to pay damages under the provision. The broader the range of potential defendants, the greater the deterrent effect of Rule 10b-5 and the likelier that plaintiffs will be compensated for their losses. Placing liability on a gatekeeper, such as a corporate auditor, may give the auditor an extra incentive to take care in ensuring the accuracy of audited financial statements. The downside, however, is that defendants may be brought in who may be lacking in culpability and who may not have had any realistic opportunity to prevent the fraud. Not all third parties make good gatekeepers. We could impose liability for all fraud on Bill Gates, for example; such a rule would do little to promote deterrence, although it would provide greater compensation.

The Supreme Court grappled with the scope of secondary liability under Rule 10b-5 in *Central Bank of Denver v. First Interstate Bank of Denver.*[24] *Central Bank* involved bonds issued in a series of offerings to finance public improvements in a planned residential and commercial development. The bonds were secured by liens on the land to be developed. As a result, the value of that land was critical to assessing the default risk of the bonds. The defendant, Central Bank, as the indenture trustee for the bonds, was charged with enforcing the covenants in the bonds, including the requirement that the value of the land securing the bonds be equal to 160 percent of the indebtedness. Questions were raised about the appraisal supplied by the developer to support the

---

24. 511 U.S. 164 (1994).

valuation of the collateral, but Central Bank failed to secure an independent appraisal before the second offering of the bonds issued. The issuer thereafter defaulted on that series of bonds.

The plaintiffs sought to bring Central Bank into the ensuing lawsuit, alleging that Central Bank had "aided and abetted" the fraud by the bonds' issuer. The Court had little difficulty in concluding that § 10(b) did not prohibit such conduct: "The statute prohibits only the making of a material misstatement (or omission) or the commission of a manipulative act. The proscription does not include giving aid to a person who commits a manipulative or deceptive act." The Court's reading of the statute was reinforced by reference to the explicit causes of action under the securities laws, none of which mentioned aiding and abetting. The Court also noted that allowing aiding and abetting as a cause of action would tend to undermine the reliance requirement of Rule 10b-5, as plaintiffs could not be said to have relied on the defendant's actions. Finally, the Court noted that aiding and abetting tended to promote "uncertainty and excessive litigation," as secondary defendants were dragged into lawsuits in an effort to extract settlements from them.

The *Central Bank* Court did not foreclose all liability against third-party defendants. Rather, if the third-party defendants themselves were primary violators of Rule 10b-5 and plaintiffs are able to demonstrate all elements of Rule 10b-5 liability against such defendants, then liability would attach. The Court wrote that plaintiffs could still bring a Rule 10b-5 action against defendants if they "employ[] a manipulative device or make[] a material statement (or omission) on which a purchaser or seller securities relies."

In *Stoneridge Investment v. Scientific-Atlanta, Inc., et al.* __ U.S. __ (2008), the Supreme Court held that plaintiffs must show reliance on the conduct of a secondary actor in order to state a Rule 10b-5 claim against them. The secondary defendants in *Stoneridge* were equipment suppliers alleged to have facilitated — via sham transactions — accounting fraud by one of their customers. The Court deemed the suppliers' business transactions, even if deceptive, too remote to have induced reliance by investors.

Despite *Central Bank*'s rejection of aiding and abetting, some areas of secondary liability remain. Even under the "bright line" rule, accountants are liable for their certifications in audited financial statements. A principal who makes a fraudulent statement through an agent can also be held liable. Logistique is thus liable for statements made by its agent, Dax. And "control persons" can be liable under § 20(a) of the Exchange Act, subject to a defense if "the controlling person acted in good faith and did not directly or indirectly induce the act or acts constituting the violation or cause of action." Some courts require the plaintiff to show that the control person had "culpable participation" in the fraud, while others put the burden of disproving this element on the defendant.

8 DAMAGES

8.1 Face-to-Face Damages

A broad range of Rule 10b-5 damages are available in face-to-face transactions. Section 28(a) of the Exchange Act explicitly excludes punitive damages and double recovery, but the usual remedies of both law and equity are available, including rescission, restitution, and the benefit of the bargain measure. Restitution requires the defendant to give up his profits. This remedy, also known as disgorgement, is the one typically used in insider trading cases, whether brought by a private plaintiff or by the SEC. Rescission allows the plaintiff to undo the transaction by returning the securities in exchange for the return of the purchase price.

Rescission is sometimes used when the fraud does not go to the underlying value of a security but rather figures in the inducement of the transaction itself. A broker, for example, may fraudulently induce an investor to purchase riskier securities than the investor wishes to hold. In such a situation, the securities market value may equal their price at the time of purchase. Nonetheless, the fraud is in the very purchase of the securities, and courts will often apply the rescission measure.

The benefit of the bargain measure, a typical remedy in contracts, is the difference between the value received and the value promised. It is rarely used in Rule 10b-5 cases, however, because of the difficulty of establishing the value promised in the purchase of a security.

8.2 Open Market Damages

The most common measure of damages in Rule 10b-5 suits is the out-of-pocket measure. The traditional measure used in tort law, the out-of-pocket measure, is simply the difference between the price paid for the security and its value at the time of purchase if undistorted by fraud. The price at the time of purchase is easy enough to determine. But what about the value at the time of purchase if fraud had not affected the market price?

For securities fraud class actions involving the secondary market price of a stock, the calculation of damages typically makes use of a *value line*, determined by the expert witnesses for the parties. The value line is derived from the amount the stock price changed when the fraud was first publicly revealed to the marketplace. This change is used as a measure of the fraud's impact on the stock value. Working backward in time, the value line is established by using the change measure to adjust the stock price. Consider the following example: Suppose Logistique's stock price drops by $20 per share when information on

Dax's fraud is first revealed to the marketplace. This $20 per share drop is used to create a value line by adjusting the stock price for Logistique downward, working backward from the date the information was revealed to the beginning of the class period. In our simple example, the stock price is adjusted just once for the $20 drop in value. Note that the adjustment to generate the value line is not necessarily a static amount because the truth may have been revealed to the market in dribs and drabs and not all at once on one date, as in our example. Once the value line is generated, damages for a security traded on any particular day during the class period can be calculated as the difference between the transaction price and the value line for that day.

Another subject for the expert witnesses will be an estimate of share turnover. The volume of trading on any given day is easily ascertained, but the amount of trading done by in-and-out traders must be estimated. In-and-out traders are investors who bought during the class period but who also sold before the revelation of the fraud and who are thus not eligible for class damages under the loss causation rule of *Dura*. The claims process will sort out who is actually entitled to collect damages, but the parties will want to have their own estimates for settlement negotiation purposes. Differing estimates of the turnover of shares can lead to wildly differing damages calculations.

Congress limited the damages available in open market fraud cases when it enacted the PSLRA. Section 21D(e)(1) of the Exchange Act states that damages

> shall not exceed the difference between the purchase or sale price paid or received, as appropriate, by the plaintiff for the subject security and the mean trading price of that security during the 90-day period beginning on the date on which the information correcting the misstatement or omission that is the basis for the action is disseminated to the market.

The rationale for this bounce back provision is that the market may initially overreact to the revelation of the fraud and that the market price may recover shortly thereafter. Congress did not think that investors should be compensated for losses that were only temporary.

As we discussed at the start of this chapter, measuring damages by the overall loss to those secondary market investors who purchased securities affected by fraud is questionable from a policy perspective. What alternatives exist to the present open market measure of damages? One could imagine simply imposing a schedule of fines on defendants involved with secondary market fraud. But any system of fines will be imprecise. Secondary market frauds vary in the amount of benefits achieved by fraud perpetrators and in probability of detection. Optimal deterrence requires calibrating fines to both the fraud benefit and the probability of its detection. Another possibility would be to impose a cap on secondary market damages. (The Canadians do this, limiting damages to 5 percent of a company's market capitalization.) Such a cap would be just as arbitrary, however, and might underdeter truly egregious secondary market frauds. Despite the exorbitant levels of current secondary market damages, finding an alternative measure for sanctions is not easy.

8.3 Proportionate Liability

Another reform introduced by the PSLRA is proportionate liability for certain defendants. The general rule under Rule 10b-5 is joint-and-several liability, that is, each defendant can be held accountable for the entire damages award. (A defendant made to pay the entire award can seek contribution from others who may also have played a role in the fraud, if the others have assets with which to pay damages.) In a large securities fraud class action, plaintiffs' attorneys face a large number of potential defendants, including individual corporate officers and directors, the corporation, and the corporate auditors. Because of their deep pockets, corporate auditors made particularly juicy targets for plaintiffs' attorneys under a joint-and-several liability regime. Even if corporate officers and directors were largely responsible for the fraud, plaintiffs' attorneys could seek the entire damage award from the corporate auditors.

Congress, responding to calls from auditors and others for reform, implemented as part of the PSLRA proportionate liability for defendants found to be only reckless violators of Rule 10b-5 (Section 21D(f), Exchange Act). Knowing violators continue to be subject to joint-and-several liability (§ 21D(f)(2)(A), Exchange Act).

Under the proportionate liability scheme, the jury is required to make a determination of the "percentage of responsibility . . . measured as percentage of the total fault of all persons who caused or contributed to the loss incurred by the plaintiff." (Section 21D(f)(3), Exchange Act.) Note that the allocation of responsibility is not limited to persons named as defendants by the plaintiff. If Dax goes to prison and Logistique is left facing the damages award alone, it can try to pin responsibility on Dax, even though he was not named as a defendant. (The proportionate liability provision creates an exception for plaintiffs with minimal net worth, but it is so narrow as to be of little practical significance.)

But can we trust the jury to make a fair allocation of responsibility? What if the jury knows that Dax is insolvent and that attributing more responsibility to Dax means that investors will simply go without compensation for their losses? The solution embodied in § 21D(f) of the Exchange Act is to rely on ignorance. Section 21D(f)(6) prohibits disclosure to the jury of the damages consequences of an allocation of responsibility.

Investors are not entirely out of luck if more culpable defendants are insolvent. Defendants who knowingly commit fraud, as mentioned above, face joint-and-several liability. The proportionate liability provision principally offers protection to potential defendants whose involvement in the fraud may have been more peripheral, such as accountants and outside directors. The effect may be to discourage plaintiffs from naming such defendants at all because they may create more distraction and expense in the litigation than the benefit they generate in the form of additional sources of recovery. Since *Central Bank* was decided in 1994 and the PSLRA was adopted in 1995, the number of accounting firms named in Rule 10b-5 class actions has dropped sharply.

⌁ 6 ⌁

Insider Trading

Ingrid is the CEO of Jungle World, Inc. Jungle World operates a chain of indoor play centers that allow children to play the role of explorers charting the rainforests. Anya is an analyst who covers recreation and leisure companies, including Jungle World. In her latest report to investors, Anya gives Jungle World a "Buy" rating. Anya's surveys indicate that the play centers are popular with children and parents alike because they combine excitement with strenuous exercise. (The kids always sleep well after a visit to Jungle World!) Anya has also done extensive analysis of demographic data; her analysis indicates that demand for recreation opportunities such as those at Jungle World is likely to go up sharply in the next three to five years. Ozzie is a retail investor (a bus driver by trade, actually). He bought Jungle World shares on the New York Stock Exchange after taking his daughter to one of the centers, where they both had a lot of fun.

Insider trading in securities markets results from the economic phenomenon of asymmetric information. Asymmetry arises when one person to a transaction knows more about the value of the securities being sold than does the other person involved in the transaction. If the securities trade in an active market, we assume that economic incentives will lead the person with superior information to *sell* when his private information tells him that the market price is too high and to *buy* when the price is too low.

Many different categories of informed investors exist in the securities markets. At one extreme, the issuer, when selling or buying securities, typically has a large information advantage relative to outside investors. For this reason, special rules apply to issuers engaged in transactions in its own securities. We discuss the rules governing an issuer's public offering of securities in Chapter 7. Corporate insiders, including the top officers and directors, also enjoy a large information advantage. Moving outside the company, analysts may develop long-term relationships with insiders such that they know more about the company than do other outside investors. Analysts and others more sophisticated than the average investor may also expend large resources to investigate particular companies, giving them an advantage.

Of course, investors lacking information may understand the incentives motivating informed traders. If the informed investors can be identified, uninformed investors may, if not too much effort is required, ask them questions before entering into a transaction, attempting to extract the information they hold. If the informed party refuses to answer those questions, the uninformed party is likely to say no to the trade or to demand a large discount. The informed may always answer the questions falsely, but the fraud laws would then come into play.

The real problem arises when the informed attempt to conceal or disguise their identity to preserve the value of their informational advantage. Concealment does not take much effort in the context of anonymous securities exchanges: People buying and selling stock over the New York Stock Exchange or Nasdaq generally do not know the identity of the person on the other side of the transaction. As a consequence, an investor such as Ozzie can do little to avoid trading on a securities exchange with investors with superior information. This anonymity makes trading on an informational advantage a practical option even for officers and directors of a firm, such as Ingrid of Jungle World, who might find it difficult to find counterparties with whom to trade if their identities were known. But this anonymity also means that those who have obtained their informational advantage through skill or hard work, for example, a particularly insightful analyst such as Anya, can capitalize on their investment in information.

Although the identity of the informed will not be generally known, uninformed investors such as Ozzie are not completely defenseless. Ozzie knows that when you trade with the smart money, you lose. Knowing that some portion of his trades will be with persons having greater information, Ozzie can discount the amount he is willing to pay for *all* shares to reflect the average loss he expects to incur when he trades with someone better informed. This discount in the secondary market eventually works its way up to the new issues market: Companies selling shares receive less than they otherwise would because outside investors discount the amount they are willing to pay for newly issued shares. That discount in the new issues market anticipates the discount investors will incur when they eventually sell the shares, because purchasers will fear they will find themselves on the losing end of a transaction with someone better informed. The bottom line is that informational advantages in the *secondary* markets generate a higher cost of capital in the *primary* market for companies such as Jungle World, so at least in theory firms have an interest in discouraging insider trading.

1 THE VALUE OF INSIDER TRADING?

Are all information advantages in the securities markets a bad thing? Uninformed (often individual) investors are at a disadvantage relative to all informed investors in the marketplace. Both the advantage enjoyed by an insider, such as Ingrid, who exploits her access to information, and that enjoyed by a

diligent analyst-investor, such as Anya, who exploits her investment insights, come at the expense of the uninformed, such as
Ozzie. Ozzie may discount shares to take into account his
information disadvantage, but this just means the issuer ultimately pays the price of the informational asymmetries in the
market.

Informational asymmetries are not all bad. As more informed
investors trade based on their information, the trades will result
in the incorporation of previously nonpublic information into
the securities market price. If Anya, for example, believes that
the shares of Jungle World are undervalued by $10 per share,
she will purchase shares of Jungle World. If she purchases a lot
of shares, the market will take the large volume of purchases as a
signal that the shares are undervalued, and the price will rise
accordingly. Once she has purchased her shares, Anya will have
a strong incentive to let the world know about her good information about Jungle World: Only by disclosing can she
maximize her profit from the price increase in Jungle World
common shares. Trading by Anya therefore leads to more informationally efficient stock prices, which is generally regarded
as a good thing (as we discussed Chapter 1).

Not all trades involving nonpublic information enhance
share price accuracy significantly. If an outside analyst works
hard and expends resources in research, the information the
outside analyst generates is arguably new and may not have
been incorporated into the securities prices absent the analyst's
research and subsequent trades. In contrast, consider an
insider such as Jungle World's CEO, Ingrid. If Ingrid trades
one week ahead of the quarterly Form 10-Q announcement of
Jungle World's earnings, the market only benefits from a slight
acceleration in when the market learns about the earnings.
This benefit is rather modest compared with the cost insider
trading may impose on uninformed investors.

Some commentators consequently have argued for a *property theory* of insider trading. Under this theory, those who

expend hard work and resources in generating new information should profit from the fruits of their labor. Those who simply purloin the information from another, such as an insider taking corporate information and trading based on this information, should not be allowed to profit.

Not all agree with the property theory of insider trading. Under the *parity of information theory* once espoused by the SEC, all investors must trade on an equal playing field. This can mean one of two possible things. Under the more stringent interpretation of this theory, no information advantages should be allowed in the marketplace. Regardless of how an investor obtained an information advantage, under the parity of information theory all information advantages should be prohibited. Under a less stringent version of the theory, all investors have the same initial equal access to information, but they may thereafter develop different information through their own hard work. Ingrid's advantage seems to be an unintended byproduct of her special access to inside information and the need to entrust firm employees with information so they can do their jobs. By contrast, Anya's advantage results from talent or hard work, not any special access to information. An insider's unequal access to information gives the insider an unerodable advantage over others in the securities markets, which may reduce outside investors' confidence.

Is hard work necessarily useful from a social standpoint? Imagine that a corporation has inside information about its future prospects. The corporation chooses to remain silent about this information. Ten separate analyst firms, realizing that learning this information will result in large trading profits, expend significant resources in interviewing the corporation's customers and suppliers and researching other sources to make an estimate of the corporation's internal information on future prospects. The first of the ten analyst firms to uncover the information will receive the lion's share of any trading profits. Each firm, consequently, will have very high incentives to expend sufficient resources to be first. Trading profits are zero sum, however, in the sense that for one person to profit, someone else must lose on the secondary market trades. The only socially useful value from the analysts' research is improvement in share price accuracy. In this scenario, the ten analyst firms' hard work is socially wasteful, because it is duplicative. The waste is particularly acute if the corporation could simply disclose the information, incorporating the information into the share price without the expenditure of analyst research dollars.

Yet another view of insider trading is the argument that insider trading serves as a form of compensation for management. If managers do a good job in increasing firm value, the managers can profit from this increase through insider trades before the positive news is disclosed. To the extent a firm internalizes the pros (efficient compensation for management) and cons (discount in share price from outside investors) of insider trading, the firm is in the best position to determine whether to allow insider trading as a form of compensation for its officers.

Is insider trading an efficient form of compensation for management? Managers may profit just as much from destroying corporate value, profiting through short sales of the company stock before revealing the information to the marketplace. It is much easier to destroy corporate value than it is to increase it. A possible solution would be to restrict management insider trades to buy orders. Even this solution, however, can hurt the company if managers systematically eschew value-maximizing but more public projects in favor of less valuable but secret projects that generate insider trading opportunities.

Given these diverse perspectives on informed trading, it is not surprising that the legal doctrine governing insider trading is not always clear-cut. One reason for this messiness is that Congress has never enacted a statute specifically prohibiting insider trading (or defining what counts as insider trading).

Insider trading has instead been treated as a species of fraud under Rule 10b-5, the antifraud rule we covered in Chapter 5, and therefore must satisfy the elements of § 10(b) of the Exchange Act. That means that the task of defining insider trading has instead been left to the SEC (with the assistance of the Justice Department) and the courts. Until recently, the SEC has avoided rulemaking in this area, preferring to develop the law of insider trading on a case-by-case basis. As a result, judicial decisions interpreting § 10(b) have defined the scope of the insider trading prohibition.

We proceed by first discussing the Supreme Court's three primary cases explicating the insider trading prohibition under Rule 10b-5. We then consider rules adopted by the SEC in the wake of those decisions, as well as the remedies for insider trading provided by Congress. Finally, we provide a brief overview of § 16 of the Exchange Act, the so-called short-swing profits rule, intended as a prophylactic measure against insider trading by certain designated classes of insiders.

2 INSIDER TRADING DOCTRINE UNDER RULE 10b-5

A trilogy of Supreme Court decisions — *Chiarella v. United States*,[1] *Dirks v. SEC*,[2] and *United States v. O'Hagan*[3] — set forth the basic contours of the insider trading prohibition. The last of these, *O'Hagan*, gives the government the broadest latitude to combat insider trading, but the Court's holding in that case only makes sense in light of its prior holdings in *Chiarella* and *Dirks*. Accordingly, we discuss these cases in the order they were decided.

---

1. 445 U.S. 222 (1980).
2. 463 U.S. 646 (1983).
3. 521 U.S. 642 (1997).

First, we need to explain a bit of terminology to help us find our way through those cases. There are two theories of why insider trading counts as fraud within the meaning of § 10(b) and Rule 10b-5: the classical theory and the misappropriation theory. Under the classical theory, so called because it has its roots in the common law of deceit, a person violates Rule 10b-5 if (1) she buys or sells a security from or to (2) a person to whom she owes a duty of trust or confidence (3) without disclosing to that person (4) material, nonpublic information in her possession. Under the misappropriation theory, a person violates Rule 10b-5 if (1) she has material nonpublic information (2) entrusted to her by a person (the "source") to whom she owes a duty of trust or confidence, (3) and she buys or sells a security (4) without first disclosing her intention to trade to the source. It is called the misappropriation theory because the person trading on the information has misappropriated it from its source.

2.1 *Chiarella*

Chiarella is the first insider trading case under the federal securities laws to reach the Supreme Court. The facts of the case, like those of many insider trading prosecutions, involved corporate takeovers. Chiarella worked as a printer for Pandick Press. Pandick's business was printing financial documents, including announcements of corporate takeover bids. Despite the efforts of Pandick and its clients to conceal the identity of the targets of these bids by using blank spaces or false names prior to the final printing, Chiarella was able to deduce the identity of the targets based on other information included in the documents. Chiarella used this foreknowledge of the bids to acquire shares in a number of the target companies, a clear violation of Pandick's company policy. He then sold the shares after the bids were announced, garnering a total profit of $30,000.

Chiarella was indicted by the U.S. Attorney and was convicted by a jury of violating § 10(b) and Rule 10b-5. The district court instructed the jury that Chiarella could be found guilty if he used material, nonpublic information when "he knew other people trading in the securities market did not have access to the same information." This instruction essentially captured the "parity of information" theory then espoused by the SEC. (Note that this theory would offer Ozzie the maximum protection because it potentially would prohibit not only insiders, such as Ingrid, but also the diligent and resourceful, such as Anya, from using their information advantage in trades with Ozzie.)

The Supreme Court found the trial court's instruction to the jury defective and reversed Chiarella's conviction. Reasoning that deception was an essential element of a § 10(b) violation, the Court's central focus was to define the circumstance that would render silence deceptive. The Court held that:

> [O]ne who fails to disclose material information prior to the consummation of a transaction commits fraud only when he is under a duty to do so. And the duty to disclose arises when one party has information that the other [party] is entitled to know because of a fiduciary or other similar relation of trust and confidence between them.

The Court found no relation of trust and confidence between Chiarella and the shareholders of the *target* firms with whom he traded. Pandick's clients were the *bidders* in these transactions, not the targets, so Chiarella acquired no duty to the target shareholders arising from his employment by Pandick. Accordingly, he had no obligation to disclose the information that he had about the future takeover bids to the shareholders with whom he traded.

The negative implication of the Court's holding is that if Chiarella had owed the target shareholders a duty, his failure to disclose that information to them before trading would have been deceptive within the meaning of § 10(b). Along the way to its holding, the Court clarified one other aspect of the duty it was recognizing under § 10(b): the fiduciary duty of disclosure extended not only to existing shareholders but also to prospective shareholders. If an insider sold shares knowing they were overvalued based on nonpublic information, nondisclosure would be fraudulent, despite the absence of an existing relationship of trust and confidence between the insider and the prospective shareholder. The requisite relationship would be created by the very sale alleged to be fraudulent. So if Ingrid were to sell some of her shares of Jungle World in advance of a disappointing earnings announcement, the investors who purchased from her would be defrauded within the meaning of § 10(b), regardless of whether they had been shareholders of Jungle World before Ingrid's fraudulent sale.

Was the Court right to reject the parity of information theory? On the one hand, one could argue that investors may lose confidence in the capital markets if they face the prospect of trading against other, more informed investors, no matter how these information advantages arose. But a strict parity of information rule would discourage any investor from researching to obtain an advantage. Share price accuracy would then depend largely (at least for firm-specific information) on the pronouncements of the company itself. Share price accuracy would correspondingly decrease.

Note though that the Court did not adopt the property rights view of insider trading, instead focusing on the presence of a fiduciary duty. A thief who purloins an information advantage may profit from this information in the secondary market so long as the thief does not owe a fiduciary duty to the investors with whom the thief trades.

The Court also rejected an alternative argument raised by the government based on the misappropriation theory. The government argued that Chiarella had deceived Pandick's clients, the bidders, by using their confidential information for his own benefit. Although Chiarella profited from trades with the target shareholders (to whom he owed no duty), the government argued that Chiarella defrauded the bidders who were the source of the information. The Court rejected this argument, however, not on the merits, but because it had not been presented to the jury. Chiarella's conviction could not be sustained on the basis of a breach of a duty to the bidders that the jury had not considered. This procedural obstacle meant that the validity of the misappropriation theory would have to wait for another day to be considered by the Supreme Court.

Insider Trading and Options Detour

One rather large loophole left by *Chiarella* was the treatment of options. Because options can be purchased with a much smaller investment than would be required to purchase a like number of shares of the underlying security, they are especially attractive to people possessing knowledge (nonpublic, of course) of the direction in which the security's price is headed, that is, insider traders. Not surprisingly, the potential for insider trading is particularly corrosive for options markets. The doctrinal problem in dealing with insider trading in the public options markets, however, is that publicly traded options are typically written by third parties, not by the issuer of the underlying securities. This means that officers and directors who owe a fiduciary duty to the company and its shareholders owe no fiduciary duty to options holders. Under *Chiarella*, if there is no duty to the option holder, the failure to disclose material, nonpublic information to that holder is not deceptive and therefore not a violation of § 10(b).

Congress closed this loophole by adding § 20(d) to the Exchange Act. Section 20(d) does not define insider trading, but it does create a duty to options holders. Under that provision, if "communicating, or purchasing or selling security while in possession of, material nonpublic information would violate" § 10(b), then "such conduct in connection with a purchase or sale of a put, call, straddle, [or] option . . . with respect to such security . . . , shall also violate" § 10(b). Thus, anyone trading options on the basis of material nonpublic information violates Rule 10b-5 if trading in the underlying security would violate Rule 10b-5. Notably, § 20(d) does not extend a similar duty to holders of debt securities. Under state corporate law, officers and directors do not usually owe a fiduciary duty to debt holders, so under *Chiarella* there would be no duty to disclose material nonpublic information to them. Section 20(d) does not change this result.

2.2 *Dirks*

An important issue arising under the classical theory was left unresolved by *Chiarella*: When would a noninsider violate Rule 10b-5 by trading on information received from an insider? In this scenario, the insider conveying the information is called the tipper, while the recipient who trades on that information is known as the tippee. The need for such a prohibition is clear: Absent an antitipping rule, an insider could evade the prohibition announced in *Chiarella* simply by channeling his trades through an accomplice. *Chiarella* blocks trades based on nonpublic material information on the part of CEO Ingrid in Jungle World's common stock. But what if Ingrid strikes a deal with her brother Tino? Under the deal, Ingrid feeds Tino material information about Jungle World, and Tino profits through secondary market trades, giving Ingrid a cut of the profits. Tino himself owes no duty to Jungle World's shareholders; do his trades violate the Rule 10b-5 prohibition on insider trading?

Dirks v. SEC was not the typical tipping case. Dirks was a securities analyst whose research focused on insurance companies. He was contacted by Secrist, a former officer of Equity Funding of America, who claimed that Equity Funding's assets were grossly overstated as a result of a massive fraud. Secrist had attempted to bring his charges of fraud to the attention of government regulators, but to no avail. Dirks did his own investigation and concluded that Secrist's allegations were true. During the course of his investigation, Dirks shared this information with his firm's clients, who sold their shares of Equity Funding. The SEC ultimately filed a complaint against Equity Funding, the *Wall Street Journal* published a front-page story about the fraud, and the company immediately went into receivership. The SEC was not done, however, with its enforcement efforts; it also filed an administrative action against Dirks. The agency found that Dirks had aided and abetted violations of § 10(b) and Rule 10b-5 by passing on the news of the Equity Funding fraud to his clients, who then sold their Equity Funding stock. The SEC censured Dirks, and the D.C. Circuit upheld the censure.

The Supreme Court reversed. Justice Powell, again writing for the Court, rejected the SEC's argument that "anyone who knowingly receives information from an insider has a fiduciary duty to disclose before trading." In the Court's view, such a broad rule "could have an inhibiting influence on the role of market analysts, which the SEC itself recognizes is necessary to the preservation of a healthy market."

The Court instead crafted a rule that imposed an insider's duty on a tippee if confidential information "has been made available to them *improperly*." The rule reads:

> A tippee assumes a fiduciary duty to the shareholders of a corporation not to trade on material non-public information only when the insider has breached his fiduciary duty to

the shareholders by disclosing the information to the tippee and tippee knows or should know that there has been a breach.

In the Court's view, use of information in these circumstances would make the tippee complicit in the tipper's breach of duty.

The requirement of a breach by an insider in disclosing the information to the tippee gave rise to another test (for breach of fiduciary duty): "The test is whether an insider personally will benefit, directly or indirectly, from his disclosure. Absent some personal gain, there has been no breach of duty to stockholders. And absent a breach by the insider, there is no derivative breach" by the tippee.

Clearly the Court has a particular kind of breach of duty in mind here: a breach of the duty of *loyalty*. A breach of the duty of care will not suffice. This test will be satisfied if the tipper receives a kickback of the profits or has an expectation of a reciprocal tip from the tippee. The personal benefit test is also satisfied, however, if the tipper "makes a gift of confidential information to a trading relative or friend. The tip and trade resemble trading by the insider himself followed by a gift of the profits to the participant."

To illustrate the distinction between loyalty and care, consider two tips by Ingrid, the CEO of Jungle World, one intentional, one unwitting. Suppose Ingrid tells her brother Tino that next quarter's earnings are not likely to meet expectations, and Tino then sells his Jungle World stock. Ingrid was motivated out of a desire to help Tino out with a useful stock tip. In that case, Ingrid will have breached her duty to Jungle World and its shareholders, and Tino will have knowingly participated in her breach by selling the stock. Both will be guilty of violating Rule 10b-5, and they will be jointly and severally liable for Tino's profits (§ 20A(c)). (And this chain can continue: If Tino passes the information along to his girlfriend Tisha, who also trades on the information, knowing that Tino received it in a breach of duty by Ingrid, Tisha will also have violated Rule 10b-5.)

Suppose instead that Ingrid, after reviewing a confidential memorandum estimating those same earnings, tosses the memo in the trash can behind her house. Pasqual, a trash collector, finds the memo and then trades on the information. On these facts, Pasqual will not have violated Rule 10b-5. (Nor will Ingrid.) Ingrid may have been careless in failing to shred the memo before discarding it, but she received no personal benefit, so she did not breach her duty of loyalty. And even if Pasqual reads "Confidential" emblazoned on the top of the memo, his knowledge will be irrelevant. Pasqual would likely have the requisite scienter for a § 10(b) violation, but there can be no fraud without a breach of the duty of loyalty by Ingrid.

In addition to tippees, the *Dirks* Court also made clear that those who receive nonpublic material information from a corporation as part of a "special confidential relationship" with the issuer become fiduciaries of the corporate shareholders. Examples include accountants, lawyers, and consultants working for a corporation.

Taken together, *Chiarella* and *Dirks* fashion a prohibition against insiders, temporary insiders, and tippees from using confidential information to trade in the shares of the company that employs them. From the SEC's perspective, however, this left a major doctrinal hole in the arsenal available to it to combat informational advantages in securities trading. What about confidential, nonpublic information obtained from outside the company that is material to the value of the company's shares and results in so-called outsider trading?

2.3 *O'Hagan*

The treatment of outsider trading is covered generally under the misappropriation theory of insider trading. The misappropriation theory finally got its turn in the Supreme Court nearly twenty years after *Chiarella* in *United States v. O'Hagan.* Jim O'Hagan was a partner in Dorsey & Whitney, a major Minneapolis law firm. Dorsey & Whitney was retained by Grand Metropolitan, a British company, to represent Grand Met in connection with its planned tender offer for Pillsbury. As is common with such offers, Grand Met was keeping its intentions confidential in an effort to keep the price of Pillsbury shares from rising in advance of its offer. (Tender offers are typically made at a substantial premium to the prior market price, creating a predictable jump in the price of the target shares when the bid is announced.) O'Hagan, however, learned of Grand Met's plans and bought a large number of call options on Pillsbury's stock, as well as 5,000 shares of the stock itself, at under $40 per share. When Grand Met announced its bid, Pillsbury's stock price rose to nearly $60 per share; O'Hagan sold his Pillsbury holdings, netting a $4.3 million profit. The Justice Department indicted O'Hagan for violations of Rule 10b-5 and obtained a subsequent jury conviction. The Eighth Circuit reversed the conviction and the government sought review in the Supreme Court.

The Court had previously accepted the proposition that an agent's use of confidential information without disclosure to his principal was fraudulent,[4] so there was little question that O'Hagan defrauded Grand Met and Dorsey & Whitney. The Court observed that "[a] fiduciary who '[pretends] loyalty to the principal while secretly converting the principal's information for personal gain,' 'dupes' or defrauds the principal." Thus, O'Hagan's failure to disclose to Grand Met and Dorsey & Whitney that he intended to trade on Grand Met's information was "deceptive" within the meaning of § 10(b).

---

4. See *Carpenter v. United States,* 484 U.S. 19 (1987) (holding that agent's use of confidential information for trading in securities violated the mail and wire fraud statutes).

The more challenging question to be decided, however, was whether this fraud was "in connection with the purchase or sale of any security" under § 10(b). Unlike the classical theory, in which the insider defrauds the shareholder who is the counterparty to the transaction by failing to disclose his confidential information, under the misappropriation theory the fraud and the securities transaction are split. The misappropriator defrauds the source of the information but trades with a shareholder to whom he may not owe any duty. Thus, there is no fraud on the counterparty to the transaction. The Court nonetheless found that the deception was "in connection with the purchase or sale" of securities. "This element is satisfied because the fiduciary's fraud is consummated, not when the fiduciary gains the confidential information, but when, without disclosure to his principal, he uses the information to purchase or sell securities. The securities transaction and the breach of duty thus coincide." Thus, O'Hagan did not defraud Grand Met and Dorsey & Whitney until the moment he placed the trades for the Pillsbury shares and options.

Consider a takeover bid by Jungle World for the shares of its competitor, Desert Isle. Summing up the Court's holding in *O'Hagan,* if Ingrid purchases Desert Isle shares in advance of Jungle World's announcement of its bid, Ingrid would be defrauding Jungle World (the source of the information) by purchasing those shares, although she would not be deceiving the Desert Isle shareholders from whom she bought the shares. Her purchases would violate Rule 10b-5 under the misappropriation theory, although the transactions would not violate the classical theory set forth in *Chiarella,* because Ingrid owes no fiduciary duty to Desert Isle or its shareholders. (Note also that trades with Jungle World shareholders, which breach a fiduciary duty owed to them by Ingrid, therefore violating the classical theory, would also breach a duty to Jungle World itself, thereby violating the misappropriation theory as well.)

Ingrid can negate the deception under the misappropriation theory, however, by announcing to the Jungle World board her intention to trade before placing her purchase order, that is, if Ingrid acts as a brazen misappropriator. Without deception, she cannot violate § 10(b). Unlike the classical theory, under which deception can only be negated by disclosure to the counterparty to the trade, the misappropriation theory requires disclosure to the source of the information, in this case, Jungle World. Even if the Jungle World board of directors orders Ingrid not to purchase the Desert Isle stock, she will still not have violated § 10(b) if she ignores their instruction. She would, however, be violating her state law fiduciary duty of loyalty.

The misappropriation theory represents a partial move toward the property theory of insider trading. The misappropriation theory prohibits trades based not only on inside corporate information but also on outside information. Prohibited outsider trading occurs when information is misappropriated from an outside source of information. The misappropriation theory therefore protects the outside source's property interest in the information. The misappropriation theory, however, is not a perfect match for the property theory. Imagine that Terry, a thief, breaks into Jungle World's offices and steals information relating to the tender offer for Desert Isle stock. When Terry trades on this information, she does not violate the misappropriation theory (despite the theft of property) because Terry does not owe any fiduciary duty to the source, Jungle World.

Combined with the classical theory of insider trading, the misappropriation theory gives us the following landscape of insider trading prohibitions under Rule 10b-5 as applicable to outsiders of a corporation. First, an outsider may be liable as a tippee under *Dirks*. Second, an outsider may be liable as an insider if the outsider is in a special confidential relationship with the issuer (such as an attorney or auditor), also pursuant to *Dirks*. Third, an outsider may be liable under the misappropriation theory if the outsider trades based on an informational advantage obtained through a deceptive breach of duty to the source of the information.

Significantly, Rule 10b-5 is not the only provision that governs informational advantages in the securities markets. Rule 14e-3 of the Exchange Act also limits trading profits based on information relating to tender offers. Rules 10b5-1 and 10b5-2 clarify the application of Rule 10b-5 to insider trading. Regulation FD limits certain informational advantages obtained through selective disclosure from an Exchange Act reporting issuer.

3 RULE 14e-3

The Supreme Court resolved another important insider trading issue in *O'Hagan*: the validity of Rule 14e-3 of the Exchange Act. As noted above, tender offers create potentially very lucrative opportunities for insider trading. After *Chiarella*, there appeared to be a very substantial gap in the prohibitions against insider trading in such situations, because the person trading with material, nonpublic information will typically have acquired it in the course of a relation with the bidder, not the target. As a result, that person will lack the duty of trust and confidence to the target's shareholders needed to invoke the protections of the classical theory. The SEC filled that gap with Rule 14e-3.

Rule 14e-3(a) prohibits trading in the target company's shares on the basis of nonpublic, material information obtained from the bidder or the target or an employee or anyone else acting on behalf of either the bidder or the target. This prohibition is bolstered by an antitipping provision (Rule 14e-3(d)). Notably, both provisions lack any requirement that the trading or the tipping be in violation of a fiduciary duty. The SEC justified this omission as eliminating a difficult evidentiary requirement that had frequently posed an obstacle to enforcement actions and prosecutions brought under Rule 10b-5. The Supreme Court upheld the SEC's authority to adopt Rule 14e-3 in *O'Hagan*.

Rule 14e-3 thus represents a move back toward parity of information for a limited, but economically important, type of informational advantage. Since information on a tender offer must, necessarily, come (perhaps indirectly) from either the target or the bidder (or an employee or agent of either), Rule 14e-3 places a blanket prohibition on trades based on such information. This prohibition applies regardless of the presence of fiduciary duty, how much effort went into uncovering the information, or whether the target or bidder authorized the trades. In other words, deception is not required to violate Rule 14e-3. Even if Anya, the analyst, learns of Jungle World's tender offer bid for Desert Isle through eavesdropping on Jungle World's communications, Anya would still violate Rule 14e-3 by trading in Desert Isle's shares. Chiarella's trades likewise would certainly have violated Rule 14e-3 if it had been in effect at the time. Despite Chiarella's lack of a fiduciary duty owed to the target company's shareholders, he traded based on information regarding a tender offer obtained from the acquiring company. The broad prohibition of Rule 14e-3, however, is limited to information relating to tender offers.

4 RULES 10b5-1 & -2

After the government's victory in *O'Hagan*, the SEC adopted two rules intended to clarify two elements of the insider trading violation under Rule 10b-5. Rule 10b5-1 clarifies what it means to trade "on the basis of" material nonpublic information. Rule 10b5-2 defines what counts as duty of trust and confidence.

4.1 Rule 10b5-1

In bringing insider trading enforcement actions, the SEC frequently met the defense that the alleged insider trader had bought or sold the securities for some reason other than on the basis of material, nonpublic information, such as a desire to fund retirement. Moreover, in recent years, predetermined stock selling plans have become increasingly popular with corporate insiders concerned about the risk of government enforcement of insider trading law, as well as securities class action exposure under Rule 10b-5. Such plans typically involve a contractual arrangement under which the insider commits to selling a certain number of shares each quarter or each year or to selling a certain number of shares in the event the securities reach a specified price. By eliminating the insider's discretion as to the timing of the sale, the plan is intended to negate any scienter on the insider's part, a necessary element for a § 10(b) violation.

Rule 10b5-1 has two operative provisions. The first defines the phrase *on the basis of* broadly in determining whether nonpublic material information motivated a securities transaction. Rule 10b5-1(b) treats a transaction as being on the basis of nonpublic information when "the person making the purchase or sale was aware of the material nonpublic information." This provision is intended to negate claims that the insider bought or sold the shares for some reason other than the material nonpublic information. Mere awareness is equated with a motivation to use the information in trading.

The second provision makes predetermined trading plans an affirmative defense to a Rule 10b-5 violation. It also specifies the terms required for that defense to be valid. The plan must be entered into before the person became aware of the material nonpublic information, and it must be reflected in a binding contract, an instruction to another person to buy or sell the security for the instructing person's account, or a written plan for the purchase or sale of securities (Rule 10b5-1(c)(1)(A)).

The contact, instruction, or plan must specify the amount of securities to be transacted, along with a date or price, or specify a formula for determining the timing and amount. Critically, the plan must not allow the insider to exercise discretion over the transactions after entering into the plan (Rule 10b5-1(c)(1)(B) & (C)). Thus, the plan must eliminate the insider's ability to time trades while in possession of nonpublic information. CEO Ingrid, for example, may set up a predetermined plan to sell 100,000 of her shares in Jungle World every month. Ingrid may not, upon later learning that Jungle World has worse than expected earnings prospects, choose to increase the programmed sales amount temporarily.

What 10b5-1 does not do, however, is limit the ability of corporate insiders to manipulate the release of corporate information to make planned trades particularly profitable. Suppose Ingrid knows that her stock plan calls for her broker to sell a number of her shares on the first Monday of each month. If Ingrid uses her authority as CEO to make sure that good news for Jungle World is released Monday morning before the markets open, she guarantees that her sales will be at a price that reflects that good news. If bad news is withheld until Tuesday morning, it will not be reflected in the price at which Ingrid sells. Minor manipulations of this sort can potentially lead to substantially higher trading profits, on average, for insiders.

Rule 10b5-1 also does not limit the ability of insiders to terminate plans while in possession of nonpublic information. The decision not to sell is outside the reach of § 10(b) because it is not "in connection with the purchase or sale" of a security. Once plans are terminated, however, insiders will face substantial uncertainty if they want to reinstate it, given the rule's requirement that the plan be adopted in "good faith."

4.2 Rule 10b5-2

The second issue addressed by the SEC in its rulemaking is what sort of "duty of trust and confidence" will give rise to the disclosure duty that triggers the misappropriation theory. Certain duties, such as the fiduciary duty owed by an officer to his company or by a lawyer to his client, are clear enough. Questions arise, however, when we push the outer reaches of the misappropriation theory. Does a son owe a fiduciary duty to his father? Does a psychiatrist owe a fiduciary duty to her patient?

Rule 10b5-2 answers questions of this sort. The rule defines "a duty of trust or confidence" to include the following:

1. An agreement to maintain information in confidence;
2. A "history, pattern, or practice of sharing confidences, such that the recipient of the information knows or reasonably should know that the person communicating the material nonpublic information expects that the recipient will maintain its confidentiality";
3. "Whenever a person receives or obtains material nonpublic information from his or her spouse, parent, child, or sibling."

(Rule 10b5-2(b).) These categories, however, are presumptions. The person receiving the information can rebut the presumption by showing that he "neither knew or reasonably should have known that the . . . source of the information expected that the person would keep the information confidential." So if Tino, Ingrid's brother, learns of material nonpublic information from her about Jungle World's intentions toward Desert Isle, Rule 10b5-2 presumes that Ingrid intended that Tino keep that information in confidence. If Tino nonetheless trades on the information, it would be his burden to show that his relationship with Ingrid was such that she would not have expected him to keep the information confidential.

Rule 10b5-2 opens up the possibility for chains of information flow, giving rise to interesting remote tippee liability. Suppose that Ingrid the CEO reveals nonpublic material information about Jungle World's improving financial prospects to Anya the analyst. Suppose that before publishing the information in her monthly public newsletter, Anya first tells her spouse Spencer about the information, telling him that it is "secret." Spencer, knowing only that Anya has good and "secret" information on Jungle World, tells his friend Felicia about the information and also tells Felicia that the information is a "secret." Felicia promises to give 50 percent of the trading profits from the information to Spencer. Felicia is Spencer's tippee. Are Spencer and Felicia liable under a tipper-tippee theory? First, we need to see if Spencer has breached a fiduciary duty in making the tip. According to Rule 10b5-2, Spencer breaches his duty of trust and confidence to Anya, his spouse. Moreover, the breach stems from Spencer's desire to profit from Felicia's trades. Note that it does not matter that Spencer owes no fiduciary duty to Jungle World nor that he does not even know that Jungle World is the ultimate source of the information. Second, we need to assess whether Felicia is aware or should have been aware of this breach. Spencer told Felicia that the information was a secret, and Felicia knows that the information is important enough to generate trading profits. It is at least arguable from these facts that Felicia should have known that Spencer must have gotten the information illicitly. Thus both Spencer and Felicia are liable under a tipper-tippee theory under *Dirks*.

Note that Rule 10b5-2 does not close the loophole of the "brazen misappropriator": the person who tells the source of the information of his intention to trade. Nor does it extend the misappropriation theory to Terry, the thief who steals material nonpublic information, or to the lucky, those who find nonpublic information carelessly disclosed by an insider.

5 REMEDIES

Although Congress has not defined insider trading, it has been considerably more active when it comes to affording remedies for the violation of the ban against insider trading. Let's start with the private remedies. Section 20A of the Exchange Act clarifies who has standing to bring a private cause of action for an insider trading violation. That section confers standing on persons who traded "contemporaneously" with the insider (but on the opposite side). Given the difficulties of matching specific trades in an anonymous exchange market, the law allows people who traded at roughly the same time to collect damages. The damages measure, however, is limited to disgorgement of the insider's profits (or losses avoided) from the insider trading. Even that amount, however, cannot be recovered if the insider has previously been required to disgorge his trading profits in an enforcement action by the SEC. As a result, § 20A is infrequently invoked.

SEC enforcement actions for insider trading are much more common. In addition to the disgorgement remedy mentioned above, the SEC can seek civil penalties under § 21A. The amount of the penalty is determined by the court in light of the facts and circumstances of the violation, but no penalty can exceed three time the profit gained or loss avoided. Penalties can also be imposed on controlling persons of the violator, but the control person can avoid liability if it is unaware of the violation. For entities involved in the securities industry, controlling persons need to show that they have adopted policies to prevent the misuse of information by their employees.

6 HOW MUST A PUBLIC COMPANY MAKE ITS DISCLOSURES?

As we have seen from its positions in the cases above, the SEC is committed, as a philosophical matter, not only to full disclosure by companies but to parity of access to that information. Material information translates into trading profits in the securities markets, and the SEC believes that the playing field should be level for investors seeking that information. The

SEC for many years sought to curtail differential access to corporate information through the insider trading prohibition of Rule 10b-5, only to have its efforts thwarted by the Supreme Court, which has adhered to a narrower interpretation of Rule 10b-5 more closely tied to the common law of deceit.

The SEC controls the timing and access to disclosures that companies make in their 10-Ks, 10-Qs, and 8-Ks, but companies can, and frequently do, make disclosures outside these filings, through press releases, conference calls, and, historically, through private discussions with analysts and institutional investors. This last category of voluntary disclosure worried the SEC. The SEC has long been concerned that the so-called smart money enjoyed more timely access to corporate information than that provided to ordinary retail investors. In the securities markets, being the first to obtain material information readily translates into trading profits. Trading profits are zero sum: If analysts and institutional investors can profit from trading on information to which they have early access, it follows that ordinary retail investors must be suffering trading losses.

The SEC's quest to promote parity of information was further fueled in the 1990s by evidence that management was using access to information to influence analyst coverage of their companies. The SEC believed that companies were coercing analysts into providing favorable coverage by threatening to withhold information from analysts who were less than enthusiastic about the company. If pliable analysts were provided with private information, their clients would be at a competitive advantage, not because the analyst was particularly insightful, but because he had access to information not available to other analysts and investors. This alleged corruption of the analyst community, essentially a form of commercial bribery, was a central factor driving the adoption of Regulation FD.

Instead of treating selective disclosure as an insider trading problem, to be regulated under the § 10(b) antifraud provision,

Regulation FD addresses it as a disclosure question. Regulation FD is promulgated under the SEC's § 13(a) authority to require disclosure by public companies, which is broader than its § 10(b) authority to regulate deception and manipulation. The innovation of Regulation FD is that it regulates the manner by which companies disclose material information, not its content.

The central provision of Regulation FD prohibits persons acting on behalf of Exchange Act reporting companies from making selective disclosure of nonpublic material information to "covered persons." (Rule 100(a) & (b), Reg. FD.) Selective disclosure is defined by its opposite, "public disclosure," which can be achieved by either (1) filing an 8-K with the information, or (2) "disclosure that is reasonably designed to provide broad, non-exclusionary distribution of the information to the public." "Persons acting on behalf" include directors, executive officers, and investor relations personnel. In the case of Jungle World, Ingrid the CEO, Francis the CFO, and Orville the outside director would clearly be included; Jungle World's mailroom clerk generally would be excluded. This helps protect the company from unauthorized selective disclosure by low-level employees; only the top tiers and investor relations personnel need be indoctrinated in Regulation FD compliance. Also excluded from this category are employees of the company who are breaching a duty of confidence by disclosing; this means that impermissible tipping of nonpublic material information by an insider to an outside tippee that violates the *Dirks* ban on insider trading does not violate Regulation FD (Rule 101(c), Reg. FD).

The last defined term important to understanding the prohibition is *covered persons,* a category which includes (1) brokers-dealers and their associated persons; (2) investment advisers and their associated persons; (3) investment companies and their affiliates; and (4) a holder of the company's securities "under circumstances in which it is reasonably foreseeable that the person" will trade on the information. (Rule 100(b)(1), Reg. FD.) The definition of covered persons also contains a number of important exclusions: (1) persons who owe the company a duty of trust and confidence (for example, attorneys, investment bankers, and accountants); (2) a person who has agreed to maintain the information in trust and confidence; and (3) credit rating agencies. (Rule 100(b)(2)(i-iii), Reg. FD.) Of course, if these persons or entities were to trade on the information disclosed to them, they would be violating Rule 10b-5. Excluded from the reach of Regulation FD are certain communications relating to public offerings, including information in the public offering registration statement, free writing prospectuses, and "oral communication[s] made in connection with the registered securities offering after the filing of the registration statement." (Rule 100(b)(2)(iv), Reg. FD.)

The rule gives a bit of wiggle room for unintentional selective disclosures, for which the company can avoid a violation of Regulation FD if it makes public disclosure "promptly." (Rule 100(a)(2), Reg. FD.) "Promptly means as soon as reasonably practicable (but in no event after the later of 24 hours or the commencement of the next day's trading on the New York Stock Exchange" after a senior official of the company learns of the nonintentional disclosure. (Rule 101(d), Reg. FD.) "Intentional" disclosures, which occur "when the person making the disclosure knows, or is reckless in not knowing, that the information he or she is communicating is both material and non-public," receive no such latitude. For intentional disclosures, public disclosure must be "simultaneous." (Rule 100(a)(1), Reg. FD.)

Consider whether any Regulation FD issues arise in the following series of hypotheticals:

1. Jungle World is a public company. Ingrid, the CEO of Jungle World, holds a meeting with suppliers of the play

equipment used in the construction of the company's play centers. None of the suppliers own Jungle World stock. At the meeting, Ingrid informs the suppliers of the company's confidential plans to expand to Canada.

Answer: Not a Regulation FD violation. We first need to consider whether Ingrid is among the defined list of those speaking on behalf of Jungle World who would fall under the scope of Regulation FD. Rule 101(c) tells us that a "senior official" is covered, bringing Ingrid, as the CEO, within Regulation FD. Second, does this communication involve material nonpublic information? Here we are told the information is "confidential" so let's assume it is nonpublic. Whether it is material or not will turn on the factors outlined in Chapter 2. For now, let's assume that information about expansion is something that reasonable investors would deem significant. Third, we ask whether Ingrid's communication is made to one of the delineated list of forbidden recipients of selective disclosure in Rule 100(b)(1). The suppliers are not broker-dealers, investment advisors, investment companies, or holders of the securities of whom it would be reasonable to foresee they would purchase or sell based on the information. Fourth, Rule 100(b)(2) contains a list of exceptions, but this analysis is unnecessary if Regulation FD does not otherwise apply. Without any other facts, the likely conclusion is that there is no Regulation FD problem with this communication.

2. Francis, the CFO of Jungle World, discusses confidential first quarter revenue numbers with a small group of mutual funds under the mistaken belief that the CEO has already disclosed this information in an earlier public press conference. Right before the next opening of the NYSE two days later, the company files the revenue numbers on a Form 8-K with the SEC.

Answer: Not a Regulation FD violation. If the CEO had in fact already disclosed the information to the public before Francis made his disclosure, the revenue numbers would likely neither be nonpublic nor material (since the information would exist in the total mix of information). Here, however, Francis only believes that the CEO disclosed earlier; in fact, the CEO had not done so. Let's assume, then, that the revenue information at the time of Francis's disclosure was both material and nonpublic. We can go through the same steps of analysis as in the first hypothetical above. First, Francis as the CFO is a "senior officer." Second, the revenue numbers are likely nonpublic and material. Third, Francis's communication is to mutual funds, which are both investment companies and likely investors with holdings in Jungle World of whom it would be reasonable to foresee they would trade on the revenue number information. (Rule 100(b)(1)). Fourth, none of the exceptions in Rule 100(b)(2) apply. Francis can nonetheless argue that his violation of Regulation FD was inadvertent, unless he was reckless in believing that the information was previously disclosed. For nonintentional violations, Regulation FD requires only that the disclosure is made "promptly." (Rule 100(a)(2)). Rule 101(d) defines promptly to mean not after the later of 24 hours or the commencement of the next day's trading on the NYSE. Here Jungle World seems to have made prompt public disclosure through its Form 8-K (see Rule 101(e)); thus there is no Regulation FD problem.

3. Ruth, an individual investor, has a 4 percent ownership interest in Jungle World. Ruth promises not to trade on Jungle World's securities for the next year and is given access to all of the company's internal books, containing a treasure trove of nonpublic material information. Seeing that Jungle World is doing better than expected, Ruth sells her stock holdings of several Jungle World competitors but keeps her promise not to trade in Jungle World shares.

Answer: Probably no Regulation FD problem. Assuming Ruth is not a broker or dealer, the only possible category of prohibited recipients of information into which Ruth may fall is that for holders of the company's securities who are reasonably expected to trade the issuer's shares on the information (Rule 100(b)(1)(iv)). Here, however, Ruth has promised not to trade Jungle World shares. Moreover, Ruth has not promised to keep the information confidential, so she has not violated the Rule 10b-5 inside trading ban.

4. Suppose Rainforest Land, Inc., a small, privately held competitor of Jungle World, raises capital in a private placement. In the private placement, Rainforest Land disclosed nonpublic material information about its financial condition to a select group of Wall Street institutional investors.
Answer: This is fine under Regulation FD. Regulation FD only applies to public companies required to register under § 12 or required to file reports under § 15(d) of the Exchange Act (Rule 101(b)). Rainforest Land is not a public company because it is privately held.

7 SECTION 16

Section 16 is the only provision of the original Exchange Act, as it was enacted in 1934, to address the problem of insider trading. It does not specifically target informed trading by insiders, as does § 10(b), but instead adopts a two-pronged prophylactic strategy intended to discourage the practice.

   The first prong involves disclosure. Section 16(a) requires that certain designated insiders disclose their transactions in the equity securities of their employer. The designated insiders of the company include beneficial owners of 10 percent or more of its equity securities, the directors, and the officers. These insiders are required to report their transactions in the company's securities on a Form 4 filed with the SEC "before the end of the second business day" following the day of the transaction (Rule 16a-3(g)(1)).

The second prong is unusual for the federal securities law in that it regulates the substance of transactions rather than merely requiring their disclosure. Section 16(b) subjects the insiders required to disclose under § 16(a) to what is called the "short-swing profits" rule. The rule works like this: If an insider buys shares of the company and sells shares of the same class within six months, any profits must be disgorged to the company. The rule also applies to the opposite sequence: If the insider sells shares and then purchases shares of the same class, the profits again must be disgorged to the company. (The provision authorizes shareholders of the company to bring suit on the company's behalf to recover the profits subject to disgorgement.)

Consider the following example. Ingrid, the CEO of Jungle World, purchases 10,000 shares of Jungle World common stock at $20 per share. Two months later, Ingrid sells the 10,000 shares at $30 per share. Even if there is no evidence that Ingrid traded based on nonpublic material information, Ingrid must disgorge her $100,000 profit to Jungle World pursuant to § 16(b).

Section 16(b) has two draconian features. The first is the damages measure; § 16(b) does not net out all transactions within the six-month period; instead, the transactions with the lowest purchase prices are matched up against the transactions with the highest sales price, each match adding to the damages measure until there are no more matches that increase the overall damages.[5] The implication of this

---

5. Imagine that Ingrid purchased 100 shares of Jungle World at $20 per share and another 100 at $40 per share, for a total expenditure of $6,000. Within six months, Ingrid then sells 150 shares at $5 per share and the remaining 50 shares at $30 per share, for a total proceeds of $2,250. Although Ingrid has lost on net, her § 16(b) damages will nonetheless be based on matching 50 shares purchased at $20 per share and 50 shares sold at $30 per share, for a damage amount of $50 \times $10/share = 500.

procedure is that an insider may have been an overall loser in his transactions during a six-month period and still be liable for § 16(b) damages.

The second harsh feature of Section 16(b) is its strict liability provision: There is no requirement that the insider have material nonpublic information at the time of the trades. The sting of strict liability is mitigated substantially, however, by the mechanical nature of the rule: Transactions more than six months apart are not subject to disgorgement. This means that most insiders can easily avoid running afoul of § 16(b) as long as they pay attention to the timing of their transactions. Moreover, the SEC has largely exempted from § 16(b) (Rule 16b-3) employees' exercise of their stock options.

One type of investor covered by § 16(b) who may have a harder time avoiding the application of the rule is the 10 percent beneficial owner. The rule sweeps in potential acquirers who may buy a toehold of more than 10 percent of a company in anticipation of a bid for control of the company. Having become 10 percent beneficial owners, if their bid is thwarted by management opposition or topped by a competitor, they could find themselves locked into a substantial investment over which they have no control for six months. The Supreme Court has eased this burden somewhat by holding that the rule has no further application after the beneficial owner has sold enough shares to drop below 10 percent.[6] It has also construed § 16(b) to be inapplicable to forced sales, such as sales made in connection with a merger.[7]

---

6. *Reliance Electric Co. v. Emerson Electric Co.*, 404 U.S. 418 (1972).
7. *Kern County Land Co. v. Occidental Petroleum Corp.*, 411 U.S. 582 (1973).

~ 7 ~

Public Offerings

Two college students, Henry and Roberta, started an Internet-based company three years ago. The company, known affectionately as Firedot, provides a virtual community in which people can congregate in a simulated online world. Firedot earns revenues from sales of "real estate" in this community, enabling participants to enjoy a permanent place to call their own in the online world. Firedot has grown rapidly and now Henry and Roberta are contemplating an initial public offering to raise capital to expand Firedot worldwide.

It takes money to make money. This truism has two important implications: (1) a discouraging thought for those without money; and (2) an unfortunate reality for many startup companies. New projects will generate profits only in the future. Microsoft may project that developing a new operating system may lead to billions of additional profits over the next decade. Developing an operating system is not cheap; Microsoft may need to invest hundreds of millions of dollars. Moreover, the potential profits from this endeavor may take years to realize. Microsoft therefore faces a timing problem. Even the most profitable projects may not get launched if a company has inadequate funding to cover a project's costs before its profits can be realized.

On a smaller scale, our two college students, Henry and Roberta, think that if they quit school they will be able to launch a new Internet-based business. If they are lucky, the business may produce profits (or, more realistically, a buy-out offer from an established company) sometime in the not-too-distant future. Although the time and energy of two college dropouts may prove sufficient to start an Internet business, most likely the two will need cash to pay for servers, routers, employee salaries, and strong infusions of caffeine. Without this cash, the two may choose not to start the business and simply stay in school.

Of course, some projects are unprofitable once the costs of developing and launching the project are taken into account. Perhaps Henry and Roberta would benefit more from staying in school even if they had the cash to launch a new business. A business plan to sell portable heaters in Austin, Texas, in June would never receive funding, and rightly so. But some business plans are more promising. Companies such as Microsoft have no trouble finding the necessary funding to launch projects they see as having a net positive present discounted value. Microsoft can simply self-finance new projects out of internally generated cash flow from its existing products.

Compare Microsoft's situation with that of our two college students. Henry and Roberta may only have a few thousand dollars between them, barely enough to start their own business. Even if their business succeeds in grabbing the attention of Internet users, profitability may be years away, because it may take longer to attract advertisers. Suppose that Henry and Roberta need $2 million to carry their business through its first two years of operation. Unlike Microsoft, Henry and Roberta do not have the resources to self-finance the business, and they are likely to have little luck in convincing a bank to loan them $2 million. (If you were a bank loan officer, would you loan money to a couple of college dropouts?) The inability of Henry and Roberta to obtain financing even for a potentially very lucrative project is not unique to startup companies. Even an established company may have difficulty raising large sums of money solely from bank financing.

What other financing options are available to companies? Companies can issue securities (becoming *issuers*), whether common stock, preferred stock, or bonds, directly to investors. Offerings of securities can take different forms. In Chapter 9 we discuss private placements of unregistered securities. In this chapter, we cover registered public offerings of securities made to the marketplace generally.

1 THE PUBLIC OFFERING PROCESS

The founders of Firedot, Henry and Roberta, would like to raise startup funds for its operations by selling common stock to investors. For entrepreneurs like Henry and Roberta, common stock offers flexibility because it does not require any immediate payments. Debt, by contrast, typically puts an immediate demand on cash flow in the form of periodic interest payments. Moreover, because Henry and Roberta plan to sell only a minority of the total outstanding shares to the public, they will retain control over the corporation. But how should Henry and Roberta, college dropouts with scant knowledge of securities regulation and financial markets, go about initiating a public offering of Firedot stock?

For most issuers, the starting point of the public offering process is finding an investment bank to serve as lead underwriter for the offering. The lead underwriter plays a particularly important role for an issuer selling securities to the public for the first time (in an *initial public offering* or IPO). The lead underwriter provides expertise in assessing market conditions, including the best timing and pricing for the offering. (Because there will typically be no existing market for the company's stock, determining its value will be a difficult process.)

The lead underwriter also assists in restructuring the corporation, if necessary, for the public marketplace. IPO issuers often clean up their corporate structure, eliminating subsidiaries and simplifying their capital structure. They will typically reduce the classes of securities to one class of common stock, getting rid of preferred stock and dual-class common stock. A simplified corporate and capital structure makes it easier for investors to value the company, reducing the risk to such investors and increasing their willingness to purchase the offered securities. Some IPO issuers also reincorporate into Delaware, the most popular state of incorporation for public companies.

The lead underwriter provides issuers with contacts with institutional investors, particularly important for issuers going public for the first time. In some types of offerings, as discussed below, the lead underwriter also plays an underwriting role by purchasing the securities from the issuer (hence the term *underwriter*), insuring that the issuer will receive a fixed amount of money from the offering.

1.1 Types of Public Offerings

The most common type of public offering is a *firm commitment offering*. In a firm commitment offering, the issuer first sells the offered securities to the underwriters at a discount; the underwriters then sell the securities to investors. In an initial public offering, the discount is typically set at 7 percent of the eventual offering price. (So if the offering price is $20, the underwriter pays the issuer $18.60 for each share.) The initial sale by the issuer to the underwriter shifts to the underwriter the risk that the offering will be poorly received by the market. Shifting this risk ensures that the company will receive a fixed and certain amount from the offering. Many investment opportunities require a minimum amount of capital to succeed. It is difficult to build a $100 million factory if the issuer raises only $50 million. Investors may worry that a company that receives less than the minimum amount of required capital will instead use the money on less promising projects (such as redecorating the CEO's office). A firm commitment offering alleviates such fears among investors, consequently increasing their willingness to purchase in the offering.

Given the risk entailed by the firm commitment offering, particularly in an IPO, investment banks seldom go solo as underwriters for a public offering. Instead, underwriters will typically form syndicates of underwriters to spread the risk of the offering. Forming a syndicate also allows for access to a broader array of investors because different underwriters may have ongoing relationships with varying groups of institutional investors.

Not all offerings involve a shift of risk from the issuer to the underwriters. In a *best efforts offering*, the underwriter does not take title to the offered securities as in a firm commitment offering. Instead, the underwriter works as the issuer's agent, earning a commission for each security sold in the offering. The risk of the offering remains with the issuer until the securities are sold to the investor. There are variants of the best efforts offering. To combat the fear among investors that an offering will fail to raise the required minimum amount to fund a particular business project, issuers may use an *all-or-nothing best efforts offering*. In an all-or-nothing offering, the investors' money is returned if the issuer fails to sell a minimum amount of securities in a specified time period.

Some offerings attempt to cut out underwriters altogether (along with the hefty commissions they receive). In a *rights offering*, the issuer sells securities directly to its current stock- holders. In such an offering, shareholders may be given rights enabling them to purchase additional shares directly from the company at a specified price. This price will often be at a discount from the current market price.

In recent years, some issuers (including most notably Google, Inc.) have turned to so-called *Dutch auctions* to sell securities in a public offering. In a Dutch auction, the offering price is set not by the underwriter and issuer but directly by the market. The issuer specifies the number of shares to be sold. Investors then submit bids specifying a desired amount of securities and the maximum price they are willing to pay for those securities. Suppose that Firedot conducts a Dutch auction for its stock and intends to sell 225,000 shares. It receives the following bids (arranged from highest to lowest price):

100,000 shares at $50 per share
125,000 shares at $45 per share
150,000 shares at $40 per share
110,000 shares at $35 per share
190,000 shares at $33 per share

The issuer chooses the highest price that will enable it to sell its desired amount of securities. If Firedot sets its price at $45 per share, it will sell 225,000 shares. In theory, the Dutch auction enables the issuer to cherry pick the top end of the market, choosing the investors who value the issuer most highly. The price of $45 per share represents the highest price Firedot may receive while still selling all 225,000 shares. Who are the investors at this top end (for example, the investors willing to pay $50 per share for Firedot)? If they are institutional investors, this valuation is perhaps realistic. On the other hand, if they are individual investors, some degree of irrational exuberance (or overconfidence) may be driving these higher bids.

1.2 Steps in the Public Offering

Before examining the public offering rules, we outline the steps in the public offering process, focusing in particular on firm commitment offerings. The public offering process revolves around a mandatory disclosure document, the registration statement. The public offering process is defined by three key events. First, the starting point of a public offering begins when the issuer is *in registration*. According to the SEC, an issuer is in registration "at least from the time an issuer reaches an understanding with the broker-dealer which is to act as managing underwriter [before] the filing of a registration statement."[1] The key phrase here is "at least." An issuer may go into registration at an earlier point in time than when an initial understanding is reached with the managing or lead underwriter. An issuer that starts active selling efforts for the offering even before locating a lead underwriter, for example, would be considered in registration.

After an issuer goes in registration, it is in the *pre-filing period*. This period lasts until the second major event, the filing of the registration statement with the SEC. During the pre-filing period, the issuer finds an investment bank to act as lead underwriter. Typically, a letter of intent is signed, indicating the lead underwriter's role in the offering and providing for the reimbursement of the underwriter's expenses during the process. The letter of intent will typically specify the underwriter's discount (as noted above, 7 percent in the case of an IPO, lower for a seasoned offering). The letter will also indicate the underwriter's agreement to handle a firm commitment offering and the issuer's agreement to cooperate in the underwriter's due diligence, which will begin in the pre-filing period. During the pre-filing period, the underwriter will help the issuer to restructure itself for the public marketplace, creating a single corporate entity with one class of common stock. The underwriter's counsel works with the issuer's lawyers in drafting a registration statement.

The *waiting period* begins with the filing of the registration statement. Typically, the lead underwriter will form the underwriter syndicate during the waiting period. The investment banks that join the syndicate will sign a syndicate agreement authorizing the lead underwriter to negotiate with the issuer

---

1. Securities Act Release No. 5180, at n. 1 (October 16, 1971).

and to perform due diligence. The issuer and the lead underwriter will also embark on a road show during the waiting period, traveling from city to city meeting with institutional investors to promote the offering. The road show allows the issuer and lead underwriter to drum up interest in the offering and gauge investors' reactions. For IPO issuers, if demand is weak, the issuer may choose to pull the offering and look for alternative sources of capital.

The SEC may review the issuer's registration statement during the waiting period. The SEC reviews all IPO registration statements, but it only selectively reviews the registration statements of seasoned issuers. After review, the SEC may comment on the registration statement and give the issuer an opportunity to respond.

The waiting period lasts until the SEC declares the registration statement "effective" and sales begin. Just prior to the effective date, the issuer and lead underwriter will determine, based on prevailing market conditions, the offering price and the number of shares to be sold. The issuer and lead underwriter will then execute a formal *underwriting agreement* that will specify the underwriter's discount, the price and shares to be sold, and the firm commitment arrangement between the issuer and the underwriters.

The offering price for IPO issuers is generally set lower than the maximum price that the market will bear, a practice known as underpricing. An IPO issuer with an underpriced stock may go public at $15 per share only to see its stock price shoot up to $25 per share on the first day of trading. Why do issuers and underwriters underprice? One theory is that underwriters purposefully underprice the shares to limit their liability exposure under the Securities Act (discussed in Chapter 8). Another theory is that investors on the first day of trading simply pay too much for the shares out of irrational exuberance. A more benign theory is that underpricing encourages liquidity in the stock, thereby promoting trading in the stock over the longer term. Initial purchasers, eager to cash in on the underpriced stock, will quickly sell their shares into the secondary market, thus encouraging brokers to focus on the resale of such shares.

The *post-effective period* begins when the SEC declares the registration statement effective. Once selling begins, the lead underwriter may stabilize the market to ensure that the market price does not drop precipitously after the offering commences. The lead underwriter may also act as a market maker for the stock, agreeing to buy and sell the securities to provide liquidity for secondary market trading. After the expiration of a specified quiet period — typically 25 days for an IPO issuer (which, as we discuss below, corresponds with the end of the prospectus delivery period for IPO issuers whose securities will be listed on an exchange) — the lead underwriter will also provide analyst research and earnings estimates for the issuer.

The following diagram depicts the various periods in the public offering process.

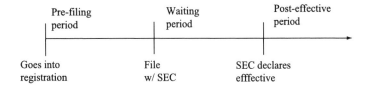

2 THE REGULATION OF PUBLIC OFFERINGS

Public offerings regulation has three goals. First, the securities laws focus on the creation of two mandatory disclosure documents: the registration statement and the statutory prospectus. The statutory prospectus is defined in § 10 of the Securities Act and contains the information found in Part 1 of the registration statement. The registration statement and statutory prospectus contain company-specific information similar to that found in the Form 10-K annual filing for Exchange Act reporting issuers. This includes information on an issuer's business, properties, material legal proceedings, management and director biographies, management discussion and analysis, principal stockholders, executive compensation, and financials, among other items. In addition, the registration statement and the statutory prospectus contain transaction-specific information about the offering, including the offering price, the number of shares, and the plan of distribution (including the underwriters and the underwriters' discount for the shares). The SEC requires that the statutory prospectus be written in "plain English" in a "clear, concise, and understandable manner," as defined in Rules 420 and 421 of the Securities Act. Part 2 of the registration statement, which is not included in the statutory prospectus, contains various exhibits and undertakings.

There are two principal registration statement forms for domestic issuers: Form S-1 and Form S-3.[2] Both forms derive their content from Regulation S-K and S-X, which specify the details of the required disclosure. Item 11(a) of Form S-1, for example, requires issuers to provide a description of their business. Rather than specify the required information further, Form S-1 directs issuers to look at Item 101 of Regulation S-K for more details.

All companies qualify for Form S-1, except for the securities of foreign governments or the political subdivisions of such governments. Form S-3 is available to domestic issuers that satisfy one of several alternative eligibility provisions. The most important category is for companies that have been reporting companies for at least one year, were timely in their periodic filings during the past year, and have over $75 million in equity held by non-affiliates. This $75 million float requirement is waived if the company is selling no more than 20% of its equity.

---

2. Small business issuers may file a more simplified registration statement under Forms SB-1 or SB-2. Foreign issuers may file a registration statement under Forms F-1 or F-3.

The disclosure specified in Regulation S-K and S-X is used both for the registration statement forms (S-1 and S-3) and the periodic disclosure forms (Forms 10-K and 10-Q, discussed in Chapter 4), thereby allowing for a practice known as *incorporation by reference*. Instead of repeating information already disclosed, Form S-1 issuers who are timely with their periodic disclosures for the prior twelve months and have filed an annual report for the most recent completed fiscal year, among other requirements, may simply refer in the registration statement to a prior SEC filing document, such as the most recent Form 10-K (a practice known as *backward incorporation by reference*). Form S-3 issuers may likewise incorporate information by reference from prior SEC filings, but they can also incorporate subsequent SEC filings after the registration statement is declared effective. The ability of a Form S-3 issuer to incorporate by reference subsequent SEC filings allows the Form S-3 issuer to keep the Form S-3 registration statement current for offerings that go on for significant periods of time, such as in shelf registration offerings, discussed below.

The second goal of the public offering process is the broad distribution of the statutory prospectus. Prior to 2005, underwriters mailing out written confirmation for securities sold in a public offering had to include a final statutory prospectus (unless a final prospectus had been previously sent). In 2005, the SEC radically reformed the public offering process. Among these reforms was a streamlined prospectus delivery requirement, known as *access equals delivery*.

The third goal of the public offering process is to channel disclosure relating to the offering through the registration statement and the statutory prospectus. The rules that restrict disclosure are called the *gun-jumping rules* and are derived from § 5 of the Securities Act. Driving the gun-jumping rules is the concept of an *offer*. Only if a communication is deemed an offer is it prohibited by the gun-jumping rules. We start with the definition of *offer*.

2.1 What Is an Offer?

Section 2(a)(3) of the Securities Act defines *offer* to include every "offer" and "solicitation of an offer to buy" a security for value. Although the definition is somewhat sparse in its guidance, the SEC has expanded on that definition.

In the SEC administrative opinion *In the Matter of Carl M. Loeb, Rhoades & Co.*[3] the SEC stated that a broad definition of an offer is necessary to control abuses that would occur as a prelude to a formal offer in the selling process. One goal of the securities laws is to slow the selling process to give investors time to digest information. Communications that "condition the public mind or arouse public interest in the particular securities" may undermine that goal. The SEC also made clear that even if the information is "news," it could still be an offer. Indeed, the risk may be even greater that investors will be thrown into a "frenzy" by information billed as news, particularly for an IPO company lacking a prior record of communications with the investing public.

The SEC has clarified the definition of an offer in a number of Securities Act releases. In Securities Act Release No. 3844,[4] the SEC makes clear that the definition of *offer* in § 2(a)(3) does more than block selling efforts by issuers and underwriters prior to the filing of the registration statement. The SEC provided a number of examples in which the issuer or the underwriters would be viewed as "conditioning the public mind." These included situations in which an underwriter mailed several thousand brochures with positive information about the issuer's industry without mentioning either the issuer or the upcoming public offering (Example 1) and one in which the underwriter sent a press release containing "representations, forecasts and quotations which could not have been supported as reliable data," often referred to as soft

---

3. 38 S.E.C. 843 (1959).
4. SEC, Oct. 8, 1957.

forward-looking information (Example 2). In contrast, a presentation by the CEO to analysts (including forward-looking information) scheduled well before the decision to make a public offering was an example of a communication deemed not an offer (Example 6). The SEC found the presentation to be unobjectionable, but it did recommend against distributing printed documents in connection with the presentation.

Why does the SEC object to forward-looking information? Investors purchase securities in the hope that their investment will yield even more money in the future. A crucial aspect in an investment decision is determining how the company will perform in the future. Consequently, forward-looking information is particularly salient for investors. On the other hand, because it is difficult to verify the accuracy of forward-looking projections, investors may be led astray more easily by this type of information.

Maintaining a strict quiet period by broadly defining an offer does not create serious problems for issuers of initial public offerings. Such issuers, prior to the offering, typically do not have a history of communicating information to the marketplace (other than communications to customers and suppliers). Exchange Act reporting issuers selling securities in a seasoned offering, however, must comply with the periodic disclosure requirements (including Form 10-K, 10-Q, and 8-K filings). Most Exchange Act reporting issuers also provide regular press releases to satisfy the demand for information from secondary market investors. Often such releases contain forward-looking information, such as projections on future earnings. Given the broad definition of an offer, Exchange Act reporting issuers face the possibility that their normal communication with investors and their SEC periodic disclosure filings may be deemed an offer and thus run afoul of the gun-jumping rules.

In Securities Act Release No. 5180,[5] the SEC downplayed the conflict faced by Exchange Act reporting issuers. In the

---

5. SEC, Oct. 16, 1971.

Release, the SEC noted that although "initiating" publicity while in registration is problematic, an issuer may continue to respond to legitimate inquiries. The emphasis in Release 5180 on avoiding "initiating" a new publicity campaign accords with the focus in Release 3844 on motivation. Although motivation is not easy to see directly, it can be inferred from actions such as the initiation of a new publicity campaign. In Release 5180, the SEC also provided a list of permissible communications, including advertisements, periodic reports, proxy statements, and answers to unsolicited inquiries. Significantly, Release 5180 did not include soft forward-looking information in the list of permissible communications.

From the SEC releases and the *Carl M. Loeb* administrative opinion, we derive several key factors informing the definition of an offer:

(1) the motivation of the communication;

(2) the type of information, particularly the presence of soft forward-looking information;

(3) the breadth and form of the communication (for example, written); and

(4) whether the underwriter is mentioned by name (or other facts about the offering).

These factors leave a good deal of uncertainty in determining whether a communication is an offer. Certain situations are clear. If an underwriter writes to solicit an offer to buy from an investor, this is clearly an offer under § 2(a)(3). If the issuer anonymously telephones an investor and simply says, "Planting trees is hard work," this is not an offer (even if somewhat odd). Between these poles is a large gray area in which an issuer or underwriter might communicate in a way that triggers some but not all of the factors above. What if an issuer, while in registration, decides to initiate a new advertisement campaign aimed at customers? What if an issuer distributes revenue projections in these ads? The uncertainty of what constitutes an offer will lead some issuers to err on the side of remaining quiet rather than risk violating the gun-jumping rules.

Deeming a communication an offer triggers the application of many of the prohibitions applicable to the public offering process. What assumptions about investors underlie the broad definition of an offer? Rational investors will give the appropriate weight to information from an issuer or underwriter about the company, its industry, and the offering. Certainly, such information is probative, but it also must be taken with a grain of salt, given the bias of the issuer and underwriters toward pushing the offering. Once the rational investors receive a statutory prospectus containing SEC-specified mandatory disclosure, investors can weigh it against information previously received from the issuer.

Implicit in the definition of an offer and the public offering rules discussed below, however, is an assumption that investors are not completely rational. Instead, some may fix on promotional material supplied by the issuer and underwriters, leading them to ignore information in the statutory prospectus. Investors may go into frenzies, paying irrationally high prices for the stock sold in the public offering. We presume the concern is primarily with individual investors. Does this view of irrational investors inform other areas of securities regulation? As we will discuss in Chapter 9, the securities laws distinguish among investors for purposes of private placements. Only investors able to "fend for themselves" are allowed to purchase in nonpublic offerings under § 4(2) of the Securities Act.

2.2 The Gun-Jumping Rules

The securities laws regulate public offerings from the time an offering goes in registration and continue into the post-effective period. The starting point is § 5 of the Securities Act. Section 5 provides the initial regulatory prohibitions that apply in the three public offering periods: the pre-filing, waiting, and post-effective periods. Both § 2(a) (providing definitions of key terms) and § 4 (providing exemptions from § 5) are important to understanding the operation of the § 5 prohibitions. In addition, the SEC has promulgated an array of rules expanding on and modifying the public offering regulations. Many of the more important rules stem from the 2005 Public Offering Reforms, promulgated to open up issuers' ability to communicate with investors during the public offering process.

The application of the gun-jumping rules often turns on the type of issuer involved in the offering. The Public Offering Reforms partitioned companies into four groups: (1) non-reporting, (2) unseasoned, (3) seasoned, and (4) well-known seasoned issuers (WKSI, or as we like to say, "wicksee"). Non-reporting companies are those not required to file periodic reports pursuant to §§ 13 or 15(d) of the Exchange Act. Unseasoned issuers include Exchange Act reporting issuers not eligible to file under Form S-3. Seasoned issuers consist of Exchange Act reporting issuers eligible for Form S-3 but not qualified for WKSI status. Issuers qualify for WKSI status in a number of possible ways, as provided in Rule 405 of the Securities Act. The most important category of WKSIs are issuers eligible to file under Form S-3 which have a worldwide market value of outstanding common equity in the hands of non-affiliates of at least $700 million. Compare the $700 million requirement for WKSI status with the $75 million equity market value requirement of Form S-3.

Before we embark on our tour through the public offering regulations, note that many of the SEC rules providing safe harbor exemptions in the public offering process do not apply in several situations. For example, investment companies and business development companies generally cannot avail themselves of the exemptions, nor can shell companies, blank check, and penny stock issuers. Business combination transactions are also generally excluded from the safe harbors. Not all safe harbors exclude all of these situations. We do not discuss these various exclusions below, lest we drown our readers in detail; check the specific safe harbor rules to determine the precise contours of these exclusions.

2.3 Pre-Filing Period

Section 5(a) prohibits all sales until the registration statement becomes effective, thus blocking sales in the pre-filing period. Section 5(c) prohibits all offers of securities prior to the filing of the registration statement. In § 5(c) we see the clearest link between the breadth of the definition of an offer under § 2(a)(3) and the prohibition against communications contained in § 5. Importantly, § 5 applies to "any person," including those not participating in the offering transactions, as long as an instrumentality of interstate commerce is used (such as the telephone or the mail).

To say that offers are prohibited during the pre-filing period is but a starting point for analysis. We next need to consider whether any of the exemptions in § 4 apply. Section 4(1), for example, exempts transactions by any person other than an issuer, underwriter, or dealer. Thus, nondealers who are not participating in the offering (such as a newspaper reporter) may freely publish information on the offering, even if the information would be considered an offer because the offering is mentioned. Section 4(4) exempts unsolicited broker's transactions. Suppose a seasoned issuer plans to sell securities in a public offering and already has common stock trading in the secondary marketplace. Section 4(4) allows the underwriters' brokers to assist investors in executing unsolicited transactions in the issuer's securities despite the § 5 prohibition.

Outside of the statutory exemptions, the SEC provides a number of exemptions by rule, allowing communication that otherwise might be considered an offer. Rule 135 allows issuers, selling security holders, and those acting on behalf of either to publish a notice on the proposed public offering. Rule 135 exempts the communication from the definition of an offer for purposes of § 5. Rule 135 requires a mandatory legend indicating that the statement is not an offer (Rule 135(a)(1)). Rule 135 then goes on to list permissible items in a notice, including, among others, the name of the issuer; the title, amount, and basic terms of the securities; the amount of the offering to be made by selling security holders (for example, insiders also selling securities in the offering); and a brief statement of the manner and purpose of the offering. The underwriters, however, must not be named (Rule 135(a)(2)).

As part of the 2005 Public Offering Reforms, the SEC freed issuers to communicate during the pre-filing period with a series of new rules: Rule 163A, 163, 168, and 169. We discuss each in turn. Because of the complexity of many of the public offering rules, we provide a series of short hypothetical question and answers for many of the rules to help clarify their operation.

Rule 163A   Rule 163A provides a safe harbor from the application of § 5(c) for any communication made by or on behalf of an issuer up to 30 days prior to the filing of the registration statement. Rule 163A imposes several conditions. First, the communication may not refer to the securities offering (Rule 163A(a)). Second, the issuer must take reasonable steps to ensure that further distribution or publication of the communication does not occur during the 30 days immediately prior to the filing of the registration statement (Rule 163A(a)). Third, an offering participant who is an underwriter or dealer, even if acting on behalf of the issuer, may not take advantage of

Rule 163A (Rule 163A(c)). The following timeline depicts the operation of Rule 163A:

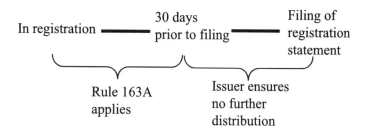

According to the SEC, "the 30-day timeframe [of Rule 163A] . . . provid[es] a sufficient time period to cool any interest in the offering that might arise from the communication."[6]

Communications exempt under Rule 163A are not considered to be in connection with a registered securities offering for purposes of Regulation FD. Recall that Rule 100(b)(2)(iv) of Regulation FD exempts from the prohibition against selective disclosure certain forms of communication in connection with a registered public offering. Rule 163A thus excludes communications from this FD exemption. What does an exclusion from an exemption mean? For an Exchange Act reporting issuer, once the Rule 100(b)(2)(iv) exemption does not apply, Regulation FD prohibits selective disclosures. For a non-Exchange Act reporting issuer, Regulation FD does not apply at all, so an exclusion from the exemption does not matter.

Consider the operation of Rule 163A in the following series of hypotheticals:

1. Firedot mails a brochure (Firedot's first such mailing) to all prior customers of the lead underwriter for Firedot's IPO. The

---

6. See 70 Fed. Reg. at 44, 740.

brochure does not mention the IPO but does tout Firedot's business success and bright future prospects. The brochure is mailed 50 days prior to the filing of Firedot's registration statement.

Answer: Fits within Rule 163A and thus does not violate § 5(c). The brochure is a communication that likely would be considered an offer despite the lack of any mention of the IPO. The discussion of Firedot's success and bright prospects combined with the timing, audience, and first-time nature of the mailing make it likely that the brochure would be seen as conditioning the market. Nonetheless, the brochure is mailed 50 days prior to the filing of the registration statement. The issuer, and not the underwriter, makes the communication, and no direct reference is made to the offering. We only need to make sure that the issuer takes reasonable steps to stop redistribution of the brochure during the 30-day period prior to the filing of the registration statement. Note that Regulation FD does not apply because Firedot is a non-reporting issuer.

2. Instead of Firedot, what if Jazzdot, a WKSI, sends the mailing in the first hypothetical?

Answer: Now we might have a Regulation FD problem. Regulation FD applies to all domestic reporting WKSI issuers, and Rule 163A specifies that the exemption under Rule 100(b)(2)(iv) of Regulation FD does not apply for communications falling under the Rule 163A safe harbor. Because the communications to the investors are selective, if they contain nonpublic material information, they would violate Regulation FD.

3. Firedot mails a brochure (Firedot's first such mailing) to all prior customers of the lead underwriter for Firedot's IPO. The brochure is mailed 50 days prior to the filing of Firedot's registration statement. The brochure, among other things, contains information on the IPO and a response card for investors to mail back their interest in the IPO.

Answer: This does not fit within Rule 163A and, without any other exemption (Rule 163A is not exclusive), violates § 5. The brochure is an offer because of the mention of the IPO and the solicitation of interest from investors. Rule 163A does not apply to communications that mention the offering (Rule 163A(a)).

4. Firedot mails a brochure (Firedot's first such mailing) to the prior customers of the lead underwriter for Firedot's IPO. The brochure is mailed 50 days prior to the filing of Firedot's registration statement. The brochure does not mention the IPO, but it does include information about Firedot's prior business success and bright future prospects. Among other things, the brochure reports that Firedot's revenues for the prior fiscal year were $100 million. In fact, the revenues were $90 million.

Answer: Rule 163A likely applies, but the issuer faces a potential antifraud problem. The difference between the reported and actual revenues is likely material. (This represents a greater than 10 percent overstatement of revenues.) The issuer would therefore face possible Rule 10b-5 liability. An interesting issue is whether the Rule 163A communication would be considered a document used in conjunction with a public offering and thus a prospectus for purposes of § 12(a)(2) liability. Unlike Rule 163 (discussed below), Rule 163A does not bring communications covered by its exemption within § 12(a)(2).

5. Firedot's lead underwriter mails a brochure to all its customers. The brochure does not mention the IPO, but it does tout Firedot's business success and bright future prospects. The brochure is mailed 50 days prior to the filing of Firedot's registration statement.

Answer: Rule 163A does not apply. The communication is the same as in the first hypothetical above, except now the lead underwriter is sending the brochure. Rule 163A does not apply to communications mailed by an underwriter of the offering (Rule 163A(c)). Why? Communications from an underwriter, even if the offering is not explicitly mentioned, may suggest that an offering is forthcoming. The presence of an underwriter also signals an intent to condition the market; there is no non-offering business purpose for the communication. Rule 163A balances allowing more communications prior to the filing of the registration statement against the fear of conditioning the marketplace.

Rule 163   Rule 163 provides a special exemption solely for WKSIs communicating during the pre-filing period. If Rule 163 applies, communications by or on behalf of a WKSI are excluded from the definition of an offer for purposes of § 5(c). Rule 163 applies to both oral and written communications, deeming written communications as free writing prospectuses and prospectuses under § 2(a)(10) relating to a public offering. By deeming a Rule 163 written communication a prospectus relating to a public offering, the SEC provides not only for Rule 10b-5 but also for § 12(a)(2) private antifraud liability.

WKSIs relying on Rule 163 must satisfy several conditions. First, written communication must include a specified legend (Rule 163(b)(1)). Second, the WKSI must file written communications under Rule 163 with the SEC "promptly" after the filing of the registration statement (Rule 163(b)(2)). Third, an offering participant who is an underwriter or dealer, even if acting on behalf of the WKSI, may not take advantage of Rule 163 (Rule 163(c)). As with Rule 163A, Rule 163 communications are not exempt under Regulation FD.

Consider the operation of Rule 163 in the following series of hypotheticals.

1. Jazzdot, a WKSI, places an advertisement during the pre-filing period in the *Wall Street Journal* detailing information

about its upcoming seasoned public offering and providing revenue and profit projections for the next five years.

Answer: This qualifies for Rule 163. Jazzdot is a WKSI. Jazzdot must provide the requisite Rule 163 legend in the advertisement. Jazzdot must also file the advertisement with the SEC promptly after filing its registration statement. No Regulation FD worries here because the advertisement is broadly disseminated through the *Wall Street Journal*.

2. Jazzdot's advertisement from hypothetical one above contains materially false representations about WKSI's plan on how to use the offering proceeds.

Answer: No Rule 163 problems (assuming all the conditions of Rule 163 are met as detailed in the answer to hypothetical one above). However, Jazzdot faces potential liability under Rule 10b-5 and § 12(a)(2) for its materially misleading information.

3. Instead of an advertisement, Jazzdot mails a brochure containing the same information as in hypothetical one above to a select group of institutional investors.

Answer: Regulation FD prohibits such selective disclosure. Rule 163(e) excludes Rule 163 communications from the exemption in Rule 100(b)(2)(iv) of Regulation FD. Thus, Regulation FD applies to such communications, since Jazzdot is a WKSI and therefore an Exchange Act reporting issuer. Note that a violation of Regulation FD is not the same as a violation of § 5(c). Section 5(c) potentially exposes Jazzdot to § 12(a)(1) private liability (as we discuss in Chapter 9). A violation of Regulation FD does not lead to any private cause of action.

4. During the pre-filing period, Jazzdot's lead underwriter places an advertisement for the offering in the *Wall Street Journal*.

Answer: This does not fit within Rule 163. Underwriters are not allowed to communicate on behalf of issuers under Rule 163 (Rule 163(c)).

Rule 168   Rules 168 and 169 give certainty to issuers who want to continue to release regularly distributed information prior to the public offering. Rule 168, limited to Exchange Act reporting issuers, provides a safe harbor for regularly released or disseminated factual business information and forward-looking information. If Rule 168 applies, the rule excludes communications from the definition of an offer for purposes of §§ 5(c) and 2(a)(10). Thus, Rule 168 allows issuers, and those working on their behalf, to communicate in the pre-filing period without violating § 5(c). In addition, once a communication is not an offer for purposes of § 2(a)(10) (the definition of a prospectus), § 5(b)(1) no longer prohibits the communication in the waiting and post-effective periods. Note that a communication that will qualify under Rule 168 will almost certainly be treated as written (including graphic communication as defined in Rule 405). Regularly released or disseminated information typically occurs through a written, broadcast, or Internet media. Another consequence of escaping the prospectus definition is that § 12(a)(2) antifraud liability does not apply to a communication that falls under Rule 168.

Rule 168 imposes a number of conditions on Exchange Act reporting issuers seeking to qualify for the safe harbor. First, only factual business or forward-looking information are permitted under Rule 168(a). Rule 168(b)(1) defines factual business information to include:

i.   Factual information about the issuer, its business or financial developments, or other aspects of its business;
ii. Advertisements of, or other information about, the issuer's products or services; and
iii. Dividend notices.

Rule 168(b)(1) specifies that factual business information includes information contained in Exchange Act reporting filings (such as in a Form 10-K).

Rule 168(b)(2) defines forward-looking information to include:

i. Projections of the issuer's revenues, income (loss), earnings (loss) per share, capital expenditures, dividends, capital structure, or other financial items;

ii. Statements about the issuer management's plans and objectives for future operations, including plans or objectives relating to the products or services of the issuer;

iii. Statements about the issuer's future economic performance, including statements of the type contemplated by the management's discussion and analysis of financial condition and results of operation . . . ; and

iv. Assumptions underlying or relating to any of the information described in paragraphs (b)(2)(i), (b)(2)(ii) and (b)(2)(iii) of this section.

Rule 168(b)(2) specifies that forward-looking information includes information contained in Exchange Act reporting filings.

Second, an offering participant who is an underwriter or dealer, even if acting on behalf of the issuer, cannot rely on Rule 168 (Rule 168(b)(3)). Third, Rule 168 does not permit disclosure of information about the public offering, nor can such disclosure be a "part of the offering activities" (Rule 168(c)). Fourth, the information under Rule 168 must be regularly released or disseminated (Rule 168(a)), and the issuer must have previously released or disseminated the same type of information in the ordinary course of business (Rule 168(d)(1)). The "timing, manner, and form" of the information must be consistent in material respects with similar past releases (Rule 168(d)(2)).

Unlike Rules 163 and 163A, Rule 168 does not mention Regulation FD. Nonetheless, note that Rule 100(b)(2)(iv) of Regulation FD does not exclude regularly released factual or forward-looking information that would qualify under Rule 168. Thus, Regulation FD applies to Rule 168 communications.

Consider the operation of Rule 168 in the following series of hypotheticals:

1. Jazzdot, a WKSI (and thus an Exchange Act reporting issuer), files its Form 10-K discussing future uncertainties and trends in the management discussion and analysis section.

Answer: This is permitted under Rule 168. Management discussion and analysis information in the Form 10-K is included in the list of allowable forward-looking information items in Rule 168(b)(2). Jazzdot must ensure that the distribution of the Form 10-K to investors uses the same timing, manner, and form as prior distributions of the Form 10-K and that such distributions were regular and in the ordinary course of business. If Jazzdot distributes its 10-K by means other than simply filing it on EDGAR, it must have used those same means in the past.

Why do we need Rule 168 at all for this hypothetical? The SEC in Securities Act Release No. 5180, discussed above, made clear that complying with periodic filing requirements would not be considered an offer at all. Nonetheless, Rule 168 affords additional certainty to issuers, which may be comforting given the negative view on soft information in SEC releases.

2. Jazzdot mails an advertisement to trade journals touting Jazzdot's products and past track record for safety and reliability.

Answer: This is permitted under Rule 168. Advertisements to customers are permitted under Rule 168(b)(1)(ii). Assuming the advertisement is regular, in the ordinary course of business, and with the same timing, manner, and form as prior communications, this mailing would be allowed under Rule 168. Rule 168, because of its exemption from the definition of a prospectus in § 2(a)(10), continues to protect such communication from § 5 even during the waiting and post-effective periods. Note that during those periods, § 5(b)(1) is the primary gun-jumping prohibition.

3. While its public offering is in registration, Jazzdot expands its mailing of an advertisement touting its products and past track record for safety and reliability to include not only trade journals but also several financial magazines.
Answer: This will not qualify for Rule 168. The expansion into financial magazines will likely not meet the same "timing, manner, and form" requirement of Rule 168(d)(2). Of course, reliance on Rule 168 is not exclusive; advertisements are generally not offers at all. However, the sudden shift to financial magazines at least raises the possibility that a court (or the SEC) may see the advertisements as attempting to condition the market and therefore as offers.

4. Jazzdot distributes a press release broadly to the securities markets as part of its regular communication with investors. The press release contains detailed projections about revenues and costs over the next several years as well as assumptions behind the projections.
Answer: The press release qualifies for Rule 168. Note that forward-looking information traditionally has been viewed as problematic by the SEC in the public offering process. The agency has generally seen it as an offer. Rule 168, nonetheless, covers forward-looking projections on revenues and costs and the underlying assumptions behind such projections (Rule 168(b)(2)(i)). We must also ensure the other provisions of Rule 168 are met: the communications are not part of the offering activities (Rule 168(c)); are released regularly in the ordinary course of business (Rule 168(a); 168(d)(1)); and are in the same time, manner, and form (Rule 168(d)(2)).

5. Jazzdot provides the press release in hypothetical four only to a select group of institutional investors.

Answer: Limiting distribution to institutional investors does not affect the application of Rule 168. However, we need to consider whether Regulation FD may prohibit such selective disclosure. Jazzdot is an Exchange Act reporting issuer and, therefore, Regulation FD applies. The Rule 100(b)(2)(iv) exemption for certain communication in a registered public offering does not apply because Rule 168 communications are not included in the list of exempted communications. Thus, Jazzdot has violated Regulation FD if it has provided material, nonpublic information to the institutional investors. Note that a violation of Regulation FD is not the same thing as a violation of § 5.

6. Instead of Jazzdot, the lead underwriter for the public offering mails the press release in hypothetical four widely to investors.

Answer: Not permitted under Rule 168. Note there is no Regulation FD problem. Rule 168(b)(3), however, specifically excludes underwriters from the class of offering participants who may distribute information pursuant to Rule 168 on behalf of the issuer.

Rule 169   Rule 169 provides a safe harbor for regularly released or disseminated factual business information for all issuers, including those that fail to qualify for Rule 168. Unlike Rule 168, Rule 169 does not require Exchange Act reporting status. Like Rule 168, Rule 169 provides that communications that qualify for its safe harbor are not treated as offers for purposes of § 5(c) (pre-filing period) and § 2(a)(10). The exclusion from § 2(a)(10) protects the communication from the application of § 5(b)(1) in the waiting and post-effective periods and § 12(a)(2) antifraud liability.

Rule 169 imposes a number of conditions. Unlike Rule 168, only factual business information is permitted under

Rule 169(a). Rule 169(b)(1) defines factual business information to include:

i. Factual information about the issuer, its business or financial developments, or other aspects of its business; and

ii. Advertisements of, or other information about, the issuer's products or services.

The other conditions under Rule 169 track those we saw under Rule 168. An offering participant who is an underwriter or dealer, even if acting on behalf of the issuer, may not rely on Rule 169 (Rule 169(b)(2)). The release of information under Rule 163 may neither contain information about the public offering nor represent it as "part of the offering activities" (Rule 169(c)).

Again, like Rule 168, the information under Rule 169 must be regularly released or disseminated (Rule 169(a)), and the issuer must have previously released or disseminated the same type of information in the ordinary course of business (Rule 169(d)(1)). The "timing, manner, and form" of the information must also be consistent in material respects with similar past releases or dissemination of information (Rule 169(d)(2)). In addition, Rule 169 is more restrictive than Rule 168. Employees of the issuer or the issuer's agents who have historically provided such information must release or disseminate the information to persons other than in their capacities as investors (for example, as customers and suppliers) (Rule 169(d)(3)).

As with Rule 168 communication, the prohibition of selective disclosure in Regulation FD potentially applies to Rule 169 communications. However, recall that Regulation FD does not apply to non-Exchange Act reporting issuers, the most common users of Rule 169. Exchange Act reporting issuers typically will use the more permissive safe harbor provision of Rule 168. So the fact that Rule 169 does not provide an exemption from Regulation FD is largely a nonissue.

Consider the operation of Rule 169 in the following series of hypotheticals.

1. During the pre-filing period, Firedot mails investors a press release discussing future uncertainties and trends in its capital expenditure needs.

Answer: This is not permitted by Rule 169. Rule 169(b)(1) does not allow the disclosure of forward-looking information, including management discussion and analysis type information. Recall that Firedot is not yet subject to periodic filing obligations under the Exchange Act, so it is obliged to provide this information. The absence of Rule 169 does not necessarily mean that we have a violation of § 5. Firedot may still attempt to argue that the press release is not an offer under § 2(a)(3). However, the discussion of future uncertainties and trends (soft information) and the SEC's traditional negative view of soft information make it likely that such communication will be viewed as conditioning the market and thus as an offer.

2. Firedot mails an advertisement to trade journals touting Firedot's products and past track record for safety and reliability.

Answer: This is permitted under Rule 169. As with Rule 168, advertisements to customers are allowed under Rule 169(b)(1)(ii). Of course, Firedot must ensure that the advertisement is regular, in the ordinary course of business, and with the same timing, manner, and form as prior communications (Rule 169(a), (d)(1), (d)(2)).

Unlike for Rule 168, Firedot must also ensure that the specific employee or agent who sends the advertisement is historically the one who provided such information. In addition, the information must be directed to persons other than in their capacities as investors (for example, as customers and suppliers) (Rule 169(d)(3)). In this case, Firedot could argue that an advertisement in trade journals is directed toward customers. Note that Rule 169, because of its exemption from the definition of a prospectus in § 2(a)(10), would continue to protect such communication from § 5, even during the waiting and post-effective periods (when § 5(b)(1) would represent the primary gun-jumping prohibition).

3. While its public offering is in registration, Firedot expands its mailing of an advertisement touting its products and past track record for safety and reliability to include not only trade journals but also several financial magazines.
Answer: This is not permitted under Rule 169. As with Rule 168, Rule 169 requires that the advertisement have the same timing, manner, and form as prior similar advertisements (Rule 169(d)(2)).

4. Firedot distributes its regular newsletter to 400 shareholders. The press release contains detailed projections about revenues and costs over the next several years as well as assumptions behind the projections.
Answer: This is not permitted under Rule 169. Even though the communication is regular, Rule 169 does not allow information directed at investors (Rule 169(d)(3)). Moreover, it does not cover forward-looking information (Rule 169(b)).

5. Firedot distributes information only to a select group of institutional investors. The communication contains detailed historical financial information.
Answer: This is not permitted under Rule 169. Note that there is no Regulation FD problem, as Firedot is not an Exchange Act reporting issuer. However, Rule 169 does not cover information sent to investors (Rule 169(d)(3)), whether broadly or narrowly. After the filing of the registration statement, Firedot could potentially still send this information if it complied with the requirements for a free writing prospectus (see the discussion below on Rules 164/433). In

the post-effective period, Firedot could attempt to treat the communication as traditional free writing under § 2(a)(10)(a) (see discussion below).

6. Instead of Firedot, but on its behalf, the lead underwriter for the initial public offering mails widely to investors the communication in hypothetical four.
Answer: Not okay under Rule 169. Rule 169(b)(2) specifically excludes underwriters from the class of offering participants who may distribute information pursuant to Rule 169 on behalf of the issuer. Thus, Rule 169 does not apply.

2.4 Waiting Period

The waiting period begins with the filing of the registration statement with SEC. Section 5(c) no longer applies, and thus offers can begin. However, § 5(b)(1) continues to prohibit "any person" from using an instrumentality of interstate commerce in transmitting a "prospectus" unless the prospectus meets the requirements of § 10. Section 10 of the Securities Act sets forth the information required (subject to SEC rule-making) in the statutory prospectus. Section 5(b)(1) clearly contemplates a broader definition of a prospectus than just the § 10 statutory prospectus (recall that the statutory prospectus is Part 1 of the registration statement). Section 2(a)(10), in turn, provides a broader definition of *prospectus* to include both "any prospectus" and a laundry list of written and broadcast communications that offer a security for sale or confirm the sale of the security.

Because § 2(a)(10) incorporates the definition of an *offer*, the definition of a prospectus is both broad and uncertain. Although not all offers are prohibited in the waiting period, any written or broadcast offer is still prohibited unless the communication meets the requirements for a formal statutory prospectus that complies with § 10. Prior to the effective date, issuers and underwriters will typically rely on Rule 430 to use a preliminary prospectus. Following Rule 430, the preliminary prospectus must contain all the same information required in a § 10(a) final prospectus, but it may omit price and price-related information (such as the underwriter discount). The implication of lifting the § 5(c) prohibition on offers in the waiting period is that issuers and underwriters may engage in oral, real-time communications with investors without running afoul of § 5. (Written offers are still prohibited by § 5(b)(1) if they do not qualify as § 10 prospectuses.) The road show, described above, is the most visible manifestation of the freer oral, real-time communication permitted during the waiting period.

The prohibition in § 5(b)(1) on prospectuses that do not meet the requirements of a § 10 statutory prospectus is only the starting point. As with the pre-filing period, the broad prohibition must be understood in light of a number of exemptions that lessen its sting. The exemptive provisions in § 4 potentially apply, including §§ 4(1) and (4), as discussed above. The SEC also provides rule-based safe harbors for communication during the waiting period (and beyond), which we canvas below.

Rule 134 Rule 134 allows issuers to issue notices announcing their public offerings. If Rule 134 applies, written communications are excluded from the definition of a prospectus under § 2(a)(10). (The notice is also excluded from the definition of a free writing prospectus in Rule 405.) Thus, if a written communication fits within Rule 134, it does not run afoul of the prospectus prohibition in § 5(b)(1).

Rule 134 written communications must meet a number of conditions. First, the communication cannot occur before the filing of registration statement with the SEC. Not that Rule 134, because it provides an exemption only from the definition of a prospectus, would have been useful in the pre-filing period in any case. Recall that § 5(c) blocks all offers in the pre-filing period, written or oral. Rule 134 only excludes from the definition of *prospectus*, not *offer*.

Second, Rule 134(a) specifies a list of permissible disclosure categories. Written communications containing information outside these categories are not permitted. Permitted information includes the legal identity and business location of the issuer, the title and price of the securities and the amount being offered, the general type of business of the issuer, the intended use of the proceeds, the type of underwriting, the names of the underwriters, the schedule of the offering (including a description of marketing events, such as the road show), and the procedures the underwriters will use to conduct the offering.

Third, Rule 134(b) provides for mandatory disclosure. The communication must include a specified legend as well as contact information for those interested in obtaining a written § 10 prospectus. The mandatory disclosures may be omitted in certain circumstances. No mandatory disclosure is required if the information contained in the Rule 134 notice is limited to only contact information for those seeking to obtain a § 10 prospectus (and the web address for the prospectus), the type of security, the price, and by whom orders will be executed. The mandatory disclosure is also not required if the written communication is accompanied or preceded by a § 10 prospectus. For electronic communications, the prospectus delivery requirement may be satisfied with an active hyperlink to the prospectus (Rule 134(f)).

Fourth, Rule 134(d) allows the solicitation of offers to buy from investors. Those seeking to solicit offers to buy must include a specified legend (dealers being solicited need not receive this), and the solicitation must be preceded or accompanied by a § 10 prospectus, including a price range if required by rule. For electronic communications, the prospectus delivery requirement may be satisfied with an active hyperlink to the prospectus (Rule 134(f)).

Consider the following questions dealing with the application of the safe harbor in Rule 134.

1. Prior to the filing of the registration statement, Firedot places a tombstone ad in the *Wall Street Journal* that contains, among other things, information on the underwriters and the road show events.

Answer: Rule 134 is not available prior to the filing of the registration statement.

2. After the filing of the registration statement, Firedot places an advertisement in the *Wall Street Journal* containing the requisite Rule 134(b) legend and contact information for the § 10(b) prospectus. The advertisement states that Firedot is planning an offering of $300 million of common stock and provides detailed projections of Firedot's revenues and costs for the next several years.

Answer: Rule 134(a) only allows certain types of information. The *Wall Street Journal* advertisement contains projections on revenues and costs, neither of which is permitted by Rule 134(a). Thus, the advertisement does not fit in the Rule 134 safe harbor.

3. After the filing of the registration statement, Firedot places a tombstone ad in the *Wall Street Journal* that discloses the underwriters and certain road show events. The ad, however, does not include any legend. (Firedot's CEO felt that such "legalese" would turn off readers of the *Wall Street Journal*.)

Answer: This tombstone ad does not meet the requirements of Rule 134. Rule 134(b) requires that Rule 134 notices include the specified legend. The Rule 134(c) exemption from the mandatory legend requirement does not apply because the ad discusses road show events (as part of the marketing of the securities) and the readers of the ad have not received a § 10 prospectus.

4. After the filing of the registration statement, Firedot places a tombstone ad on the *Wall Street Journal* Web site that contains information on the underwriters and the road show events. The ad, however, does not include any legend. (Firedot's CEO felt that such "legalese" would turn off readers of the *Wall Street Journal* Web site.) Firedot does include a hyperlink at the bottom of the Internet ad that links viewers to the § 10 preliminary prospectus.

Answer: This ad is okay under Rule 134. While similar to hypothetical three above, here we have the inclusion of a hyperlink to the § 10 prospectus. Rule 134(f) tells us that a hyperlink to the § 10 prospectus meets the prospectus delivery requirement for Rule 134(b) purposes in the case of electronic communications. If the prospectus has been delivered, we do not need to tell investors where to go to get a prospectus.

5. Firedot delivers a valid Rule 134 tombstone notice (containing information on its upcoming public offering) solely to a select group of institutional investors.

Answer: This selective disclosure is okay. Rule 100(b)(2)(iv)(E) of Regulation FD exempts Rule 134 communications related to a registered public offering.

6. The two lead underwriters for Firedot's offering deliver a valid Rule 134 tombstone notice (containing information on the public offering, the required legend, and contact information on where to obtain the statutory prospectus) to all the investor-clients of the two underwriters. The Rule 134 notice also includes a response postcard that investors may return indicating their interest in purchasing securities in the public offering. The postcard provides a telephone number and address for investors who wish to obtain a § 10 prospectus.

Answer: This is not permitted. Rule 134(d) allows the solicitation of offers to buy. Rule 134(d), however, requires that a § 10 prospectus precede or accompany the solicitation.

Rule 433. As part of the 2005 Public Offering Reforms, the SEC drastically opened up the ability of the issuer and offering participants to make written communications relating to a public offering. The SEC established a new category of communication known as free writing prospectuses. Rule 405 defines a free writing prospectus expansively to include written communications that offer for sale a security subject to a registration statement, even if the communications do not qualify as a § 10 statutory prospectus.

Rules 164 and 433 allow issuers to use free writing prospectuses without worry about § 5 constraints. Rule 164(a) specifies that an issuer or other offering participant, including any underwriter or dealer, may use a free writing prospectus after the filing of a registration statement. If the conditions of Rule 433 are met, Rule 164(a) deems the free writing prospectus a § 10(b) prospectus for purposes of § 5(b)(1). Although the requirements for Rule 164 are therefore found primarily in Rule 433, note that Rule 164 provides a number of cure provisions for immaterial or unintentional failures to meet: the filing requirements of Rule 433 (164(b)); the legend requirement of Rule 433 (164(c)); and the record retention requirement of Rule 433 (164(c)).

Rule 433 provides that free writing prospectuses that meet the requirements set forth in Rule 433 are deemed prospectuses under § 10(b) for purposes of § 5(b)(1). Somewhat oddly, Rule 433 also provides that a free writing prospectus also qualifies as a § 10(b) prospectus for purposes of §§ 2(a)(10)(a) and 5(b)(2). However, both §§ 2(a)(10)(a) and 5(b)(2) require the delivery of a § 10(a) prospectus, making it irrelevant that Rule 433 deems a prospectus to be a § 10(b) prospectus. Perhaps the SEC is merely emphasizing that a final prospectus must be delivered. Nonetheless, the real importance of Rule 433 is in deeming free writing prospectuses as § 10(b) prospectuses for purposes of § 5(b)(1). Recall that § 5(b)(1) prohibits the transmission of any prospectus that does not meet the requirements of § 10, but a § 10(b) prospectus counts.

Compare how Rule 433 operates with the other safe harbor provisions discussed above. Rule 134, for example, excludes qualifying communication from the definition of a prospectus and thereby from the reach of § 5(b)(1). Rule 433 does the opposite: A qualifying communication from an issuer or offering participant is deemed not only a prospectus but a § 10(b) prospectus. Both avenues generate the same result: Section 5(b)(1) does not prohibit the communication. Why the different approaches? One answer lies not with § 5(b)(1), but with § 12(a)(2) antifraud liability. As we will discuss in Chapter 8, § 12(a)(2) applies only for communications "by means of a prospectus" in the context of a public offering. Free writing prospectuses falling under Rule 433 both are prospectuses and are specifically "deemed to be public" (Rule 433(a)). Thus, § 12(a)(2) antifraud liability applies to free writing prospectuses.

Rule 433 imposes a number of requirements. First, for all types of issuers, Rule 433 applies only after the filing of a registration statement with the SEC containing a prospectus meeting the requirements of § 10. (In the case of an IPO issuer, the prospectus must contain a price range for the offering.) (Rules 433(b)(1), (2).)

Second, Rule 433(b) imposes a prospectus delivery requirement on certain issuers. WKSIs and seasoned issuers that qualify for Form S-3 have no prospectus delivery requirement. For non-reporting and unseasoned issuers, however, offering participants transmitting a free writing prospectus must ensure that a § 10 prospectus precedes or accompanies the communication (Rule 433(b)(2)(i)). Rule 433(b)(2)(i) removes the prospectus delivery requirement if a § 10 prospectus has already been provided, as long as it contains no material difference from the current § 10 prospectus. Rule 433(b)(2)(i) also provides that a § 10(b) preliminary prospectus may be used to satisfy the prospectus delivery requirement only in the waiting period. Once a § 10(a) prospectus becomes available in the post-effective period, offering participants must transmit the § 10(a) final prospectus to meet the prospectus delivery requirement of Rule 433(b)(2)(i). Finally, in the case of electronic communications, the SEC permits delivery of the most recent § 10 prospectus through an active hyperlink.

Third, Rule 433(c) restricts the information that can appear in a free writing prospectus. The free writing prospectus must not contain information that conflicts with information in the registration statement, the § 10 prospectus (or any prospectus supplement that is part of the registration statement), or any information in the issuer's periodic and current reports filed with the SEC pursuant to §§ 13 or 15(d) of the Exchange Act (for example, the periodic disclosure filing requirements of Exchange Act reporting issuers). (Rule 433(c)(1).) Rule 433(c)(2) also requires that free writing prospectuses must include a specified legend as well as an e-mail address for use by those interested in obtaining the statutory prospectus and other documents filed by the issuer with the SEC (and, optionally, the issuer's Web site or another Internet address at which the documents may be found).

Fourth, Rule 433(d) imposes a filing requirement with the SEC. The free writing prospectus must be filed no later than the date of first use. Issuers face the most comprehensive filing requirement. Issuers must file all "issuer free writing prospectuses" (Rule 433(d)(1)(i)(A)). Rule 433(h) defines an issuer free writing prospectus (FWP) to include those "prepared by or on behalf of the issuer or used or referred to by an issuer." Any FWP that the issuer itself sends out to investors would qualify as an issuer free writing prospectus. Issuers must also file any issuer information that is contained in the FWP prepared by or on behalf of any other offering participant, such as an underwriter (Rule 433(d)(1)(i)(B)). Importantly, information that the other offering participant generates based on the issuer-supplied information is not included within the scope of "issuer information." Thus, if an issuer provides internal financial numbers to an underwriter, and the underwriter develops and distributes its own financial projection based on the numbers, the financial projections are not issuer information and therefore do not trigger the filing requirement. Finally, the issuer must file a FWP containing a description of the final terms of the issue's securities in the offering (Rule 433(d)(1)(i)(C)). This has become one of the most common uses for free writing prospectuses.

Offering participants, other than the issuer, must file their free writing prospectuses with the SEC, but only if distributed "in a manner reasonably designed to lead to its broad unrestricted dissemination" (Rule 433(d)(1)(ii)). What counts as broad unrestricted dissemination? If an underwriter mails an offering circular containing detailed financial projections to all doctors in California, that mailing would count as broad and unrestricted dissemination. But what if the underwriter mails the same circular to its own brokerage clients? The SEC does not treat communications by underwriters to their own investor-clientele as broad, unrestricted dissemination, a real advantage for underwriters with long client lists.

In cases where a free writing prospectus does not contain "substantive changes" from a FWP previously filed with the SEC, the issuer or other offering participant does not need to file the new FWP (Rule 433(d)(3)). Likewise, the requirement to file "issuer information" does not apply if the information was previously filed with the SEC (Rule 433(d)(4)).

Special filing rules apply if the free writing prospectus is an electronic road show. The default rule is that electronic road shows need not be filed with the SEC (Rule 433(d)(8)(i)). However, the presumption changes for electronic road shows if a non–Exchange Act reporting issuer is offering common equity or convertible equity securities. Electronic road shows for such securities must be filed with the SEC

(Rule 433(d)(8)(ii)), with one exception. If a bona fide electronic road show is available without restriction (for example, on the Internet), the filing requirement is excused. Rule 433(h) defines a *bona fide electronic road show* to mean a road show that "contains a presentation by one or more officers of an issuer or other persons in an issuer's management." Rule 433(h)(5) goes on to require "if more than one road show that is a written communication is being used" then it must include "discussion of the same general areas of information . . . as such other issuer road show or shows for the same offering that are written communications." Many issuers have taken advantage of the ability to post electronic road shows for all investors to view. As of the writing of this book, investors could, for example, view electronic road shows at *www.retailroadshow.com*.

Fifth, if an issuer or other offering participant does not file the free writing prospectus with the SEC, Rule 433(g) imposes a record retention requirement. The issuer or other offering participant must retain all non-filed FWPs for three years following the initial bona fide offering of the securities. The three-year period corresponds to the statute of limitations for fraud claims under the Securities Act.

Lastly, Rule 433(f) establishes a special regime for media free writing prospectuses. The special regime applies only if information is provided, authorized, or approved by an issuer or other offering participant for use by a media source. (A media source is a person in the business of publishing, radio or television broadcasting, or otherwise disseminating written communication.) The issuer or offering participant must file the media source written communication with the SEC within four business days after learning of the publication or dissemination of the communication (subject to certain exceptions). If these conditions are met, Rule 433(f) exempts the media FWP from the application of Rule 433(b)(2)(i) (prospectus delivery), 433(c)(2) (legend), and 433(d) (filing). To be excused from these requirements, the media source may not receive payment or other consideration from the issuer or other offering participant for the written communication or its dissemination (Rule 433(f)(1)(i)). What if a media source receives compensation from the issuer or other offering participant? Such media sources are treated as offering participants and accordingly must comply with the rules for FWPs that apply for other offering participants.

Assume for the following hypotheticals on free writing prospectuses that Jazzdot is a WKSI and Firedot is a non-reporting (IPO) issuer. Both companies are registering common stock for sale in a public offering.

1. Jazzdot mails a free writing prospectus during the waiting period that contains information on its upcoming seasoned offering, including projections of financial results for the next five years. Jazzdot fails to include a § 10(b) prospectus in its mailing.

Answer: This is permitted under Rule 433. Jazzdot is a WKSI and thus does not need to deliver a prospectus with or prior to the FWP (Rule 433(b)(1)). Note that, unlike Rule 134, a free writing prospectus does not limit the type of information (other than the consistency requirement of Rule 433(c)(1)). Jazzdot must include the requisite Rule 433(c)(2) legend and file the issuer FWP by the date of first use (Rule 433(d)(1)(i)(A)).

2. Firedot e-mails a free writing prospectus during the waiting period that contains information on its upcoming offering, including projections of financial results for the next five years. Firedot fails to include a § 10(b) prospectus as an attachment with the e-mails, but it does include a hyperlink at the bottom of every e-mail to the most recent statutory prospectus.

Answer: This is permitted under Rule 433. Firedot is a non-reporting issuer and thus must make a prospectus delivery (Rule 433(b)(2)) (which must include a price range, since Firedot is registering an IPO). The SEC note to

Rule 433(b)(2), however, indicates that including an active hyperlink to the current statutory prospectus is sufficient to meet the prospectus delivery requirement. Firedot must include the requisite Rule 433(c)(2) legend. Lastly, Firedot must file the issuer FWP by the date of first use (Rule 433(d)(1)(i)(A)). How many investors do you think will actually click on the active hyperlink when presented with a free writing prospectus?

3. Firedot e-mails a free writing prospectus during the post-effective period that contains information on its upcoming offering, including projections of financial results for the next five years. Firedot fails to include a § 10 prospectus as an attachment with the e-mails, but it does include a hyperlink at the bottom of every e-mail to the last preliminary prospectus used in the waiting period.

Answer: This is not permitted under Rule 433. The response is the same as in hypothetical two above, except that the FWP is mailed in the post-effective period and the hyperlink is to a preliminary prospectus. Rule 433(b)(2) tells us that, after the effective date, a § 10(a) *final* prospectus must precede or accompany a FWP.

4. Jazzdot gives its previously filed free writing prospectus (containing financial information) to its lead underwriter in the waiting period. The underwriter republishes the issuer's financial information in the underwriter's own free writing prospectus and includes its own set of projections, synthesized from the issuer-supplied financial information. The underwriter's free writing prospectus is delivered to all prior customers of the underwriter's brokerage division.

Answer: This is permitted under Rule 433. Jazzdot is a WKSI, so the underwriter does not need to deliver a prospectus under Rule 433(b)(1). The underwriter must meet the information requirements of Rule 433(c), including the requisite legend. The free writing prospectus contains both issuer information (the supplied financial information) and underwriter-created information (the projections). The issuer does not need to file the issuer information because it is contained in a prior FWP filing with the SEC (Rule 433(d)(4)). The underwriter does not need to file its FWP because the FWP is distributed only to the underwriter's prior brokerage customers. According to the SEC, this is not "broadly disseminated" (Rule 433(d)(1)(ii)). Because the underwriter has not filed its FWP, it must retain the FWP for three years (Rule 433(g)).

5. Firedot posts a recorded file copy of its road show presentation to institutional investors on its Web site, where it is freely available to all. Firedot does not file the recorded presentation with the SEC.

Answer: This is permitted under Rule 433. The recorded transmission of the road show is an electronic free writing prospectus. Because Firedot is a non-reporting issuer, the road show must include an active hyperlink to the current statutory prospectus (Rule 433(b)(2)). Firedot must also include the required legend and ensure that the road show information is consistent with the information in Firedot's registration statement (Rule 433(c)). Firedot does not, however, need to file the electronic road show with the SEC. Although non-reporting issuers of common stock normally must file the electronic road show, assuming the road show posted on the Internet for any person to view qualifies as a bona fide version of the road show (Rule 433(h)(5)), Firedot is exempt from this filing requirement (Rule 433(d)(8)). Instead, Firedot must retain a copy of the electronic road show for three years, pursuant to Rule 433(g).

6. To drum up publicity, Roberta, Firedot's CEO, gives an interview to *Investors' Newsletter*, a weekly circular with a large investor readership. *Investors' Newsletter* publishes the interview almost verbatim. Shortly before the interview is

published, Firedot purchases $20,000 of new advertisements in *Investors' Newsletter*. Assume that a § 10 prospectus was not mailed to the recipients of the *Investors' Newsletter*.

Answer: This probably will not qualify for Rule 433. Although *Investors' Newsletter* is a media source, it likely does not meet the requirements for Rule 433(f). The timing of the new ad purchase makes it at least a possibility that the media source will be viewed as receiving compensation for publishing the interview. If the media source is a compensated participant in the offering, it must meet the various Rule 433 requirements, including the prospectus delivery requirement for non-reporting issuers (such as Firedot) under Rule 433(b)(2), the information requirements of Rule 433(c), and the filing requirement for offering participants engaged in broad dissemination of the FWP under Rule 433(d)(1)(ii). The prospectus delivery requirement, in particular, makes compliance with Rule 433 improbable.

2.5 The Process of Going Effective

Section 8(a) of the Securities Act specifies that the registration statement becomes effective on "the twentieth day after the filing thereof or such earlier date as the Commission may determine." At first glance, it would appear that an issuer may simply wait twenty days for an offering to go effective without any input from the SEC. Issuers, however, voluntarily wait for the SEC to give its approval before going effective. Pursuant to Rule 473, issuers typically file a delaying amendment with the registration statement. The delaying amendment will ensure that the registration statement does not go effective until the SEC gives its approval. In practice, the issuer and its underwriters file an acceleration request with the SEC a few days prior to the desired effective date for the offering.

Why wait for SEC approval? The statutory structure conflicts with market realities. First, § 8(a) provides that any amendment to the registration statement resets the filing date for purposes of the twenty-day clock for registration statements to become effective. Those who wish to use this provision of § 8(a) must therefore file a complete registration statement and avoid amending the registration statement for twenty days. However, no issuer will want to set the price of an offering (a mandatory item of information for the registration statement, absent an SEC exemption such as that under Rule 430A) until just before sales commence.

Second, obtaining SEC approval may be a good thing for issuers. Many issuers view the process of obtaining SEC approval — including comments from the SEC — as a useful review that reduces the risk of later antifraud liability. Better for the SEC to find problems before sales commence than for plaintiffs' attorneys to find problems after the offering.

Third, issuers may voluntarily delay the effective date for fear that refusing to do so may send a red flag to the SEC. The SEC has formal powers to refuse to allow a registration statement to go effective if it determines (after notice and a hearing) that the registration statement is "on its face incomplete or inaccurate in any material respect" (§ 8(b)). The SEC's refusal power under § 8(b) is limited by the need to give notice to the issuer no later than ten days after the filing of the registration statement. More importantly, the SEC may issue a stop order at any time suspending the effectiveness of a registration statement (after notice and a hearing) (§ 8(d)).

2.6 Post-Effective Period

In the post-effective period, § 5(a) no longer applies and sales can begin. Despite the removal of the § 5(a) prohibition on sales in the post-effective period, the gun-jumping rules continue to have bite. In particular, § 5(b)(1) continues to block all prospectuses that do not satisfy § 10. Section 5(b)(2) also prohibits the transmission of securities for sale unless preceded or accompanied by a § 10(a) prospectus. Three aspects of the gun-jumping rules are important during the post-effective period: the prospectus delivery requirement, access equals delivery, and the duty to update the prospectus and the registration statement.

2.6.1 *Prospectus Delivery* The prospectus delivery period is derived from the intersection of a number of provisions. Recall that § 5(b)(1) applies to any person and any transaction in which a prospectus is transmitted using an instrumentality of interstate commerce. Section 2(a)(10), in turn, defines a prospectus to include, among other things, a written sales confirmation.

The inclusion of written sales confirmation in the definition of a prospectus is crucial. In most securities transactions, the physical security certificates are not transmitted, but instead sit in a central location, like the Depository Trust Corporation. Electronic notations reflect ownership in the centralized pool of securities. Investors who purchase or sell securities receive only a written sales confirmation when the transaction closes. Because the written sales confirmation is a prospectus, it must satisfy § 10 or run afoul of § 5(b)(1). This prohibition disappears, however, pursuant to § 2(a)(10)(a), when a § 10(a) prospectus accompanies or precedes the transmission of the written sales confirmation. If § 2(a)(10)(a) applies, the written sales confirmation is excluded from the definition of a prospectus and thus is not prohibited under § 5(b)(1). Prospectus delivery is required to exempt the delivery of a sales confirmation. The exemption in § 2(a)(10)(a) establishes the prospectus delivery requirement in conjunction with § 5(b)(1) and the general scope of the prospectus definition under § 2(a)(10). The upshot is that, although § 5(b)(2) requires the transmission of a § 10(a) statutory prospectus with securities transmitted for sale, in practice the real teeth of the prospectus delivery requirement occurs through the operation of § 5(b)(1) and the inclusion of written confirmations of sales in the definition of a prospectus under § 2(a)(10). Got that?

One can question the benefit to an investor of receiving a final statutory prospectus with a sale confirmation. The cow has left the barn: The securities purchase decision has already been made when the investor receives the prospectus. One response is that the statutory prospectus, thus sent to at least some segment of the market, and may affect overall demand. The SEC has imposed a more pragmatic response on brokers. Rule 15c2-8(b) of the Exchange Act requires brokers participating in an IPO to send a copy of the preliminary prospectus at least 48 hours prior to sending the sales confirmation.

Note that the exemption afforded by § 2(a)(10)(a) covers more than written confirmation of sales. Once in the post-effective period, under § 2(a)(10)(a) issuers and other participants in an offering may distribute any document that otherwise would be a prospectus (that is, a written document providing information on the offering or soliciting offers to buy), as long as they precede or accompany the document with a § 10(a) statutory prospectus, a practice we refer to as *traditional* free writing. Of course, issuers and offering participants may also continue to use Rules 164 and 433 to distribute selling documents as free writing prospectuses. Does either the exemption under § 2(a)(10)(a) (traditional free writing) or Rule 164 and 433 (free writing prospectuses) dominate the other? The answer here is no. Traditional free writing under § 2(a)(10)(a) does not impose the legend, filing, or record retention requirements of Rule 433. For seasoned issuers or WKSIs, free writing prospectuses under Rule 433 do not require prospectus delivery.

With an understanding of the basis of the prospectus delivery requirement (the operation of § 2(a)(10)(a) in conjunction with § 5(b)(1)), we can now determine the time period during which the prospectus must be delivered. Section 5(b)(1) applies at all times after the filing of the registration statement. Without an exemption, the prospectus delivery period would be open ended. Your intuition, however, should tell you that this cannot be the result. How can ordinary secondary market investors selling securities to other investors (sometimes years after the public offering by which the securities made their way to the market) satisfy the prospectus delivery requirement? The Securities Act limits the duration of the prospectus delivery requirement through a series of exemptions in § 4. The most important exemptions are found in §§ 4(1), 4(3), and 4(4).

Section 4(1) exempts any transaction not involving an "issuer, underwriter, or dealer." Exemption from § 5 eliminates the prohibition of § 5(b)(1), and thus written sales confirmations may be sent (as well as other written documentation and offers) without delivering the prospectus. As we will discuss in Chapter 9, § 4(1) is a transaction exemption and not an exemption for particular securities market participants. Thus, even if an investor is not an issuer, underwriter, or dealer, if one of these entities is participating in the transaction, the § 4(1) exemption is not available. Many ordinary secondary market transactions take place through a broker. Unfortunately, § 2(a)(12) defines a dealer to include not only those in the business of buying and selling securities for their own account, but also those who act as agent for others (that is, brokers). Despite the inclusion of ordinary brokers as dealers, most courts (as typified in the *Ackerberg v. Johnson* case discussed in Chapter 9) do not treat the presence of a broker as making § 4(1) inapplicable. Ordinary secondary market transactions executed with the assistance of a broker, therefore, fall within § 4(1) and do not need to meet the prospectus delivery requirement.

Section 4(3) exempts securities dealers from § 5. Importantly, § 4(3) is not available for dealers who continue to act as underwriter for a public offering or who are selling part of an unsold allotment of securities in a public offering. They must deliver a prospectus with the confirmation for as long as the offering continues. Section 4(3) exempts other dealers from § 5 as long as their transactions do not take place during a specified blackout period during which § 4(3) is unavailable. The blackout period extends for a specified number of days from the effective date *or* the first date on which the securities were bona fide offered to the public, whichever is later. The SEC has shortened the blackout period through Rule 174; the period now varies with the type of issuer:

- 0 days: Issuer already is a public reporting company (Rule 174(b));
- 25 days: Issuer's securities will be listed on a registered national securities exchange or included in certain electronic interdealer quotation systems (Rule 174(d));
- 40 days: Issuer is engaged in a seasoned offering and does not meet Rule 174(b) or (d) (a very small category); and
- 90 days: Issuer is engaged in an initial public offering and does not meet Rule 174(b) or (d).

Rule 174 carries over the underwriter's exception to a § 4(3) exemption; dealers acting as underwriters in an offering as well as dealers otherwise participating in an offering and selling unsold allotment securities face an indefinite prospectus delivery requirement. For all other dealers, the prospectus delivery requirement extends in the post-effective period until one of the four specified ending dates above.

Section 4(4) exempts brokers participating in an unsolicited broker's transaction from the prospectus delivery requirement. Section 4(4) provides a useful exemption for brokers associated with investment banks still acting as underwriters and thus unable to make use of § 4(3). The availability of § 4(4) allows brokers of a participating underwriter to provide liquidity for secondary market resales even while public offering sales continue. Although brokers for a participating underwriter may have an undue incentive to push sales, the § 4(4) requirement that transactions be unsolicited to qualify for the exemption blunts this fear.

2.6.2 Access Equals Delivery   Do investors really read the statutory prospectus? Does compelling the distribution of the final § 10(a) statutory prospectus with the written sales confirmation effectively distribute information to the marketplace? We suspect that the answer may vary with the type of company. A number of analysts typically follow seasoned issuers, or WKSIs, and WKSIs' securities will have a liquid (and presumably informationally efficient) secondary market. Simply posting the statutory prospectus at a centralized, well-known Web site, such as EDGAR, will rapidly disseminate the information throughout the marketplace via analysts and secondary market trading. For IPO issuers without analyst coverage or a secondary resale market, information reaches the market more slowly. Brokers may read the statutory prospectus and pass on their advice to investor-clients. Some investors, particularly institutional investors, may analyze the prospectus before deciding whether to invest. After that, information is disseminated throughout the marketplace more by happenstance, depending on the research and analysis of specific investors. Broader distribution of the prospectus may play a more important role under these circumstances.

As part of the 2005 Public Offering Reforms, the SEC moved to radically reduce the burden of the prospectus delivery requirement for issuers. Under newly promulgated Rule 172, the SEC effectively eliminated the prospectus delivery requirement for the transmission of written sales confirmation and notices of allocations of securities (Rule 172(a)) and securities for sale (Rule 172(b)). Delivery is still required, but if Rule 172 is satisfied, access to the final prospectus is deemed to be the equivalent of delivery.

Rule 172(c) imposes certain conditions to satisfy access equals delivery. First, the registration statement must be effective and not subject to any proceeding or examination under §§ 8(d) or (e) (Rule 172(c)(1)). Second, none of the issuers, underwriters, or participating dealers may be subject to a proceeding under § 8A (which provides for SEC cease-and-desist proceedings) (Rule 172(c)(2)). Third, the issuer must file a § 10(a) statutory prospectus with the SEC or make a "good faith and reasonable" effort to file within the time period specified in Rule 424. In the event the time period is exceeded, the issuer must file the prospectus as soon as practicable (Rule 172(c)(3)). This Rule 172(c)(3) filing requirement does not apply for dealers in transactions "requiring delivery pursuant to § 4(3)" (Rule 172(c)(4)). Of course, § 4(3) does not directly require delivery of the prospectus: Section 5(b)(1) and § 2(a)(10)(a) require the delivery. Still, the SEC reference to § 4(3) implicates all dealers who otherwise would face a prospectus delivery requirement for written confirmation of sales; during the prospectus delivery time period, § 4(3) does not provide an exemption from § 5.

The following hypotheticals illustrate the operation of Rule 172.

1. Imagine that Firedot at the start of the post-effective period mails a selling brochure touting its great prospects and the opportunities for investors in its public offering.

Answer: Absent an exemption, this is clearly a prospectus that does not meet the requirements of § 10 and therefore violates § 5(b)(1). One possible exemption is through the § 2(a)(10)(a) traditional free writing provision, which requires that a § 10(a) prospectus precede or accompany the brochure. Rule 172 does not eliminate the need for prospectus delivery to bring a communication within the § 2(a)(10)(a) exemption. By its own terms, Rule 172 only applies to written confirmation of sales and notices of allocations of securities as well as the transmission of securities for sale under § 5(b)(2).

2. Firedot's underwriter mails sales confirmations to investors purchasing directly from the underwriter in Firedot's initial public offering.

Answer: Absent an exemption, the sales confirmation is a prospectus not conforming to § 10 and thus violates § 5(b)(1). Prior to 2005, issuers and underwriters could avoid the § 5(b)(1) prohibition by mailing a § 10(a) prospectus before, or together with, a written sales confirmation. Rule 172(a) today provides that written sales confirmation may be transmitted without a § 10(a) prospectus. We only need to make sure the various requirements of Rule 172(c) are met (including that the issuer has filed a § 10(a) prospectus with the SEC or has made a good faith and reasonable attempt effort to do so). This is the situation that access equals delivery is intended to cover. Now underwriters sending out confirmation of sales generally do not need to include the statutory prospectus. Delivery is presumed from access to the prospectus on EDGAR.

3. At the effective date of its IPO, Firedot included a statutory prospectus with the registration statement that omitted price and price-related information pursuant to Rule 430A. Firedot failed to file with the SEC a § 10(a) prospectus that included the required price and price-related information pursuant to Rule 424(b)(1). HighGrowth, Inc., a dealer unaffiliated with Firedot's IPO, buys and sells Firedot stock on the secondary market within the first week after the IPO commences. Does HighGrowth need to send a statutory prospectus together with written confirmation of sales as it sells Firedot stock?

Answer: No. Rule 172 provides access equals delivery even for unaffiliated dealers. Moreover, Rule 172(c)(4) makes clear that the requirement of a filed § 10(a) prospectus with the SEC under Rule 172(c)(3) does not apply to dealers. Presumably, given the reference to § 4(3), this latitude is only for dealers not acting as underwriters in the offering.

Despite the presence of Rule 172, the prospectus delivery period is still relevant in the post-effective period. As noted above, Rule 172 does not eliminate prospectus delivery for traditional free writing communication under § 2(a)(10)(a), other than a written confirmation of sales or a notice of allocation of securities. The prospectus delivery period is important for the operation of Rule 173, a companion provision also promulgated by the SEC as part of the 2005 Public Offering Reforms. Rule 173(a) provides that during the prospectus delivery time period (as defined by § 4(3) and Rule 174), the underwriters and dealers selling in transactions representing a sale by the issuer or an underwriter must include a notice that the sale is pursuant to a registration statement if a statutory prospectus would have been delivered but for the operation of Rule 172. If no underwriter or dealer is involved in the transaction, the issuer must supply the notice (Rule 173(b)).

Although the SEC still requires that a notice be sent, this burden is far less onerous than the prospectus delivery requirement. Prior to the 2005 Public Offering Reforms, failure to comply with the prospectus delivery requirement could potentially violate § 5. As we will see in the next chapter, all transactions in a public offering are integrated; thus any violation of § 5 in one particular part of the offering leads to a § 5 violation for the entire offering, exposing the issuer and underwriters to potentially massive liability under § 12(a)(1). After the 2005 Public Offering Reforms, underwriters and dealers still must deliver notices. However, failure to comply with the notice requirement does not undermine the ability to rely on the Rule 172 access equals delivery provision (see Rule 173(c)). Although an SEC enforcement action is possible for failure to comply with the Rule 173 notice requirement, violating Rule 173 does not give rise to § 12(a)(1) liability for violating § 5.

So why require notice at all? As we will see in the next chapter, § 11 provides a private liability provision for material misstatements and omissions in the registration statement.

Private plaintiffs must meet strict standing requirements to bring a § 11 action. Specifically, the plaintiff-investors must be able to trace the securities purchased back to the allegedly fraudulent registration statement. The provision of notice provides prospective plaintiffs proof sufficient to meet this tracing requirement.

Still get it? Here's a summary.

(1) A writing sales confirmation is a prospectus (§ 2(a)(10)).
(2) Section 5(b)(1) prohibits the transmission of the written sales confirmation because it is a prospectus that does not meet the requirements of § 10.
(3) Section 2(a)(10)(a) excludes the written sales confirmation from the definition of a prospectus if preceded or accompanied by a § 10(a) prospectus (thus giving rise to the prospectus delivery requirement).
(4) Various exemptions from § 5 exist, removing the prospectus delivery requirement. Section 4(3) provides an exemption for dealers not acting as underwriters for unsold allotments after a specified time period (the prospectus delivery period).
(5) Rule 172 allows that access equals delivery, thus eliminating physical delivery of the prospectus. Instead, Rule 173 imposes a notice delivery requirement during the prospectus delivery period. Failure to comply with Rule 173 does not violate § 5.

2.6.3 Updating in the Post-Effective Period   Businesses are not static: A company may change its CEO, move into new markets, sell new products, and so on. When does a company making a public offering need to update its statutory prospectus or registration statement to reflect this new information?

Although the statutory prospectus is Part 1 of the registration statement, after the effective date, the two documents may take on separate lives. The registration statement must be accurate only as of the effective date of the offering. The statutory prospectus is sent repeatedly to investors (or is deemed delivered under the Rule 172 access equals delivery provision) during the prospectus delivery period. The statutory prospectus must be accurate each time it is delivered. Changes the issuer makes to the statutory prospectus (referred to as *stickering* the new information) are not necessarily reflected in the registration statement previously filed with the SEC. Updating the statutory prospectus does not necessarily entail amending the registration statement. Only when the issuer files the prospectus with the SEC (pursuant to Rule 424(b)) is the information contained in the prospectus reincorporated into the registration statement. This reincorporation results in a new effective date for the registration statement.

Updating the Statutory Prospectus   When must a statutory prospectus be updated? An updating duty may arise from several sources. First, § 10(a)(3) provides that, after nine months from the effective date of the registration statement, the statutory prospectus may not contain information more than sixteen months old "so far as such information is known to the user of such prospectus or can be furnished by such user without unreasonable effort or expense." Of course, this duty is implicated only if the statutory prospectus is still in use.

Second, the threat of antifraud liability provides a more immediate incentive to update the prospectus. The prospectus must be accurate at all times, since sales occur during the prospectus delivery period. If the prospectus is inaccurate at the time of its use, investors may sue using either Rule 10b-5 or § 12(a)(2) antifraud liability. (We cover § 12(a)(2) in Chapter 8.) Thus, if information in the prospectus changes materially while the prospectus is being used, continuing to use the prospectus exposes the issuer to antifraud liability. Rather than face such liability, the issuer will, at a minimum, sticker the corrected information onto the prospectus.

Updating the Registration Statement Having updated the prospectus, must the issuer file it with the SEC? Filing includes the prospectus as part of the registration statement, thereby resetting its effective date. Why does it matter whether updates appear in the statutory prospectus or the registration statement? As we will see in Chapter 8, special private antifraud liability provisions attach to the registration statement (§ 11 of the Securities Act) and prospectus (§ 12(a)(2)). Section 11 represents a more powerful cause of action for plaintiffs, but it applies only to the registration statement, the accuracy of which is measured as of the effective date. Issuers and other offering participants would rather avoid updating the registration statement and resetting the effective date if possible.

The primary duty to update the registration statement comes from Rule 424(b). Rule 424(b)(3) requires filing if a prospectus contains a "substantive change from or addition" to the information in previously filed prospectuses. What counts as "substantive"? The term means something more than mere materiality. But how much more? Easy examples include a change in control, a change in the CEO, or a restatement of past financials: the sort of events that would require an 8-K. But the exact contours of "substantive" are unclear.

For many offerings, updating is simply not an issue. Prior to going effective and initiating sales in an initial public offering, underwriters will assemble a list of investors interested in purchasing the offering, a practice known as *book building*. The underwriter will then price the offering such that the offering will sell quickly to investors in the book. Typically, the offering will be completed the same day it is declared effective by the SEC. Moreover, the SEC has long interpreted § 6(a) as requiring that registered securities be sold promptly.

Many issuers must be able to sell a public offering on an extended and intermittent basis. The SEC has relaxed its position on delayed offerings for a special class known as shelf registration offerings. (We discuss shelf registration below.) With the provision of extended and intermittent offerings, updating becomes an important issue.

The following table summarizes the gun-jumping regime.

Pre-Filing Period	Waiting Period	Post-Effective Period
§ 5(a), (c) § 2(a)(3) — Offer § 4 exemptions	§ 5(a), (b)(1) § 2(a)(3) — Offer § 2(a)(10) — Prospectus § 4 exemptions	§ 5(b)(1), (b)(2) § 2(a)(3) — Offer § 2(a)(10) — Prospectus § 4 exemptions
Rule 135 Notice Rules 163A, 163, 168, 169	Rule 134 Notice Rules 164, 433, 168, 169	Rule 134 Notice Rules 164, 433, 168, 169
		§ 4(3) + Rule 174 (Prospectus delivery)
		Rules 172, 173 § 2(a)(10)(a) — Traditional free writing
		Updating requirements

3 SHELF REGISTRATION

What sorts of issuers need or want to sell securities on a delayed basis? First, imagine a WKSI with a liquid secondary market, a large number of analysts, and a rich information environment for its securities. Arguably, investors in the securities of such a WKSI do not need the protection of the gun-jumping rules. Such rules impede information flow to the detriment of investors in an otherwise well-informed market. Although we saw that the gun-jumping rules do make a number of accommodations for WKSIs, we can question whether any of the remaining gun-jumping provisions are cost effective.

Second, imagine pre-IPO investors owning so-called restricted shares (a topic covered in Chapter 10) of an issuer that has recently done an IPO. Before they can sell a large volume of those shares in the secondary market, they must be registered (thus eliminating their restricted status) or find an exemption from § 5. Such investors often negotiate for the issuer to register the sales but may not be sure of when they will actually sell the securities. Sales could take place one month, six months, or even two years from now. Rather than having to reregister the securities every time a sale takes place, the issuers and the selling investors would benefit from being able to register the securities for sales over time.

The SEC responded to the needs of such issuers with shelf registration. The starting point for understanding shelf registrations is Rule 415 of the Securities Act. Rule 415 provides that securities may be sold on a continuous or delayed basis, provided its conditions are met. The first condition, provided in Rule 415(a)(1), is that the registration statement pertains to one of several specified types of offerings. These offerings include securities sold by persons other than the issuer, such as our pre-IPO investors above (Rule 415(a)(1)(i)). Thus, insiders or other selling securities holders with restricted shares may make use of Rule 415(a)(1)(i) to sell their holdings at a later time without needing the issuer to reregister the securities.

Another category of shelf registration covers securities issued upon the exercise of outstanding options, warrants, or rights or the conversion of outstanding securities (Rule 415(a)(1)(iii), (iv)). Issuers face a problem if they sell debt securities convertible into stock at the discretion of the debt securities holder. Section 2(a)(3) provides as follows:

> The issue or transfer of a right or privilege . . . giving the holder of such security the right to convert such security into another security . . . which right cannot be exercised until some future date, shall not be deemed to be an offer or sale of such other security; but the issue or transfer of such other security upon the exercise of such right of conversion or subscription shall be deemed a sale of such other security.

Thus, each time an investor converts the debt into stock at some future date, the issuer has "sold" the stock to the investor on that date. Rule 415(a)(1)(iv) allows the issuer to register the underlying conversion stock under a shelf registration statement to cover the future deemed sales as conversions occur.

Another category covers securities registered on Form S-3 to be offered or sold on an immediate, continuous, or delayed basis by the issuer or certain entities affiliated with the issuer (Rule 415(a)(1)(x)). What is the rationale for this category? Form S-3 issuers, particularly WKSIs, can communicate relatively freely during the public offering process. Rule 163, for example, allows WKSIs to engage in oral and written offers in the pre-filing period. Nonetheless, the public offering process still limits WKSIs and other Form S-3 issuers. For example, free writing prospectuses must be filed with the SEC under both Rule 163 and Rules 164/433. The same arguments that led the SEC to relax the public offering rules for WKSIs (and non-WKSI Form S-3 issuers) also justify the application of shelf registration for such issuers. Larger issuers whose securities trade in liquid secondary markets typically enjoy the coverage of a number of sell-side analysts. The analysts provide a source of information and expertise for investors in the marketplace. Moreover, such issuers also often have an extensive history of SEC filings. And the liquid market helps ensure that publicly available information is incorporated into the stock market price.

Rule 415 limits the time available for certain shelf offerings. Rule 415(a)(2) provides that certain shelf registered offerings (those covered in Rules 415(a)(1)(viii) and (ix)), not registered on Form S-3, may only register an amount of securities "expected to be offered and sold within two years from the initial effective date of the registration." Note that the two-year time limitation does not apply to the shelf offerings discussed above under Rule 415(a)(1)(i), (iii), (iv), and (x). Form S-3 issuers who qualify under Rule 415(a)(1)(x) do not need to finish their offering within two years.

Rule 415 also requires issuers to update the information in their registration statement. Rule 415(a)(3) requires issuers making a shelf registration to furnish an undertaking pursuant to Item 512(a) of Regulation S-K. The next section provides a detailed discussion of updating in the shelf registration context.

Rule 415(a)(4) applies only to "at the market" offerings of equity securities by or on behalf of an issuer. Such offerings can only be made under Rule 415(a)(1)(x) (that is, they must be registered on Form S-3). Rule 415(a)(4) defines an *at the market offering* as "an offering of equity securities into an existing trading market for outstanding shares of the same class at other than a fixed price."

Rule 415(a)(5) and (6) require certain shelf issuers to reregister. WKSIs are treated more leniently than are other issuers. Shelf registration statements for WKSIs are termed "automatic shelf registration statements" (see definition in Rule 405). Rule 415(a)(5) provides that securities registered on an automatic shelf registration statement and securities under Rule 415(a)(1)(vii), (ix), and (x) may be offered and sold only for a maximum of three years after the initial effective date. This limitation is more apparent than real for Rule 415(a)(1)(x) offerings. To continue sales under Rule 415(a)(1)(x), the issuer must file a new registration statement on Form S-3. Because of incorporation by reference, the issuer may simply refer to information in prior filed documents, leaving only transaction-related information to be included in the Form S-3. (We will see below under Rule 430B that most transaction-related information can be omitted for shelf-registered offerings until an actual sale takes place.) The newly filed registration statement is automatically effective under Rule 462(e) for WKSIs, thus avoiding any delay or break in the offering for such issuers. Even for non-WKSIs, securities under the prior registration statement may continue to be offered and sold until the new registration statement becomes effective or 180 days after the three year limitation, whichever comes first. In the case of a continuous offering of securities, securities can be sold until the new registration statement becomes effective without the 180-day limitation.

Rule 415(a)(6) allows issuers to transfer unsold securities and unused filing fees from the prior registration statement to the new registration statement. For WKSIs, filing fees are even more favorably treated. WKSIs, pursuant to Rule 456(b), may pay filing fees on a pay-as-you-go basis when they actually sell securities from the shelf.

The following questions illustrate the operation of Rule 415.

1. Firedot, a Form S-1 IPO issuer, registers to sell common stock intermittently over the next year, if and when it needs capital.

Answer: This is not permitted by Rule 415. Only S-3 issuers may use Rule 415(a)(1)(x). None of the other categories in Rule 415(a)(1) apply. Intermittent sales do not qualify as "continuous" for purposes of Rule 415(a)(1)(ix).

2. Firedot registers to sell common stock commencing promptly and continuing over the next year on a continuous basis through sales on Nasdaq.

Answer: This is still not permitted by Rule 415. At first glance, it may seem like Rule 415(a)(1)(ix) may apply. But sales onto Nasdaq at other than a fixed price are considered "at the market." Issuers will not want to fix the price of their offering if they sell over any period of time because market conditions may change. Rule 415(a)(4) requires at the market offerings of equity securities by or on behalf of the issuer to fall under Rule 415(a)(1)(x), thereby limiting the category to Form S-3 issuers.

3. Firedot files a shelf registration statement covering occasional sales of common stock onto Nasdaq by Firedot insiders over the next four years.

Answer: This is permitted by Rule 415, under Rule 415(a)(1)(i). The two-year requirement of Rule 415(a)(2) does not apply to Rule 415(a)(1)(i) shelf offerings. The issuer must make an Item 512(a) undertaking pursuant to Rule 415(a)(3). Although the offer is for equity securities at the market, Rule 415(a)(4) does not apply because the offering is not by or on behalf of the issuer. Lastly, the three-year reregistration requirement of Rule 415(a)(5) does not apply to Rule 415(a)(1)(i) offerings, so four years is fine.

4. Jazzdot, a WKSI, files an automatic shelf registration statement to sell common stock intermittently over the next four years.

Answer: This offering qualifies under Rule 415(a)(1)(x). The two-year limit of Rule 415(a)(2) does not apply to Rule 415(a)(1)(x) offerings. The issuer must make an Item 512(a) undertaking pursuant to Rule 415(a)(3). Rule 415(a)(4) does not matter because the offering is already under Rule 415(a)(1)(x).

The three-year limitation of Rule 415(a)(5) does apply to Rule 415(a)(1)(x) offerings, but a WKSI need only file a Form S-3 again before the expiration of the three years. The new registration statement will become effective automatically under Rule 462(e), allowing a continuous offering of indefinite duration.

3.1 The Base Prospectus

One of the most critical issues for shelf registration is changes in business circumstances. Suppose Firedot, Inc., now several years after its IPO and a well-known seasoned issuer, files a shelf registration form on January 1. Firedot will not want on January 1 to disclose the offering price, number of shares offered, the underwriters, or other information relating to a plan of distribution that may occur well into the future.

Suppose eight months later, on September 1, Firedot decides to do a shelf takedown and sell $50 million of common stock through the shelf registration statement. During the interim between January 1 and September 1, Firedot's share price may fluctuate; Firedot may seek to employ a new lead underwriter or negotiate more advantageous terms; and so on.

The SEC affords flexibility with respect to transaction-related information by allowing shelf registration issuers to file a *base prospectus* under Rule 430B. Rule 430B applies only to certain types of shelf registration, including Rule 415(a)(1)(x) shelf offerings. For our discussion, we focus on Rule 415(a)(1)(x), available only to Form S-3 issuers. Issuers registering under Rule 415(a)(1)(x), among others, may omit from the base prospectus information that is "unknown or not reasonably available to the issuer pursuant to Rule 409" (Rule 430B(a)). (Rule 409 expands on the types of information considered unknown and not reasonably available.) Rule 430B(a) also provides that WKSIs may further omit details such as "whether the offering is a primary offering or an offering on behalf of persons other than the issuer, or a combination thereof, the plan of distribution for the securities, a description of the securities registered other than an identification of the name or class of such securities, and the identification of other issuers."

What can WKSIs omit that non-WKSI Form S-3 issuers cannot? Information relating to price and the plan of distribution are not known at the filing of the base prospectus, so even a non-WKSI Form S-3 issuer could omit this information. Nonetheless, WKSIs take comfort from the certainty that such information can be excluded. Moreover, even if an issuer knows whether selling security holders will also sell securities under the shelf registration, the specific securities it will sell, and other affiliated issuers that will participate in the offering (such as a subsidiary corporation of the issuer), a WKSI issuer need not disclose such information in the base prospectus.

Once a base prospectus qualifies under Rule 430B, the Rule tells us that the prospectus qualifies as a § 10 prospectus for purposes of § 5(b)(1). Thus, issuers (and others) may freely distribute the base prospectus without fear of running afoul of § 5. Now suppose that eight months have passed, and Firedot wants to sell common stock from the shelf on September 1. Can Firedot continue to use the base prospectus under Rule 430B? Rule 430B(c) says that the base prospectus does not satisfy the requirements of either § 5(b)(2) (relating to the delivery of a prospectus with securities for sale) or § 2(a)(10)(a) (the traditional free writing exemption). Thus, issuers seeking to transmit securities for sale or engage in traditional free writing (such as sending a written sales confirmation) must add the previously omitted information to the Rule 430B base prospectus, typically through a prospectus supplement, for it to qualify as a § 10(a) prospectus.

But wait; Rule 172, discussed above, allows issuers to avoid the prospectus delivery requirement for the transmission of a written confirmation of sales. Might an issuer and its underwriters avoid updating the base prospectus with price and price-related information if all it sends to investors is a written sales confirmation? The quick answer is no. Rule 172(c)(3) requires that a § 10(a) prospectus be filed with the SEC. Rule 430B provides that the base prospectus applies for § 5(b)(1), but it does not satisfy the § 10(a) prospectus requirement of Rule 172(c)(3). Recall, however, that Rule 172(c)(3) does not apply to dealers other than underwriters.

Can the underwriter look to § 4(3) for an exemption to transmit a prospectus supplement providing the previously omitted Rule 430B information? After all, for Form S-3 issuers listed on a national securities exchange (such as the NYSE or Nasdaq), the prospectus delivery period is zero days under Rule 174(b). This applies only to dealers no longer acting as underwriters, however, so underwriters must still comply with § 5.

Moreover, investor demand will pressure an issuer to provide a prospectus supplement with the previously omitted price and price-related information. Investors in shelf offerings expect a standardized disclosure package. Issuers failing to transmit a prospectus supplement with price and price-related information will likely get a chilly response from investors.

Once the issuer starts using an updated prospectus (a prospectus supplement together with the base prospectus), Rule 424(b)(2) requires the filing of the new prospectus with the SEC. Filing with the SEC incorporates the new prospectus as part of the registration statement. Filing therefore exposes the information in the new prospectus to potential § 11 liability. Rule 430B(d) provides issuers other alternatives for updating the information in the prospectus, which is treated as "part of an effective registration statement." In addition to a Rule 424(b) filing, an issuer may make a post-effective amendment to the registration statement or may incorporate the information by reference from a prior periodic or current report filed with the SEC.

The following questions illustrate the operation of Rule 430B.

1. Jazzdot, a WKSI, omits management's biography from the base prospectus filed as part of its automatic shelf registration statement.
Answer: This is not permitted under Rule 430B. The WKSI may omit only information specified in Rule 430B(a). Management's biography is certainly known to Jazzdot's own management and thus cannot be excluded from the base prospectus.

2. Jazzdot omits the plan of distribution (including price) for any future shelf takedown sales from the base prospectus filed as part of the automatic shelf registration statement. Also omitted is the specific class of securities to be sold.

Answer: This is not permitted under Rule 430B. The WKSI may omit information on the plan of distribution under Rule 430B. Even a non-WKSI may be able to omit such information if the issuer has not settled on the plan at the time of filing (Rule 430B(a)). However, the WKSI must include information on the class of securities registered (Rule 430B(a)). Note that pursuant to Rule 413(b), the WKSI may include new classes of securities at any time in an automatic shelf registration statement through a post-effective amendment. Moreover, pursuant to Rule 462(e), such post-effective amendments are automatically effective. Thus, adding new classes of securities is relatively painless for the WKSI issuer.

3. Two years after the filing of the initial automatic shelf registration statement, Jazzdot's lead underwriter distributes a valid Rule 430B base prospectus together with a glossy brochure detailing the benefits of investing in Jazzdot.

Answer: Absent an exemption, this violates § 5(b)(1). The glossy brochure is a prospectus under § 2(a)(10). The traditional free writing exemption in § 2(a)(10)(a) requires a § 10(a) statutory prospectus. However, Rule 430B(c) explicitly states that a Rule 430B base prospectus only satisfies the requirements of § 5(b)(1) (and therefore implicitly may not be used for § 2(a)(10)(a)).

4. Two years after filing the initial automatic shelf registration statement, Jazzdot's lead underwriter sends a valid Rule 430B base prospectus together with securities sold through the shelf offering.

Answer: Absent an exemption, this violates § 5(b)(2). Section 5(b)(2) requires that a § 10(a) statutory prospectus precede or accompany securities transmitted for sale. Rule 430B(c) explicitly states that a Rule 430B base prospectus only satisfies the requirements of § 5(b)(1).

5. Six months after the start of the Jazzdot's shelf registration offering, the CEO of Jazzdot resigns and a new CEO is hired. The underwriter continues sending out the original Rule 430B base prospectus.

Answer: This potentially violates § 12(a)(2) and Rule 10b-5. To avoid possible antifraud liability, Jazzdot should update the base prospectus. This would typically be done by filing a Form 8-K, which will be incorporated by reference, disclosing the management shift.

3.2 Updating in the Shelf Context

The passage of time during a shelf registration affects the business as well as information relating to price and the plan of distribution. Corporate officers may turn over, the products sold may change, new competitive risks may arise in the marketplace, and so on. Information an issuer included in the initial shelf registration statement may become inaccurate.

Consider whether the prospectus must reflect the changed information. As we saw in the non-shelf context, antifraud liability under both Rule 10b-5 and § 12(a)(2) may lead an issuer to update the prospectus. A failure to update may result in later antifraud lawsuits from eager plaintiffs' attorneys if the new information is material. In addition, § 10(a)(3) requires that after nine months from the effective date the issuer must update any information more than sixteen months old. Once the prospectus is changed (typically by stickering it), we need to ask whether the registration statement must be updated. Recall that Rule 424(b)(3) requires the issuer to file substantive changes or additions to the prospectus with the SEC as part of the registration statement, thereby updating the registration statement as well.

On top of the updating rules that apply to the non-shelf situation, Item 512(a) provides an additional layer of updating requirements for shelf offerings. Consider the three main provisions of Item 512(a).

- Item 512(a)(1)(i) requires issuers that update the prospectus pursuant to § 10(a)(3) to also include the updated prospectus as part of the registration statement.
- Item 512(a)(1)(ii) provides that the issuer must update both the prospectus and the registration statement with information that represents a "fundamental" change to the information in the registration statement. What counts as a fundamental change? It clearly means something more than material information. Possibilities include accounting restatements, changes in control, a change of top executive officers, or a change in accountants. The SEC considered formalizing the definition of a fundamental change to include such categories of changes, but it has not yet provided definitive guidance. The precise definition of *fundamental* remains uncertain.
- Item 512(a)(1)(iii) focuses on changes to the plan of distribution, including the underwriters, the underwriters' discount, and so on. For this limited set of information, Item 512(a)(1)(iii) sets a lower threshold, mere materiality, triggering a duty to include the information as part of the registration statement. Although Item 512(a)(1)(ii) does not specify that the information relating to the plan of distribution must be reflected in the prospectus, issuers will include such information in the prospectus for a number of reasons. If the plan of distribution information was previously omitted under Rule 430B, all the same reasons for updating the prospectus discussed above for Rule 430B base prospectuses apply. Even if the plan of distribution had previously been included in the prospectus, continued use of the old prospectus after a material change has occurred in the plan of distribution opens the issuer up to potential antifraud liability.

Issuers may make the required update to the registration statement using an amendment to the registration statement. Item 512(a)(1) also provides that Form S-3 issuers may incorporate by reference to filings with the SEC, thereby updating information in the registration statement as well. Issuers may also include the information by filing a prospectus with the SEC pursuant to Rule 424(b).

4 OTHER ISSUES

Although we have touched on many of the key aspects of the public offering process and its regulation, our analysis has been far from comprehensive. The following sections touch briefly on other important areas of concern.

4.1 Securities Analysts

Analysts play an important role for secondary market trading. Sell-side analysts, associated with brokerage firms, provide the secondary marketplace with information on the issuers they cover. Of course, investors can obtain information directly through SEC filings for Exchange Act reporting issuers and through their own research. Sell-side analysts add to this information through the synthesis of issuer-supplied information with information about competitors, the economy, and other factors relevant to the valuation of a company. Through this synthesis, sell-side analysts provide investors with earnings projections and summary recommendations on whether to buy a particular security. Buy-side analysts, in contrast, work for particular institutional investors and provide their research solely to those institutional investors.

In the case of an issuer with a preexisting secondary market for its shares (typically an Exchange Act reporting issuer), analysts providing research for use in the secondary market may worry that the provision of research may "condition" the primary market and therefore be treated as an offer for purposes of § 5. The SEC has provided a number of exemptions for research by analysts affiliated with brokerage firms. These exemptions are found in Rules 137, 138, and 139 of the Securities Act. Non-affiliated, independent analysts may escape the reach of § 5 simply by using § 4(1) for transactions not involving an issuer, underwriter, or dealer.

4.2 Market Stabilization

Once the offering becomes effective, underwriters focus on more than simply selling shares. The securities' prevailing price in the secondary market is of paramount importance. If the secondary market price drops below the offer price, investors will be unwilling to purchase securities from the underwriters. Those institutional investors who purchased shares from the underwriters at the now higher than market price will face losses in reselling the shares into the secondary marketplace. Understandably upset, these investors may be wary of buying shares from the underwriters in the future. Not only will the underwriters lose their reputations among institutional investors, they will also suffer loss of reputation among future potential issuers, who will question the underwriters' expertise in pricing an offering.

Underwriters have a number of ways to avoid the problems caused when the secondary market price drops below the offer price. Underwriters may seek to underprice an offering below the projected market price, reducing the risk that the offer price will be higher than the market price. After an offering starts, underwriters may purchase securities in the secondary market in an attempt to prevent or retard a drop in the price of the securities below the offer price. This practice is known as *market stabilization.* In certain instances under Regulation M, distribution participants — including underwriters, brokers, and dealers — and their affiliated purchasers can bid for a distributed security in the secondary market. Among other limitations, these bids must be at or below the public offering price. Stabilizing bids may be made only to avoid a decline in the market price, not to increase the price above independent bids in the market. Regulation M exempts from its prohibitions certain securities that meet a minimum trading volume and public float criteria. Also exempted are passive market making activities.

In practice, some market incentives discourage stabilization. Regulation M requires that "[a]ny person displaying or transmitting a bid that such person knows is for the purpose of stabilizing shall provide prior notice to the market on which such stabilizing will be effected" (Rule 104(h)(1) of Regulation M). Disclosing to the marketplace that the price of recently offered securities is being stabilized may signal that stabilization is pushing the market price artificially high. Alternatively, stabilization may signal the underwriters' lack of confidence in the market price. Either signal may lead to the very downward market price trend that the underwriters had sought to avoid.

4.3 Lock-Up Agreements

Company insiders, including employees, their friends, and their families, as well as venture capitalists in certain startup companies selling shares in an IPO, will often sign lock-up agreements with the issuer and the underwriters in an offering. Most lock-up agreements specify that the insiders will not sell shares into the public marketplace for 180 days after the start of the public offering. Insiders' sales into the marketplace too soon after the start of an offering may drastically increase the number of securities available. Underwriters fear that such sales could trigger a drop in the secondary market price, especially problematic if the drop is below the offer price. Although the SEC does not require or specify the contents of a lock-up agreement, it does require that the registration statement and prospectus disclose the existence of such agreements.

∼ 8 ∼

Civil Liability Under the Securities Act

zTunes, Inc., manufactures a line of portable music players. zTunes recently raised $100 million in capital through a registered public offering of common stock. zTunes's prospectus said that it would use the proceeds from the offering to fund the introduction of a new zPod player. zTunes also reported in its audited financials that its net profits for the past fiscal year amounted to $50 million. Three months after the close of the offering, zTunes revealed that it had secretly taken out loans of $25 million and used the proceeds to artificially boost its revenues, inflating its net profits for the past fiscal year. zTunes also disclosed that it would direct the bulk of the public offering proceeds toward paying off the loans rather than launching the new zPod player.

Fraud has an obvious effect on investors. Investors buy securities expecting to receive even more money in the future. Investors look to disclosures from the issuer, among other sources of information, to estimate the future returns from those securities. If that information is wrong, investors may pay too much.

How do issuers benefit from misleading investors? In our discussion of Rule 10b-5 in Chapter 5, we discussed fraud in the context of secondary market transactions. The managers of a company may wish to inflate the value of a company in the eyes of the investing public as a means of boosting the managers' stock-based compensation or to postpone financial insolvency. Managers may profit from fraudulent information via insider trading, as we discussed in Chapter 6.

The incentive to commit fraud is even more powerful when an issuer or its major shareholders are selling securities. In a primary transaction, fraud that inflates the value of a company's securities also inflates the proceeds from the offering. zTunes, for example, raised $100 million because of its representations. If zTunes had instead told investors that it was unprofitable and needed money to pay down its past debts, it is likely that investors would have been far less interested in the zTunes public offering. The underwriters might have had a difficult time bringing the offering to market at all.

As we saw in Chapter 7, the federal securities laws counter this greater risk of fraud when issuers and insiders sell securities directly to investors by requiring detailed disclosure via a registration statement and statutory prospectus. Detailed information, however, is meaningless unless it is credible. The Securities Act supplements the general antifraud prohibition of Rule 10b-5 with two specialized civil liability provisions, §§ 11 and 12(a)(2). Section 11 targets inaccuracies in the registration statement and § 12(a)(2) targets misstatements in the prospectus. The securities laws also enforce the gun-jumping rules through private liability under § 12(a)(1) for any violation of § 5. In this chapter, we discuss these civil liability provisions of the Securities Act.

1 SECTION 11 LIABILITY

Section 11 of the Securities Act provides investors a civil liability provision for material misstatements or omissions in the registration statement for a public offering. Although investors can also file a Rule 10b-5 action alleging fraud in the registration statement, § 11 provides a powerful alternative source of liability. As we will discuss below, plaintiffs need only show the presence of a material misstatement or omission in a registration statement. Compare that burden with Rule 10b-5, for which plaintiffs must demonstrate scienter, reliance, and causation. Despite these advantages, § 11 does not dominate Rule 10b-5 as a civil liability provision. Among other things, § 11 severely restricts standing for investors to bring a claim. The measure of § 11 damages is also capped at the public offering price, limiting compensation for those who purchase the securities in the secondary market at a price greater than the offering price. If the secondary market price does not go below the offering price, § 11 affords no recovery at all, even if a security has fallen sharply from its secondary market highpoint.

1.1 Standing

Section 11 covers only securities registered pursuant to a registration statement and provides that only "any person acquiring" such securities may sue (the *tracing* requirement). Consider zTunes, Inc., which went public five years ago and has recently sold additional securities through a seasoned public offering. Suppose that zTunes overstated its revenues significantly; those inflated revenue figures are included in the audited financials of the registration statement. A material misstatement in a registration statement for a public company such as zTunes may affect not only the investors who purchase in the offering but also investors who buy the company's securities in secondary market trading at a high market price. Section 11, however, excludes investors who cannot show that they purchased the specific securities sold through the registration statement containing the alleged material misstatement or omission.

Section 11 liability thus discriminates among different vintages of securities trading in the secondary market, based on the registration statement (if any) by which the securities were initially offered to the public. Some zTunes, Inc., common stock may be from the IPO vintage, while other common stock may trace to the registration statement for the seasoned offering. All vintages of common stock, however, enjoy the same rights to dividends, assets in liquidation, and voting authority to elect directors and decide other matters. Moreover, the shares are equally affected by fraud in the current registration statement. Investors ordinarily will not even know the specific vintage of stock they have purchased, particularly if the shares are purchased through a brokerage account with the stock held in the brokerage firm's street name.

The disparate treatment for different vintages of stock becomes even more problematic when we factor in the strict tracing rules that federal courts apply in determining whether an investor purchased stock covered in the specific registration statement alleged to be misleading. *Abbey v. Computer Memories, Inc.*[1] demonstrates the tracing requirement for standing. Computer Memories, Inc. (CMI) sold 2 million common shares in a seasoned public offering in 1983. At the time, CMI already had 9 million common shares outstanding. An investor, Abbey, purchased 9,000 CMI shares in the secondary market shortly after the offering. Despite his inability to point to any specific CMI share, Abbey argued that he met the tracing requirement for § 11 standing. Given that 18 percent of the outstanding shares (2 million of the 11 million total outstanding) came from the 1983 offering, it was highly probable that at least *one* of Abbey's 9,000 shares met the tracing requirement. The court rejected Abbey's probability-based argument as mere "circumstantial" evidence. To put Abbey's argument in perspective, suppose we told you that the chance of rain on any given day was 18 percent. What are the chances that rain will occur on at least one of the next 9,000 days (almost

---

1. 634 F. Supp. 870 (N.D. Cal. 1986).

25 years)? Nonetheless, probabilistic evidence alone was insufficient for the *Abbey* court to demonstrate tracing.[2]

In sum, § 11 liability is severely curtailed for issuers selling stock in a seasoned public offering. Investors who purchase directly from underwriters in the offering (and can document such purchases) will meet the tracing requirement. Those who purchase shares through brokers in the secondary market (where multiple vintages of shares trade) will be unable to trace under § 11 and must look to Rule 10b-5 liability.

When will secondary market purchasers be able to trace for § 11? Different bond offerings typically have unique combinations of interest rates and terms, so tracing will be straightforward. For common stock, companies that have no other shares trading in the secondary market at the time of their registered public offering — as will typically be the case in an initial public offering — provide no tracing problem for investors. Note that, even here, tracing may become an issue if the IPO issuer earlier sold shares in a private placement that were later resold into the secondary market without a registered offering. (We discuss resales of private placement stock in Chapter 10.) This problem has now been ameliorated by Rule 173, which requires underwriters to provide notice to shareholders that they have purchased in a public offering.

What justifies the § 11 tracing requirement? As the *Abbey* court mentions, investors can still rely on Rule 10b-5. We may fear the power of § 11 liability, given that plaintiffs do not need to prove scienter, reliance, or causation requirements for their case in chief, as we discuss later. We may also believe that initial public offerings pose the greatest risk of fraud; tracing may act indirectly to focus the bite of § 11 mostly on IPO-related fraud in the registration statement.

---

2. Abbey also advanced a tracing theory based on his ownership of a fractional interest in the "fungible mass" of CMI shares held by the DTC. The court rejected the fungible mass theory as too broad; if it had accepted the theory, all secondary market purchasers would have § 11 standing.

1.2 Defendants

Unlike Rule 10b-5, the list of potential § 11 defendants is straightforward, set forth in § 11(a). Potential defendants include:

(1) those who signed the registration statement (§ 11(a)(1));
(2) directors (§ 11(a)(2), (3));
(3) various experts who prepared or certified a part of the registration statement (§ 11(a)(4));
(4) underwriters (§ 11(a)(5)); and
(5) controlling persons of any of the above (§ 15).

A seemingly conspicuous omission from the list of potential § 11 defendants is the issuer and its top executive officers. Section 6(a), however, requires that the issuer, the chief executive officer, and the chief financial officer, among others, sign the registration statement. Section 11(a)(1) then includes these signatories as potential § 11 defendants.

Directors at the time of the filing of the registration statement, as well as those named in the registration statement as being or about to become directors, are potential § 11 defendants under §§ 11(a)(2) and (3). Section 11(a) does not distinguish between inside directors (directors employed by the issuer) and outside directors (directors not employed by the issuer and who, in some cases, are also independent in the sense that they lack any consulting or other financial relationship with the issuer). Section 11(a)(2) and (3) also make no distinction based on the length of time a person has served as a director. In theory, directors may be instated the day the registration statement is filed and find themselves liable under § 11 for a misstatement in the registration statement. No one, however, forces a person to become a director of a company, particularly not on the day the registration statement is filed. As we discuss below, § 11 provides a due diligence defense, however, that looks at the defendant's experience with the issuer, among other factors.

Experts are potential defendants under § 11(a)(4) only for the part of the registration statement they certify. The most common example of an expert is the auditor of the audited financial statements contained in the registration statement.

Underwriters, brought in by § 11(a)(5), include the large Wall Street investment banking firms that finance firm commitment offerings, such as Goldman Sachs, Merrill Lynch, and Morgan Stanley, as well as many smaller regional broker-dealers. Section 2(a)(11), however, defines underwriters to include not only those who purchase securities from the issuer with a view to the distribution of the securities to the public but also those who offer or sell for the issuer in such a distribution. As we will discuss in Chapter 9, the concept of underwriter is potentially quite broad. Nonetheless, the principal targets of this provision are the investment banks that form the underwriting syndicate.

Lastly, control persons face potential § 11 liability pursuant to § 15 of the Securities Act. The most common situation for control person liability is when a third party controls the issuer, for example, a parent-subsidiary relationship. Control persons are jointly and severally liable with the controlled defendant, but § 15 also provides a defense: Control persons are not liable if they "had no knowledge of or reasonable ground to believe in the existence of the facts by reason of which the liability of the controlled person is alleged to exist." This defense for control persons is in addition to the defenses available to the controlled defendant.

Recall that in *Central Bank of Denver* (covered in Chapter 5), the Supreme Court, in the course of rejecting aiding and abetting liability under Rule 10b-5, relied on Congress's decision not to include aiding and abetting liability in the express liability provision of § 11. However, § 11 implicitly includes a concept of aiding and abetting in its delineated list of defendants: There is no requirement that defendants make a statement. The public certainly could view those who sign the registration statement as vouching for its content. Underwriters, however, do not sign the registration statement. An underwriter's liability as a primary violator is tenuous under Rule 10b-5; under § 11(a)(5), an underwriter's liability is clear. Perhaps Congress did include a form of aiding and abetting in § 11, even though the statute does not use those precise words? Section 11 differs from Rule 10b-5, however, in putting potential defendants clearly on notice of their status.

1.3 Elements of the Cause of Action

Section 11 provides investors with standing to sue specified defendants for damages if the registration statement relating to their purchased securities contains an "untrue statement of a material fact or omitted to state a material fact required to be stated therein or necessary to make the statements therein not misleading." Thus, plaintiffs' only burden of proof in a § 11 action is to show a material misstatement or omission.

After the issuer has disclosed an earnings statement covering a period of at least twelve months after the effective date of the registration statement, any subsequent purchasers must also show reliance. Even here, § 11 states that "such reliance may be established without proof of the reading of the registration statement by such person." In practice, because of the stringent tracing requirements for standing, purchasers one year after the effective date may face difficulty proving standing.

Although plaintiffs in a § 11 action do not need to show loss causation, § 11(e) provides a loss causation defense. Defendants bear the burden of proof of showing an absence of loss causation. Nonetheless, plaintiffs will face additional legal costs in rebutting the defendants' defense.

Section 13 provides the statute of limitations for § 11. Under § 13, plaintiffs must bring a § 11 action "within one year after the discovery of the untrue statement or the omission, or after such discovery should have been made by the exercise of reasonable diligence." Section 13 also provides a statute of repose: No action may be brought "more than three years after the security was bona fide offered to the public." In comparison, Rule 10b-5 provides that plaintiffs must bring a Rule 10b-5 action within two years after the discovery of the fraud (or when discovery should have occurred through reasonable diligence) and in no case more than five years after the occurrence of the fraud.

The following table reports a comparison of the elements of a § 11 cause of action compared with a Rule 10b-5 action.

Elements	Section 11	Rule 10b-5
Misstatement or Omission	Yes	Yes
Materiality	Yes	Yes
Scienter	No	Yes
Reliance	After 1 year	Yes
Loss Causation	Defense	Yes
Statute of Limitations	1/3 year	2/5 year

The lack of any requirement to show scienter and reliance (at least for purchasers within one year of the effective date) provides § 11 plaintiffs with a powerful cause of action. Consider the Rule 10b-5 counterparts. We saw in Chapter 5 that after the enactment of the PSLRA, plaintiffs pursuing a Rule 10b-5 action must plead with particularity information with respect to the scienter of the defendants. Determining facts specific to the situation of particular defendants that would give rise to a strong inference of scienter is often difficult, particularly in the absence of an obvious smoking gun. Although Rule 10b-5 does allow for a showing of fraud on the market to demonstrate reliance, the fraud on the market theory requires a liquid secondary market with a relatively efficient stock market price. For IPO issuers, in particular, the secondary market at the time of the offering may not have sufficient liquidity to ensure the requisite efficient pricing to justify the fraud on the market presumption. Section 11 allows plaintiffs to bring a cause of action when it might not be feasible under Rule 10b-5.

1.4 Defenses

From the perspective of plaintiffs, § 11 provides a powerful cause of action. Although plaintiffs bear the burden of proof in showing materiality, the § 11 cause of action does not require a showing of reliance, causation, or scienter. Defendants, however, do not necessarily face liability once plaintiffs demonstrate a material misstatement in the registration statement. Instead, § 11(b) provides a number of possible defenses for defendants other than the issuer. The most powerful defense is the due diligence defense provided under § 11(b)(3).

Defendants, other than the issuer, can escape liability under § 11 by meeting their burden of proof in showing due diligence. The due diligence defense turns on two factors: (1) whether the defendant is an expert or non-expert, and (2) whether the material misstatement or omission is present in an expertised or non-expertised section of the registration statement. The following table breaks down the due diligence requirements based on these two factors.

Due Diligence Defense Requirements

	Non-Expertised	Expertised
Expert	No Liability: § 11(a)(4)	Reasonable investigation, reasonable ground to believe and did believe as truth: § 11(b)(3)(B)
Non-Expert	Reasonable investigation, reasonable ground to believe and did believe as truth: § 11(b)(3)(A)	Reasonable ground to believe and did believe as truth: § 11(b)(3)(C)

There is no due diligence defense for experts with respect to non-expertised sections of the registration statements because experts only face liability for the sections of the registration statement they prepared or to which they certified. For example, an independent auditor is liable only for material misstatements and omissions in the audited financial statements in the registration statement.

Examining the rest of the table, note that there are two forms of the due diligence defense. First, for experts with respect to expertised sections and non-experts with respect to non-expertised sections, the due diligence defense requires that the defendants "(1) after reasonable investigation, (2) had reasonable ground to believe and did believe, that the (3) statements therein were true and that there was no omission to state a material fact required to be stated therein or necessary to make the statements therein not misleading." The key to this first form of the due diligence defense is the reasonable investigation requirement. Unfortunately, what constitutes reasonable investigation is a key uncertainty for participants in a public offering. Some refer to this form of the due diligence defense as the "reasonable investigation" defense or, somewhat confusingly, simply the "due diligence defense."

Second, for non-experts with respect to an expertised section of the registration statement (for example, an underwriter with respect to a material misstatement in the audited financial statements), the due diligence defense requires that the defendants had: "(1) no reasonable ground to believe and did not believe, (2) at the time such part of the registration statement became effective, that the statements therein were untrue or that there was an omission to state a material fact required to be stated therein or necessary to make the statements therein not misleading." The lack of a reasonable investigation requirement leads some courts to refer to this defense simply as the "reliance defense." Non-expert defendants are entitled to rely on the work of experts unless they have reason to believe there are inaccuracies.

Why are there two forms of the due diligence defense under § 11(a)(3)? The presence of an expert bolsters the credibility of the expertised section. As long as an auditor has performed a competent audit, having others perform their own investigation will add only marginally to the veracity of the disclosed information. This assumption points out the limits of the reliance defense and, indirectly, the definition of *expert*. To be comfortable with the reliance form of the due diligence defense, we need to be sure that the designated expert really performs a thorough investigation on which others may reasonably rely.

So who are the experts in a public offering? Auditors are experts with respect to audited financial statements. In performing an audit, auditors go through a well-specified process (following Generally Accepted Auditing Standards, or GAAS). The GAAS consists of ten auditing standards, covering the field work performed by auditors and the standards for reporting financial information in accordance with the Generally Accepted Accounting Principles (or GAAP). Auditors are not the only possible experts. If the issuer is involved in exploration for new mineral deposits, geologists would qualify as experts and their mineral reports would be considered an expertised section of the registration statement. The issuer's attorneys also typically provide expert opinions as to whether the offered stock was validly issued under state corporate law (a ministerial task).

In addition to offering their opinion on the validity of the stock issuance, the issuer's attorneys often draft the registration statement. As part of this role, the issuer's attorneys collects information about the issuer's business, properties, principal stockholders, management, directors, and so on. Given their central role in drafting the registration statement, should we consider the issuer's attorney an expert for the narrative portions of the registration statement? If the issuer's attorneys are deemed experts, this means that the *other* defendants are freed of the reasonable investigation requirement. Although the thorough audit that auditors perform may justify excusing other defendants from investigating audited financial statements, it is doubtful that the issuer's attorneys have the expertise to provide the same level of reassurance for the other portions of the registration statement. Not surprisingly, the issuer's attorneys are not treated as experts for the entire registration statement.

Once we have determined the type of defendant (expert or non-expert) and the part of the registration statement in question (expertised or non-expertised), we can then assess whether the due diligence (or reliance) defense applies. Unfortunately, the courts have provided little guidance on this point, leaving considerable uncertainty. In large part this uncertainty derives from the fact-specific nature of the defense. Due diligence may vary based on, among other things, the type of issuer, the type of security, the type of defendant, the knowledge and expertise of the defendant, and the presence of red flags that may have suggested a problem.

The seminal court opinion on the due diligence defense is *Escott v. BarChris Construction Corp.*[3] In the early 1960s, BarChris, a builder of bowling alleys, issued convertible debentures in a public offering. BarChris's business did not fare well, and it went bankrupt, defaulting on the debentures; the purchasers of the debentures filed a § 11 suit. After determining that the registration statement contained material misrepresentations, the court turned to the issue of whether the defendants in the action had met their due diligence defense.

The *Escott* opinion provided a number of important lessons regarding the due diligence defense.

---

3. 283 F. Supp. 643 (S.D.N.Y. 1968).

- Top executive officers will have a particularly hard time showing reasonable belief given their central position, making it difficult for them to meet either of the two types of due diligence defenses;
- For expertised sections of the registration statement, outsiders may rely on experts without investigation;
- For non-expertised sections, the extent of investigation required of outsiders will turn on the outsiders' expertise (underwriters) and position relative to the issuer;
- Simply relying on the oral representations of top officers is *not* a reasonable investigation;
- At a minimum, reasonable investigation requires looking at easily verifiable information found in written documents (corporate board minutes, contracts, and so on);
- Defendants need not perform a full audit to meet the due diligence defense.

Left unanswered by *BarChris*, however, is the precise level of investigation required. The gap between a full audit and simply looking at board minutes and major contracts is a large one. The challenge for underwriters is to know which contracts will be deemed major in the context of subsequent litigation.

In *Feit v. Leasco Data Processing Equipment Corp.*,[4] a shareholder of Reliance Insurance Company (the target company) exchanged his stock for the newly issued shares of Leasco (the acquiror) in a tender offer. In connection with the tender offer, Leasco filed a registration statement with the SEC and distributed a statutory prospectus for the issue of the new shares. The target shareholder-plaintiff alleged that Leasco's registration statement failed to disclose that Reliance had $100 million of "surplus surplus" available to it (which would come under Leasco's control after the tender offer). After holding that the omitted information relating to the $100 million surplus

---

4. 332 F. Supp. 544 (E.D.N.Y. 1971).

surplus was material, the court tackled the due diligence defense of Leasco's directors and of the underwriters participating in Leasco's exchange offering. The court noted that the due diligence defense is particularly challenging for insiders: "*BarChris* imposes such stringent requirements of knowledge of corporate affairs on inside directors that one is led to the conclusion that liability will lie in practically all cases of misrepresentation. Their liability approaches that of the issuer as guarantor of the accuracy of the prospectus." The director defendants failed to meet these stringent requirements.

The court then turned to the due diligence defense asserted by the underwriters of the exchange offering. The court first noted that, among the various offering participants, only the underwriters and the auditor had the expertise and ability to undertake a thorough independent investigation and to take an adverse role against the issuer. At a minimum, the court held, underwriters must read board minutes, look at important contracts, and investigate any inconsistencies between those documents and management representations. The court then found that the underwriters had met their due diligence defense. Among other things, the underwriters had

- made a thorough review of all available financial data;
- independently examined Leasco's audit and the report of an actuary on Reliance;
- made "searching" inquiries of Leasco's major bank;
- studied the corporate minutes, records, and major agreements of Leasco;
- reviewed the proposed registration statement line-by-line.

Does *Feit v. Leasco* provide a checklist for underwriters and other possible § 11 defendants seeking to satisfy the requirements of a due diligence defense? Although such a checklist would provide much appreciated certainty to the ranks of corporate directors and underwriters involved in public offerings, the amount of due diligence investigation required varies based not only on the factors identified in Rule 176 (type of issuer, security, defendant, and so on) but also on the presence of certain red flags.

In re WorldCom Securities Litigation[5] involved a massive accounting fraud at WorldCom. WorldCom, a large telecommunications company, had grown rapidly during the 1990s through a series of acquisitions. In 2000 and again in 2001, WorldCom raised capital in two public bond offerings registered for the shelf (Rule 415) using Form S-3. The Form S-3s (and prospectus supplements) for the offerings incorporated by reference financial statements from previously filed Form 10-Ks. On June 25, 2002, WorldCom announced that it had understated its expenses by billions of dollars and would need to restate its reported financial results. A substantial expense for WorldCom was the amount it paid to other telecommunication companies to secure access to their communication lines, known as *line costs*. (WorldCom needed access to these companies' lines to help it develop a comprehensive data and phone network.) One measure of a communication company's financial health is the ratio of these line costs to revenue (known as the E/R ratio). Plaintiffs alleged, among other things, that WorldCom (under the instructions of its chief financial officer, Scott Sullivan, and chief executive officer, Bernard Ebbers, both of whom went to federal prison for securities fraud) converted line costs that should have been treated as current expenses into capital expenses. The effect of this conversion was to shift line costs from an expense against the current year's income to that of future years, improving profit numbers for the current year. The shift also improved the E/R ratio.

WorldCom's disclosure of the accounting restatement triggered a flurry of class actions against, among others, the

---

5. 346 F. Supp. 2d 628 (S.D.N.Y. 2004).

underwriters of WorldCom's bond offerings. Several of the underwriter defendants moved for summary judgment. In deciding on the summary judgment motion, the court distinguished between the expertised and non-expertised portions of the plaintiffs' complaint.

With respect to the audited financial statement (an expertised section of the registration statement), the underwriters argued that they were entitled to rely on the audit by Arthur Anderson, meaning that they would only need to show an absence of actual knowledge of the fraud and that they had a reasonable belief in the financial statements' accuracy. The court rejected the underwriters' summary judgment motion, focusing on the fact that WorldCom's E/R ratio was significantly lower than the ratios of its competitors. Even though the E/R ratio was public knowledge and no one suggested at the time that the E/R ratio indicated accounting fraud, the court held that the discrepancy between the E/R ratios of WorldCom and its competitors was a potential red flag. The presence of a red flag would give rise to a duty to investigate further; reliance on the auditors was insufficient.

The court's focus on the E/R ratio is particularly notable for the light it sheds on the potential scope of what may constitute a red flag. The real focus should be on companies with elevated likelihood of fraud or other disclosure inaccuracies. Treating a fact as a red flag has the consequence of imposing an investigation duty on non-expert defendants, even for expertised sections of the registration statement. Is the E/R ratio discrepancy a smoking gun indicating that something is awry with the company's disclosures? Financial numbers and ratios are rarely identical for different companies, even within a particular industry. It is hardly surprising when firms in the same industry have different costs and profitability. One may wonder, therefore, whether accepting a differing E/R ratio standing alone as a potential red flag (for the jury to decide later at trial) potentially collapses the reliance defense into the reasonable investigation version of the due diligence defense.

After rejecting the reliance defense for the expertised portions, the court turned to the non-expertised section of the registration statement, in this case the unaudited interim financial statements. The underwriters argued that they relied reasonably on two comfort letters provided by Arthur Anderson, WorldCom's auditor. WorldCom's two offerings were shelf registration offerings. Because of the fast pace of such offerings, disclosures are typically incorporated by reference from prior filed documents. In addition, underwriters (or more accurately, the underwriters' counsel for WorldCom) develop long-term, continuous learning on shelf-registration issuers; that continuous learning depends on the ability to rely reasonably on other intermediaries, such as auditors.

The court rejected the underwriter's argument that less due diligence is required for a shelf registration due to the fast pace and time pressures of such offerings. The court reaffirmed that to meet the due diligence defense for the non-expertised portion of the registration statement, the underwriters must demonstrate reasonable investigation. Comfort letters may be part of a reasonable investigation, but they are not sufficient standing alone. Moreover, the court noted that "Underwriters perform a different function from auditors. They have special access to information about an issuer at a critical time in the issuer's corporate life, at a time it is seeking to raise capital. The public relies on the underwriter to obtain and verify relevant information and then make sure that essential facts are disclosed." In rejecting the summary judgment motion, the court also noted that many of the underwriters had internally downgraded WorldCom's credit rating prior to the 2001 offering and had taken steps to limit their exposure as WorldCom's creditors. The underwriters argued that, even with reasonable investigation, the fraud would have gone undiscovered. The court rejected this argument, noting that "[w]ithout a reasonable investigation, of course, it can never be known what would have been uncovered or what additional disclosures would have been demanded."

1.5 Section 11 Damages

Section 11 provides a precise formula to determine damages. Under § 11(e), damages are equal to the difference between two numbers. The first number is the amount paid for the security, not exceeding the price at which the security was offered to the public. The second number is one of three alternatives, the choice of which turns on whether a particular investor sold the securities and, if so, when. These alternatives are

> (1) the value thereof as of the time such suit was brought, or (2) the price at which such security shall have been disposed of in the market before suit, or (3) the price at which such security shall have been disposed of after suit but before judgment if such damages shall be less than the damages representing the difference between the amount paid for the security (not exceeding the price at which the security was offered to the public) and the value thereof as of the time such suit was brought.

Consider the first number. If zTunes sells securities in its registered public offering at $50 per share and an investor purchases the securities later in the secondary market at $75 per share, the first number is equal to $50. (Assume that the investor is able to trace back to the registered public offering; if not, the investor lacks standing.) The investor cannot recover damages for any amount paid above the public offering price, even if the investor suffers a loss on this amount. Suppose the second number is the value at the time the suit was filed and is equal to $0. The investor who purchased at $75 will have suffered an investment loss of $75 per share. The § 11(e) damage measure, however, will give the investor a maximum of $50 per share damages.

One way of thinking of this § 11(e) cap on damages is as an irrebuttable loss causation defense. Section 11(e) assumes that any loss attributable to a purchase price above the public offering price is *not* due to any material misstatement or omission in the registration statement, but to some exogenous cause. Put another way, any material misstatement or omission in the registration statement is assumed to boost the share price up to the public offering price, but no further. Is this assumption justified?

Consider the second number in the damages formula. If the investor does not sell, but instead holds the purchased securities to the end of suit, the second number is equal to the value at the time of the filing of suit. After the filing of a securities class action, the stock market price of the sued company typically drops. Even if the company is ultimately found not liable, litigation puts a cloud over the company, hurting relationships with customers and suppliers. In addition, company management faces the distraction of defending themselves and the company. Finally, the company incurs large litigation costs in the form of attorneys' fees, expert witness fees, and so on. Setting the second number in the § 11(e) damage measure at the value at the time of the filing of suit eliminates these subsequent losses from the damages figure. To the extent the filing of a suit is a public announcement of problems in the registration statement, setting the determination of value at the filing of suit also cuts off any later stock price movements resulting from subsequent, unrelated disclosures.

Why does § 11(e) provide multiple alternatives for the determination of the second number? Consider a chain of investors (all able to trace back to the registration statement) who purchased zTunes common stock prior to the filing of suit. Investor 1 purchases from an underwriter at $50 per share. Investor 2 purchases from Investor 1 at $30 per share. Investor 3 purchases from Investor 2 at $20 per share. Suppose the value at the time of the filing of suit is $10 per share. The total loss, from the public offering price of $50 down to the $10 value at the filing of suit, equals $40 per share. All three investors in our example have standing to sue under § 11 for the same share, which has traveled through the hands of each. To determine the second number in the damage measure under § 11(e), the $40 total damages per share must be apportioned among these three investors as follows:

Investor 1 = $50 (purchase price) − $30
(price at which sold prior to suit filing) = $20

Investor 2 = $30 (purchase price) − $20
(price at which sold prior to suit filing) = $10

Investor 3 = $20 (purchase price) − $10
(price at which sold prior to suit filing) = $10

The three investors together can collect a total of $40 in damages. Not all possible chains of post-offering transactions results in as clean an apportionment of damages. Suppose Investor 1 purchases from an underwriter at $50 per share, Investor 2 purchases from Investor 1 at $5 per share, and Investor 3 purchases from Investor 2 at $40 per share. Suppose the value at the time of the filing of suit is $10 per share and that filing occurs sometime after Investor 3's purchase. The total loss from the public offering price of $50 down to the value at the filing of suit is equal to $40 per share.

Investor 1 = $50 (purchase price) − $5
(price at which sold prior to suit filing) = $45

Investor 2 = $5 (purchase price) − $40
(price at which sold prior to suit filing) = None

Investor 3 = $40 (purchase price) − $10
(price at which sold prior to suit filing) = $30

Now the total damages are equal to $75, even though the total drop in value for the particular stock was $40. What happened? Investor 1's damage measure alone is greater than the $40 total drop in value from the public offering price to the value at the suit filing time. While Investor 2 actually profited from her purchase of zTunes stock, this profit is not used to offset Investor 3's loss. This seemingly excessive damage measure may be ameliorated by the loss causation defense. Suppose, for example, that the material misstatement in the registration statement was publicly revealed immediately before Investor 2 purchased her shares. A defendant could then make the argument that the drop in stock price that Investor 3 suffered was due to another unrelated factor and therefore barred by the loss causation defense of § 11.

Finally, consider an investor (able to trace) who sells her zTunes common stock after the filing of suit. Suppose the investor purchased the shares earlier at $40 per share and that the value at the filing of suit was $10 per share. If the investor sells the shares after the filing of suit at $5 per share, her damages equal $30 per share ($40 − $10). Despite the investor's actual loss of $35 per share, § 11(e) limits the damages to the $40 purchase price minus the $10 value at the time of the filing of suit, the same damage measure used for those who hold on to their shares until judgment in the suit. Limiting damages by using the value at the suit filing acts to remove from the damage calculus unrelated factors that may cause the stock price to drop after the filing of suit. By contrast, if the investor instead sells the shares after the filing of suit at $20 per share, her damages are $20 per share ($40 − $20). The § 11 damage measure only compensates the investor for the actual amount of loss suffered (similar to damages if the investor had sold prior to the filing of suit). But what if unrelated factors caused the price increase to $20 per share after the filing of suit (for example, the economy overall grew more than expected)? This unrelated factor is not ignored; instead, damages are reduced because of this increase. Why this asymmetry?

Given the importance of the value at the time of the filing of suit in calculating § 11 damages, how should we determine value? The simplest method would be to look at the market price at the suit filing date. If the company's shares trade in an efficient market, we can expect the market price to incorporate all publicly available information relevant to the company's value. But what about nonpublic information? And what if the market is not efficient, but instead displays bubbles and other irrationalities? Some courts will accept arguments that value at the filing of suit is not the same as the market price on that date. In *Beecher v. Able*,[6] a federal district court accepted the defendant's arguments that panic selling after the announcement of disappointing short-term financial results at Douglas Aircraft, combined with the company's good long-term prospects, meant that the Douglas Aircraft's value was higher than the market price at the filing of suit. Was the *Beecher* court correct in placing little to no weight on what it characterizes as "temporary" short-term conditions, instead placing almost all the weight of evidence on Douglas's long-term prospects? As we discussed in Chapter 1, investors invest money to obtain even more money in the future. If a company's problems truly are short-term and its long-term prospects remain sound, the overall market price of an investment will change only slightly, because the expected net present value of its future cash flows will only be marginally affected. The court's acceptance of the defendant's panic selling theory is also open to criticism. Although the court is perhaps correct that markets generally exhibit rational pricing yet go through phases of irrationality (think Internet bubble in the late 1990s), how does the court know irrationality is driving the market at any particular time? And, perhaps more importantly, can the court measure the magnitude of the irrationality? Although the market price may reflect irrationalities and deviate from fair value, courts that substitute their assessments of value for the market's may be worse.

1.6 Loss Causation

Once the damage measure is calculated according to the formula provided in § 11(e), § 11(e) then adds an additional step:

> If the defendant proves that any portion or all of such
> damages represents other than the depreciation in value of

---

6. 435 F. Supp. 397 (S.D.N.Y. 1975).

such security resulting from such part of the registration statement, with respect to which his liability is asserted, not being true or omitting to state a material fact required to be stated therein or necessary to make the statements therein not misleading, such portion of or all such damages shall not be recoverable.

Commonly referred to as the loss causation defense, this defense allows defendants, who bear the burden of proof, to reduce their liability by demonstrating that other causes were responsible for the plaintiffs' stock losses. There are two possible other causes: (a) overall market and industry movements, and (b) firm-specific information not related to the alleged material misstatement or omission.

In *Akerman v. Oryx Communications, Inc.*,[7] the Second Circuit addressed the loss causation defense under § 11(e) relating to misrepresentations contained in the registration statement for Oryx's initial public offering. Among other things, the court rejected the statistical evidence offered by both the plaintiffs and the defendants on loss causation relating to overall market movements. Defendants introduced evidence comparing the stock price performance of one hundred companies that went public contemporaneously with Oryx. However, the court pointed out that the defendants' study did not control for the differing characteristics between the one hundred companies and Oryx that could affect stock price movement (for example, technology, product, profitability, and so on). Plaintiffs introduced evidence comparing Oryx's stock price performance with the performance of the over-the-counter composite index. The court similarly rejected the plaintiffs' evidence as failing to control for the differing characteristics of the OTC composite index companies that could also affect stock price movement.

---

7. 810 F.2d 336 (2d Cir. 1987).

Lacking expertise of their own, courts will often allow expert witnesses (typically moonlighting finance professors) to offer opinions on the stock price movement of the issuer upon the first public revelation of the material misstatement or omission using the event study methodology we discussed in Chapter 5. What are the common steps in demonstrating loss causation?

1. The first date the public learns of the inaccuracy in question is determined. The change in the company's share price around this date is computed.

2. The change in the company's share price is adjusted against a benchmark. The benchmark controls for other exogenous factors outside the company that may affect the company's share price. Typically, litigants will perform an event study utilizing estimates of how the company's stock would be expected to move relative to the entire market to create a benchmark for the expected returns during the event study time period. The expected return is subtracted from the change in the company's share price to give the adjusted change in the company's share price (sometimes referred to as the excess return).

3. Given the excess return, litigants then assess whether firm-specific factors other than the inaccuracy in question may have led to the share price change. For example, on the date of Oryx's public revelation of its accounting misstatement, Oryx may have also disclosed that it expected record earnings growth. Good information announced on the same date may have drowned out the negative impact on Oryx's share price of the public revelation of the accounting misstatement. Courts often have difficulty separating the impact of various firm-specific information events that occur contemporaneously.

1.7 Indemnification, Contribution, and Joint and Several Liability

Section 11 provides for joint and several liability with two exceptions. First, the liability of underwriters is capped under § 11(e) at "the total price at which the securities underwritten by him and distributed to the public were offered to the public." If an underwriter member of a syndicate of underwriters underwrote only $10 million of a $500 million offering, under § 11(e) that particular underwriter would face liability only up to the $10 million. Second, § 11(f) shields outside directors from joint and several liability. Outside directors benefit from the proportionate liability regime of § 21D(f) of the Exchange Act we examined in Chapter 5.

Given the presence of joint and several liability for most defendants and the desire of underwriters, in particular, to avoid liability altogether, participants in public offerings routinely sign contractual agreements shifting liability exposure through indemnification clauses. In *Eichensholtz v. Brennan*,[8] the Third Circuit dealt with the question of how much to allow parties to adjust their liability under § 11 through indemnification agreements. The Third Circuit held that no express or implied right to indemnification exists under the securities laws. The court went further, however, essentially voiding the contractual indemnification rights the underwriters had negotiated with ITB. The court held that indemnification conflicts with the policies underlying the securities laws. Both acts seek to protect investors, not underwriters. The court stated, "If the court enforced an underwriter indemnification provision, it would effectively eliminate the underwriter's incentive to fulfill its investigative obligation."

Could indemnification of underwriters benefit investors? If underwriters were protected from liability, presumably underwriters would demand a lower risk premium, thereby reducing the cost of capital. The court ignored this possibility, however, focusing instead on investor protection; if underwriters were relieved of potential § 11 liability, they might not perform due diligence with as much zeal. If we are concerned about reducing the incentive of underwriters to perform due diligence,

---

8. 52 F.3d 478 (3d Cir. 1995).

should private liability insurance policies also be forbidden? Many participants in a registered securities offering, including underwriters, purchase liability insurance. In the case of judgment at trial or settlement, the underwriters then pay little or nothing out of their own pockets. Of course, the underwriter may face higher insurance premiums in the future, so the underwriter still has some incentive to perform due diligence to uncover problems in the offering.

2 SECTION 12(a)(1)

Unlike §§ 11 and 12(a)(2), civil liability under § 12(a)(1) does not require a material misstatement or omission. Instead, § 12(a)(1) requires a violation of § 5. Section 12(a)(1) therefore enlists private plaintiffs to encourage issuers (and other defendants discussed below) to comply with the § 5 gun-jumping requirements covered in Chapter 7.

2.1 Standing and Defendants

Unlike § 11, which required purchasers to trace securities back to a particular registration statement, § 12(a)(1) limits standing to bring suit to those who purchase in an offering that violates § 5. Also in contrast to § 11, § 12(a)(1) does not delineate a list of permissible defendants. Instead, the purchaser is allowed to bring suit against any person who "offers or sells a security in violation of section 5."

The Supreme Court in *Pinter v. Dahl*[9] addressed the scope of who "offers or sells a security in violation of section 5." Pinter, an oil and gas producer, sold securities to Dahl. Dahl not only invested but told other investors about the venture and assisted the investors in completing the subscription-agreement

---

9. 486 U.S. 622 (1988).

form. Dahl received no commission from Pinter for assisting in these sales of securities. Unfortunately for Dahl and the other investors, Pinter's business failed, and the securities proved worthless. Dahl and the other investors brought suit against Pinter seeking rescission under § 12(a)(1). Following the best defense is a good offense strategy, Pinter counterclaimed against Dahl, contending that Dahl was a statutory seller under § 12(a)(1) and thus liable in contribution to Pinter for the claims of the other investors.

The Supreme Court defined a statutory seller for purposes of § 12(a)(1) liability to include (1) those who are in contractual privity and pass title or other interest of security to the purchaser, and (2) those who solicit offers to buy for value. Not all those encouraging a purchase qualify as a statutory seller under the *Pinter* formulation. The Court stated that the scope of solicitations of offers to buy for value does not include those whose motivation is solely to benefit the buyer of the securities. In contrast, those who are motivated "at least in part by a desire to serve his own financial interests or those of the securities owner" are soliciting for offers to buy for value and thus would count as statutory sellers for purposes of § 12(a)(1) liability. Although Dahl received no commission, the Court did not find that dispositive on whether Dahl was motivated "at least in part by a desire to serve his own financial interests or those of the securities owner." The Court remanded for further determination on Dahl's motive.

Unlike § 11, which provides a defined list of potential defendants, the view of solicitation in § 12(a)(1) focuses on the functional role played by offering participants. As the *Pinter* Court put it, "The solicitation of a buyer is perhaps the most critical stage of the selling transaction. It is the first stage of a traditional securities sale to involve the buyer, and it is directed at producing the sale. In addition, brokers and other solicitors are well positioned to control the flow of information to a potential purchaser."

Does the *Pinter* Court's solicitation test offer predictability in application? On the one hand, those who are paid agents of the issuer and are actively involved in selling (such as underwriters) are relatively easy to identify. But what about Dahl, who was not directly compensated by Pinter for bringing in additional investors? Perhaps Dahl benefited from his efforts. More investors meant more money and a greater likelihood that the investment would succeed or, at the very least, a larger pool in bankruptcy if the venture did not pan out. On the other hand, maybe Dahl really was trying to help other investors get in on a "sure thing." An easy bright-line fix to the uncertainty problem would be to limit the definition of statutory seller for purposes of § 12(a)(1) to those who are paid by the issuer. But such a fix may lead opportunistic promoters to hide their compensation from the issuer.

An important issue in applying § 12(a)(1) rescission liability is whether a purchaser who buys in a transaction in which a § 5 violation occurs may sue not only the immediate statutory seller but also those who sold to the immediate seller. In a firm commitment offering, an issuer sells securities to its underwriters. The underwriters in turn sell to investors in the marketplace. These investors may then resell to other investors in secondary market trading. According to the *Pinter* Court, "One important consequence of this provision is that § 12(1) imposes liability on only the buyer's immediate seller; remote purchasers are precluded from bringing actions against remote sellers. Thus, a buyer cannot recover against his seller's seller."

Purchasers in the secondary market would be able to sue only the person from whom they purchased the securities. Those who purchased directly from an underwriter could sue the underwriter, but not the issuer. The underwriter would then have standing to sue the issuer. An outside investor who purchased from another outside investor, however, would not have standing to sue the selling investor because

§ 4(1) would exempt the resale transaction from § 5, eliminating § 12(a)(1) liability for the resale. Thus, § 12(a)(1) limits the scope of liability primarily to those who purchased directly from the issuer or one of its underwriters.[10]

2.2 Elements of the Cause of Action

Section 12(a)(1) civil liability requires that plaintiffs demonstrate an offer or sale of a security in violation of § 5. In order to meet their burden, plaintiffs in many cases will only need to show that they purchased securities and that the offering was not registered. It will then be the defendant's burden to show that the offer and sale were exempt from registration. There are no other elements to the plaintiff's cause of action.

2.3 Defenses

Consistent with the minimal elements to the plaintiff's cause of action, § 12(a)(1) provides no defenses for defendants. Section 12(a)(1) is designed as a crush-out mechanism to ensure compliance with § 5. Moreover, as we will discuss more fully in Chapter 9, the securities laws encompass a broad definition of *transaction*. If a § 5 violation occurs in one part of a transaction, potentially the entire transaction could become subject to § 12(a)(1) liability. Thus, if an issuer mistakenly sends a free writing prospectus in the pre-filing period and the issuer cannot otherwise find an exemption that applies, the free writing prospectus will violate § 5 and any sales that eventually take place under the offering will

---

10. Issuers in a shelf registration must make an undertaking under Item 512(a)(6) of Regulation S-K. The undertaking explicitly provides that the issuer is a statutory seller with respect to certain forms of communication for purposes of § 12, among other Securities Act provisions, to those purchasing in the "initial distribution" of the securities. Thus, in a shelf registration the initial investors purchasing from the underwriters may in fact be able to sue the issuer, although subsequent purchasers in the secondary market do not have this ability.

likewise violate § 5. If an issuer sells securities in violation of § 5 to one set of investors (perhaps because traditional free writing was sent out in the post-effective period without an accompanying statutory prospectus), all other investors in the public offering can sue the issuer for violating § 5.

All is not so bleak, however, for issuers that violate § 5 prior to the effective date of the registration statement. Such a violation can be *cured* if the issuer waits for a sufficient period after the violation before proceeding with its offering. The SEC sometimes imposes a 30-day waiting period as a sanction for violating § 5. The rationale for the waiting period is that it will allow any "conditioning of the market" to be dispelled before any sales actually take place. Any subsequent sales then occur in a separate transaction from the earlier improper offer in violation of § 5.

2.4 Remedies Under Section 12(a)(1)

Section 12(a)(1) provides for rescission or rescissionary damages. Rescission allows the investor to return their securities to the issuer and receive the consideration paid for the securities, subject to adjustments for any income earned on the securities and for interest. If the investor has already sold the securities, the investor may obtain rescissionary damages equal to the price paid minus the price obtained upon sale (again with the adjustments noted above).

Section 12(a)(1), however, provides no adjustment for loss causation, in keeping with the provision's crush-out deterrence purpose. Why provide crush-out damages greater than the issuer's benefit from violating § 5? Neither § 11 nor § 12(a)(2) (as discussed below) provide such disproportionately large damages. Crush-out damages work best when the chance of court error (for example, mistakenly penalizing a party that did not violate the legal provision in question) is low. Because of the bright-line rule quality of § 12(a)(1) — a § 5 violation either does or does not exist — § 12(a)(1) lends itself to crush-out damages. The assumption is that courts (or juries) will make fewer errors in determining whether a § 5 violation occurred as compared with whether a material misstatement or omission exists under § 11. Is this assumption correct? Recall that the definition of an *offer* for purposes of § 5 is quite ambiguous, even with the new safe harbors promulgated as part of the SEC's 2005 public offering reforms.

Consider the operation of § 12(a)(1) in the following hypothetical. zTunes raised $100 million in a registered firm commitment public offering. In the offering, zTunes sold common stock to Goldbuck Brothers, an investment bank, at a price of $45 per share. Goldbuck Brothers resold the securities to the general public. During the public offering, assume that zTunes violated § 5 by failing to distribute the final statutory prospectus together with free writing under § 2(a)(10)(a) and no other exemption applies. Determine the § 12(a)(1) damages in each of the following hypotheticals.

1. Goldbuck Brothers sold stock in the offering to Diane at $50 per share. Diane resold her shares at $60 per share to Ken. Ken then resold the shares at $20 per share to Kyle.
Answer: Ken cannot sue under § 12(a)(1) because Diane's resale is exempt under § 4(1). Diane can sue Goldbuck Brothers, the underwriter in the offering, but has no damages as she sold her shares at a profit. Similarly, the underwriter has no damages against zTunes because it also sold its shares at a profit.

2. Goldbuck Brothers sold stock in the offering to Lita at $50 per share. Lita resold her shares at $40 per share to Lauren. Lauren then resold the shares at $20 per share to Olivia.
Answer: Lauren cannot sue under § 12(a)(1) because Lita's resale is covered under the § 4(1) exemption from § 5. Lita can sue Goldbuck Brothers, the underwriter in the offering.

Now Lita can obtain rescissionary damages equal to $10 per share (her $50 consideration paid for the shares minus the $40 for which she sold each share). Goldbuck Brothers can now turn around and sue zTunes under § 12(a)(1), since zTunes passed title to Goldbuck Brothers (and thus was in privity of contract). The rescissionary damage measure will equal $5 per share (based on the $45 consideration paid minus the $40 total amount received after taking into account the $10 payment back to Lita).

3 SECTION 12(a)(2)

Although it is a statutory companion to § 12(a)(1), § 12(a)(2) provides civil liability more akin to § 11. Section 12(a)(2) focuses on material misstatements or omissions that occur relating to offers and sales of securities "by means of a prospectus or oral communication."

3.1 Standing and Defendants

Standing to sue under § 12(a)(2), as with § 12(a)(1), requires that the plaintiff purchased securities from a potential statutory seller-defendant. Due to the common roots of §§ 12(a)(1) and 12(a)(2), most courts apply the same definition of *statutory seller* when determining potential defendants for both provisions.

One difference between the scope of potential defendants between the two provisions deals with the issue of remote sellers. Recall that the *Pinter* Court explicitly prohibited purchasers from suing remote sellers for purposes of § 12(a)(1). So if Xavier sells to Yale who sells to Zeke, Zeke may sue only Yale and not Xavier (unless Xavier directly solicited Zeke). The SEC in Rule 159A of the Securities Act, nonetheless, treats the issuer as a statutory seller for purposes of § 12(a)(2), regardless of the underwriting method. Rule 159A brings in certain types of communications, including the preliminary or final statutory prospectus, certain free writing prospectuses, and any other communication made by the issuer to purchasers of the securities. Thus, if an issuer sells securities to an underwriter who in turn resells to investors (that is, a firm commitment offering), the investors may sue the issuer under § 12(a)(2) pursuant to Rule 159A, even though there is no contractual privity between the issuer and the investors. Rule 159A restricts its application only to those purchasers in the "initial distribution" of securities. Thus, while investors who purchase directly from an underwriter may sue the issuer under § 12(a)(2), subsequent investors who purchase through resale transactions in the secondary market are out of luck.

3.2 Narrowing the Scope of Section 12(a)(2)

The Supreme Court in *Gustafson v. Alloyd Co.*[11] addressed the scope of § 12(a)(2) liability. Prior to *Gustafson*, there was a debate as to whether § 12(a)(2) applied to communications in secondary market transactions and private placements. Because § 2(a)(10) provides such a broad definition of *prospectus* and § 12(a)(2) applies where securities are offered or sold "by means of a prospectus," arguably § 12(a)(2) could apply to both private placements and secondary market transactions. *Gustafson* resolved this debate on the scope of § 12(a)(2).

Gustafson and two others bore the sole shareholders of Alloyd, Inc. Gustafson negotiated a sale of all the Alloyd shares to Wind Point Partners II, LP, and a number of individual investors (through a new corporation, Alloyd Holdings, Inc., formed to purchase the shares of Alloyd). Among other things, the purchase agreement provided that if the year-end audit and financial statements after the sale revealed a discrepancy

---

11. 513 U.S. 561 (1995).

between the estimated value at the time of the contract and the actual value, an adjustment would be made to the party disadvantaged by the discrepancy. After the sale, the year-end audit showed that Alloyd's actual earnings were less than the estimates and, under the contract, the purchasers could claim an adjustment of $815,000 from Gustafson and his coshareholders. Instead of pursuing their contract rights, the purchasers brought an action for rescission under § 12(a)(2), claiming that the purchase agreement was a prospectus and that financial data of Alloyd at the time of the contract had been materially inaccurate.

Justice Kennedy, writing for the Court, held that the purchase agreement did not constitute a prospectus and therefore § 12(a)(2) did not apply. Kennedy began his analysis, not with the definition of prospectus in § 2(a)(10), but with § 10 of the Securities Act. Section 10(a) provides that "a prospectus relating to a security . . . shall contain the information contained in the registration statement." From this, Kennedy inferred that the term *prospectus* must have one consistent meaning throughout the Securities Act. Only a prospectus within that consistent meaning would qualify for § 12(a)(2) liability. Kennedy also pointed to the parallel structure in the Securities Act between the requirements for a registration statement and a § 10 statutory prospectus, on the one hand, and liability under §§ 11 and 12(a)(2), on the other. Moreover, the central purpose of the Securities Act was to regulate public offerings. Given this central purpose, Kennedy was skeptical "that § 12[a](2) creates vast additional liabilities that are quite independent of the new substantive obligations the Act imposes." As one last nail in the argument that there may be different kinds of prospectuses under the Securities Act, Kennedy noted that the Act does not speak in terms of a "formal" or "informal" prospectus, but instead uses the term "prospectus" throughout.

Kennedy's opinion does not, however, consider § 5(b)(1). Recall that § 5(b)(1) makes it unlawful for any person "to . . . transmit any prospectus relating to any security with respect to which a registration statement has been filed under this title, unless such prospectus meets the requirements of section 10." This prohibition seems difficult to square with the proposition that the Securities Act does not contemplate two types of prospectuses. If there is only one type of prospectus, with the same meaning in § 10 and § 12(a)(2), then why not also in § 5(b)(1)? But if *prospectus* means a § 10 prospectus, how could it violate the requirement in § 5(b)(1) that "such prospectus meets the requirements of section 10"? Clearly, § 5(b)(1) contemplates that some prospectuses may *not* meet the requirements of § 10, otherwise the prohibition under § 5(b)(1) would never apply.

Turning at last to § 2(a)(10), the definitional provision for a prospectus, Kennedy encountered another difficulty. Section 2(a)(10) does not refer to § 10. Focusing on the presence of circulars, advertisements, and other components of the § 2(a)(10) definition of prospectus, all of which imply "wide dissemination," Kennedy interpreted § 2(a)(10) as defining prospectus to mean "a document soliciting the public to acquire securities."

Kennedy's detour to § 2(a)(10) is puzzling to the extent he moves away from his initial arguments for one definition of *prospectus* as given in § 10 of the Securities Act. Now, according to Kennedy, a prospectus may encompass documents used to solicit the public in a public offering, a broader concept than a § 10 statutory prospectus. Kennedy justifies the detour as necessary to "prevent[] a seller of stock from avoiding liability by calling a soliciting document something other than a prospectus." But this shift by Kennedy once again creates two types of prospectuses in the Securities Act: a § 10 statutory prospectus, and a § 2(a)(10) prospectus used as part of a solicitation in a public offering. Because *prospectus* refers to a document that is part of a solicitation in a public offering, Kennedy concludes that the contract of sale (drawn up as part of the privately negotiated sale of the stock of Alloyd, Inc.) was not a prospectus and that § 12(a)(2) did not apply.

Gustafson's focus on communications used in the solicitation of a public offering puts considerable stress on the definition of a public offering. Kennedy's reference to the parallel between a registration statement and a prospectus suggests that Kennedy had only registered public offerings in mind for the application of § 12(a)(2) liability. Justice Ginsberg, however, wrote in her dissent, "I understand the Court's definition of a public offering to encompass both transactions that must be registered under § 5 and transactions that would have been registered had the securities involved not qualified for exemption under § 3." Among other exemptions, the SEC has promulgated Regulation A under § 3(b), providing for a form of nonregistered mini-public offering for certain non-Exchange Act reporting issuers. Rules 504 and 505 of Regulation D are also promulgated under § 3(b), as we discuss in Chapter 9. All of these offerings may fall under § 12(a)(2).

One last loose end: Section 12(a)(2) applies to oral as well as written communications. Although in theory § 12(a)(2) could apply to oral communications even outside the context of a public offering, the *Gustafson* Court noted that "the phrase 'oral communication' is restricted to oral communications that relate to a prospectus."

3.3 Elements of the Cause of Action

Although § 12(a)(2) does not explicitly require that plaintiffs demonstrate reliance or loss causation, courts have interpreted the "by means of" language of the provision as requiring a weak causal link between the prospectus and the investor's losses. The Seventh Circuit in *Sanders v. John Nuveen & Co.*[12] for example, held that the "by means of" language in § 12(a)(2)

---

12. 619 F.2d 1222 (7th Cir. 1980).

requires some causal connection between the misrepresentation or omission and the plaintiffs' purchase, but this causation requirement does not require reliance. Nor are purchasers required to demonstrate that they even obtained the prospectus. The court justified this weak causal link by referencing the Securities Act's legislative history, which had this to say about statements made in the course of selling securities: "[A]lthough they may never actually have been seen by the prospective purchaser, because of their wide dissemination, [these statements] determine the market price of the security." The court made clear, however, that an active trading market (similar to that required in the fraud on the market presumption of reliance) is not required to meet the weak causation requirement of § 12(a)(2). Even without a market, the court asserted that the price of the offered securities will still depend on the market perception of the issuer and thus be affected by the fraud: "In the case at bar, publication of [the issuer's] true financial condition would have caused a total collapse of the market for its notes."

We are left with the following puzzle from *Sanders*. Without an active trading market, how would fraud in a prospectus affect the market price? Perhaps the mere existence of a market price suggests that some form of price discovery is occurring in the market. And, as the court points out, if fraud were uncovered, this information would reach the various investors participating in this market, causing the market for the issuer's securities to collapse.

3.4 Loss Causation Defense

Section 12(b) provides defendants with a loss causation defense in a § 12(a)(2) action similar to that found in § 11. Under the defense, defendants bear the burden of proving that a portion or all of the amount recoverable under § 12(a)(2) is not due to the material misstatement or omission at issue in the prospectus.

The initial measure of damages under § 12(a)(2) is quite different from that under § 11. Section 12(a)(2) provides for rescission or rescissionary damages. If investors have held on to their securities, they may receive the full consideration originally paid for the securities (with adjustments for interest less any income received from the securities, such as dividends). So an investor who paid $75 per share for zTunes stock would, under § 12(a)(2), receive $75 (with adjustments) back. Section 11, as we have seen, will pay only the difference between the purchase price (but no more than the public offering price) and, among other measures, the value at the filing of suit. So if the investor paid $75 per share but the zTunes public offering price was $50 and the value at the time of the filing of suit was $20, the damage measure under § 11 would equal $30 (the $50 public offering price minus the $20 value at the filing of suit).

Despite this initial difference between the damage measures under § 12(a)(2) and § 11, loss causation works to align the two. Suppose the first public announcement of the material misstatements in the registration statement and prospectus for zTunes's offering occurred on November 1 and resulted in an immediate $25 drop in the company's stock market price (adjusted for overall market movements). Defendants may use this price drop as evidence that the value of the material misstatement for investors was only $25 per share and that no other part of the stock market price drop is attributable to the material misstatements. Of course, plaintiffs will argue otherwise. But if the court accepts the defendant's version of the facts, under the loss causation defense both the §§ 11 and 12(a)(2) damage measures will be limited to only $25 per share of zTunes stock, despite the starting point of $75 under § 12(a)(2) and $30 under § 11.

3.5 Reasonable Care Defense

Defendants in a § 12(a)(2) action also enjoy a reasonable care defense. The defendant bears the burden of proof of demonstrating that the defendant did not know nor, in the exercise of reasonable care, could have known of the untruth or omission. An interesting question in considering the § 12(a)(2) reasonable care defense is how the defense relates to the § 11 due diligence defense. Recall that § 11 contained both a due diligence defense, requiring reasonable investigation, reasonable belief, and actual belief in the accuracy of the registration statement, and a reliance defense, requiring only reasonable belief and actual belief. Is "reasonable care" more like the due diligence or reliance forms of the § 11 defenses? Or is it something in between?

The rationale for the reliance form of the due diligence defense under § 11 depends on the presence of an expert third party upon whom other parties may rely. As we discussed above, designating a defendant as an expert for an expertised portion of the registration statement reduces the other defendants' requirements for meeting their due diligence defense (requiring only the reliance form of the defense). Because of the expert's ability and investigation, others may reasonably rely even without investigation. Section 12(a)(2), in contrast, makes no such fine distinctions between different portions of the prospectus. If we assume that § 12(a)(2) contemplates only one type of "reasonable care" defense, then adopting the reliance form of the § 11 due diligence defense for § 12(a)(2) would cause potential problems.

Consider sections of the prospectus for which no expert provides certification, such as the description of properties, management biography, discussion and analysis of future capital needs, and so on. To the extent Congress intended § 12(a)(2) defendants to perform a gatekeeping function in preventing fraud, applying the reasonable investigation form of the § 11 defense to determine what reasonable care requires for § 12(a)(2) makes more sense. If we equate reasonable care with reasonable investigation, all defendants in a § 12(a)(2) action must then engage in at least some investigation to meet their defense. If our policy goal is to encourage third party gatekeepers, this reasonable investigation formulation of the reasonable care defense provides the greatest incentives for gatekeeping. Courts have generally held that the reasonable care defense in § 12(a)(2) is more akin to the form of due diligence defense requiring reasonable investigation.[13] Of course, if an expert has certified a portion of the prospectus, a non-expert may argue that its "reasonable care" consisted of relying on the expertise of the expert.

---

13. See, for example, *Software Toolworks,* 50 F.3d at 621 (9th Cir. 1994) (noting that the two articulations of due diligence are "similar," if not identical).

～ 9 ～

Exempt Offerings

Ionix, a privately held corporation, manufactures x-ray machines for use at airport security checkpoints. Recently, Ionix invented a new security technology that allows airport security screeners to identify prohibited items in passenger carry-on luggage more accurately. Carl, the CEO, founder, and largest shareholder of Ionix, is excited about the market prospects for the new technology. Carl realizes, however, that Ionix needs $10 million to develop a prototype of the machine to demonstrate for airport managers. Wary of the cost and hassle of going through a public offering, Carl would like to sell common stock through an exempt offering to investors.

Companies always have the option of selling securities through a registered public offering pursuant to § 5 of the Securities Act. Registration requires the issuer to put together a mandatory information package in the form of a registration statement and statutory prospectus, to comply with the gun-jumping rules, and to face heightened civil liability under §§ 11 and 12 of the Securities Act. In this chapter, we consider the provisions in the securities laws that allow issuers to offer and sell securities other than through a registered public offering.

We begin with the statutory exemption for offerings not involving a public offering under § 4(2) of the Securities Act, that is, a private placement. Most issuers do not structure private placements by relying directly on § 4(2); rather, they use one of the available safe harbors. Nonetheless, we start our analysis with § 4(2) doctrine to illuminate an important issue: why the securities laws provide *any* capital raising alternative to the registered public offering. After all, Congress and the SEC could require all issuers selling securities to register the sale as a public offering. Not all issuers, investors, and offered securities are the same, however. As we discuss below, the securities laws take these differences into account by exempting some offerings from § 5.

The bulk of the chapter then covers the SEC's safe harbor exemptions in Regulation D of the Securities Act. Regulation D provides much needed guidance for issuers attempting to avoid the registration requirements of § 5. We complete our tour through exempt transactions with a brief discussion of the exemption under Regulation A for mini-public offerings. We also touch upon exemptions for intrastate offerings, international offerings made outside the United States, and exempt securities.

1 SECTION 4(2)

Section 4(2) of the Securities Act exempts issuers from § 5 if they sell securities other than through "any public offering." Through a § 4(2) nonpublic, private placement issuers can avoid the registration, gun-jumping, and prospectus requirements of § 5. These advantages of § 4(2) are undercut to some extent, however, by the lack of certainty in the application of the exemption.

Certain types of offerings clearly fall under § 4(2). Consider Ionix and Carl. Suppose Carl, the CEO and largest shareholder of Ionix, decides to invest his own money in Ionix in return for more shares of Ionix common stock. A sale of shares to one investor, Carl, who also is the CEO and largest shareholder of Ionix, is plainly not a "public offering" of shares. At the other extreme, suppose Ionix offers its shares broadly, using general advertising, including a number of cable TV ads enticing investors to "buy, buy, buy" the shares. This plainly would be a public offering.

Between these two poles lies a gray region. Consider the following three situations.

1. Ionix offers and sells its common shares to all Ionix employees who have obtained an MBA degree. Over 100 employees qualify under this criterion; their positions range from executive vice presidents to newly-hired marketing associates.
2. Ionix offers its common shares at a job conference attended by approximately 300 economics Ph.D. graduate students seeking their first academic jobs. Because the students all aspire to academic positions, they are all dirt poor. Ten of the offerees eventually purchase a total of $1 million of the Ionix stock, borrowing the money for the purchases from their relatives.
3. Carl wants to share the upside possibilities of investing in Ionix with members of his family. Carl has Ionix offer common stock to everyone who attends his family reunion. Of the 30 family members who attend the gathering, five decide to purchase a total of $50 million of common stock.

Are any of these situations not public for purposes of § 4(2)? A plain language approach would be one way of answering this question. According to *Webster's Dictionary* the word *public* means "accessible . . . to all members of the community." Under the dictionary approach, any restriction, such as an offering only to those with red hair, would exclude an offering from being considered public. Such an approach, however, does not offer any solid policy basis for distinguishing public from nonpublic offerings.

An alternate approach to defining *public* looks to whether the protections of § 5 are necessary. If § 5 applies, we have seen that the issuer faces (1) mandatory disclosure, (2) gun-jumping rules, and (3) heightened civil liability provisions. Moreover, once an issuer sells securities through a registered public offering,

§ 15(d) of the Exchange Act makes the issuer a public reporting company. The provisions of the Sarbanes-Oxley Act will also apply to the issuer. One can approach the issue of whether an offering is public by asking this question: Do investors in an issuer's offering need the various protections afforded under § 5 and the Exchange Act's regulation of public companies?

Two considerations are relevant in answering this question. First, the protections under § 5 and public company status are costly. Issuers, of course, face the direct cost of complying with the regulatory requirements. But public offering and public company status may also become a distraction for managements attempting to ensure compliance. Moreover, it forces the company to open its books and operations to outsiders. Significantly, many of these costs are fixed: They do not vary with the size of the offering or of the company. Issuers selling a modest amount of securities may find that the high fixed costs of the public offering process exceed its benefits. Second, the benefits of § 5 and the public company provisions may vary depending on the type of investors sought in an offering. Offerings made solely to sophisticated investors who can assess the merits and risks of an investment without the assistance of regulatory protections have less need for mandatory disclosure, gun-jumping rules, and heightened civil liability.

Based on this reasoning, the securities laws take a functional approach to determining when an offering requires the protections afforded under § 5 and is therefore public. In 1935, the SEC General Counsel provided an opinion in which he delineated five factors to consider when deciding whether an offering constituted a public offering for purposes of § 4(2): (1) the number of offerees; (2) the relationship of the offerees to each other and to the issuer; (3) the size of the offering; (4) the number of units offered; and (5) the manner of the offering.[1]

---

1. Securities Act Release No. 285 (January 24, 1935).

If all five factors point in the same direction, issuers enjoy a measure of certainty in determining whether an offering is public. Suppose Ionix offers and sells 1,000 shares of common stock for $100,000. The shares are sold in a privately negotiated transaction with two executive vice presidents of Ionix. In this case, the small number of offerees, their position with the issuer, the small size of the offering, the small number of shares, and the lack of public promotion of the offering, all point to a private, nonpublic offering. The sales to the executive vice presidents likely qualify under § 4(2) for an exemption from § 5.

But what if Ionix offers and sells one million shares of common stock for $100 million in privately negotiated transactions with the same two executive vice presidents of Ionix? Although the number of offerees remains small, they both work for the issuer, and the manner of the offering is private, the size of the offering and the number of units are now quite large. When the 1935 factors diverge, the determination of whether an offering is public or private may be little more than guesswork.

In addition to this uncertainty in application, do the 1935 factors capture the proper policy balance in determining the types of offerings that should escape the protections of § 5? Suppose Ionix sells 1,000 shares of common stock for $100,000 in a privately negotiated transaction with two now-retired employees of Ionix. Neither retiree has much investment experience; both are investing because they got a hot stock tip from one of their former coworkers. The retirees used to work in Ionix's mailroom; they have put their entire life savings into the Ionix stock. In this case, under the 1935 factors, the small size of the offering, the private manner of sales, the limited number of offerees, and their relationship with each other and to the company as coworkers all point toward treating the offering as private. Nonetheless, the presence of inexperienced retiree-investors raises substantial investor protection concerns.

In response, one could argue that the relationship to the issuer in the preceding example (as mailroom coworkers) is not the sort of relationship contemplated under the 1935 factors. Still, all the other factors point toward a private offering. Moreover, even a focus on the relationship to the issuer may not quite capture our concerns with respect to the needs of investors. A wide range of investment experience and expertise exists among investors without any relationship to the issuer, such as outside investors. Both Goldman Sachs, a large Wall Street investment bank, and a retired music teacher from Iowa may consider investing in Ionix. Most people would say, however, that Goldman Sachs has a far lower need for the protections of the registered public offering process as compared with the retired music teacher.

The Supreme Court adopted a different test of whether an offering is public in *SEC v. Ralston Purina Co.*[2] Ralston Purina offered and sold its common stock to some of its employees, including artists, clerical assistants, copywriters, electricians, and stock clerks. The Court held that the functional policy goal of registration under § 5 should govern what types of offerings are considered nonpublic and therefore exempt pursuant to § 4(2). If investors can "fend for themselves," the Court reasoned, they do not need the protections of § 5. Although the Court did not completely reject the use of the 1935 General Counsel factors, the Court found that they were not dispositive. Under the *Ralston Purina* formulation, an offering even to a small number of investors may constitute a public offering if the investors cannot "fend for themselves." As an example of a nonpublic offering, the Court cited an offering to executive officers of an issuer who have access to the same information normally provided in a registration statement in a public offering. One procedural point: The Court held that the burden of proof lies with the party seeking an exemption from § 5.

---

2. 346 U.S. 119 (1953).

After *Ralston Purina*, at least three issues remain open under § 4(2). First, can investors other than executive officers of an issuer "fend for themselves"? Second, what role does information play in determining whether investors can "fend for themselves"? In particular, are investors who are merely provided information similar to that in a registration statement, but who otherwise have no access to the internal information of a company, able to "fend for themselves"? Third, do the 1935 factors carry any weight after *Ralston Purina*?

The case law providing additional guidance on what is a public offering is limited, primarily because the SEC provides the Regulation D safe harbor for issuers selling securities in a private offering. As a result, relatively few offerings rely exclusively on § 4(2). A leading case is *Doran v. Petroleum Management Corp.*[3] Petroleum Management Corp. (PMC) offered and sold interests in an oil drilling limited partnership through an unregistered offering. Doran invested in the offering. Unfortunately for PMC and Doran, the limited partnership interests did not perform as expected. Doran filed suit against PMC for selling unregistered securities in violation of § 5. PMC defended on the ground that its offering was exempt under § 4(2).

The *Doran* court held that in determining the application of § 4(2), courts must weigh not only the 1935 factors as "guideposts" but also the legislative purpose to protect investors. Among the 1935 factors, the court noted that the "the number of offerees and their relationship to the issuer" most closely matched the purpose of protecting investors, but the need of the offerees for the protection of the securities laws was also relevant, as emphasized in *Ralston Purina*.

In assessing the need for investor protection, *Doran* did not limit its review to purchasers but included all offerees. Thus, Doran's considerable experience investing in oil limited partnerships was not dispositive. The question was whether the

---

3. 545 F.2d 893 (5th Cir. 1977).

issuer's offering — viewed as one transaction — qualified for § 4(2). If the transaction as a whole fails to qualify for § 4(2) because some of the offerees are unable to "fend for themselves," then even sophisticated purchasers may sue for violations of § 5. Under § 12(a)(1) of the Securities Act, all purchasers in the offering are allowed to rescind if there has been a § 5 violation for any offeree. The harshness of this result contributes to the crush-out quality of § 12(a)(1) that we discussed in Chapter 8.

The inquiry into the offerees' need for protection requires an examination of (1) the sophistication of the offerees, and (2) the information available to the offerees. Sophistication alone is not enough. As the *Doran* court put it, "Just as a scientist cannot be without his specimens, so the shrewdest investor's acuity will be blunted without specifications about the issuer." Information can be made available to investors either through direct disclosure of information equivalent to that found in a registration statement or, alternatively, through *access*. The court defined access as "a relationship based on factors such as employment, family, or economic bargaining power that enables the offeree effectively to obtain such information." If information is made available through access, as opposed to disclosure, the relationship of the offerees to the issuer and the sophistication of the issuer take on enhanced importance.

If the issuer must provide information equivalent to that in a registration statement (whether by disclosure or through access) to qualify for § 4(2), why not just do a public offering? Even if similar information must be disclosed, issuers in a § 4(2) private placement avoid other requirements that accompany a registered public offering. Private placement issuers do not need to follow the gun-jumping rules, nor do they face the enhanced civil liability provisions under §§ 11 and 12 of the Securities Act. Of equal importance for non-reporting issuers, selling securities through an exempt transaction does not trigger the public company reporting obligations under

§ 15(d) of the Exchange Act. (Although they must take care to keep the number of shareholders of any class of equity securities below 500, lest they trigger § 12(g).)

Despite the guidance provided in *Ralston Purina* and *Doran*, determining what types of offerings qualify as private under § 4(2) remains tricky. What type of access counts as making information available under *Doran*? *Doran* makes clear that sophistication alone does not guarantee access, but it also suggests that "economic bargaining power" may lead to access. The realities of the marketplace suggest that sophisticated investors understand the importance of information and will simply refuse to purchase unless provided with adequate information. This may give sophisticated investors as a group economic bargaining power that allows them to force disclosure.

Who counts as a sophisticated investor? Determining sophistication is not easy. We could require each offeree to take an exam testing investment expertise. Such a test, however, would be costly, and it might not accurately capture investment sophistication. Those who can do well on an exam may not necessarily make good investors. One could also imagine requiring potential investors to sit through oral interviews with finance professors and investment bankers to get a more nuanced sense of the investor's sophistication. Although perhaps more accurate, such a procedure would be prohibitively expensive if it were applied to all offerees.

Perhaps we could use more objective criteria to determine sophistication, such as years of prior investment experience, net worth, annual income, and so on. Unfortunately, easy-to-apply factors (such as net worth and income thresholds) tend to correlate poorly with investment sophistication. Simply because an investor is wealthy does not mean the investor is sophisticated regarding investment. Some investors may become wealthy through inheritance, others because they have talents unrelated to the financial markets. Of course, the wealthy can better withstand the risks of investments: They can afford to take a loss. On the other hand, the wealthy and unsophisticated are prime targets of fraud. Alternatively, the wealthy may be more likely to hire investment advisors, essentially renting sophistication through third party agents. Although the policy goal of restricting § 4(2) exempt offerings solely to investors who can "fend for themselves" makes sense, issuers relying on § 4(2) face the daunting task (and burden of proof) of demonstrating that all of their offerees possess that sophistication.

2 REGULATION D

The SEC has used its broad rulemaking authority to provide several safe harbors for issuers seeking exemptions from the requirements of § 5. Three of these safe harbors are found in Regulation D of the Securities Act (encompassing Rule 501 through 508). Regulation D provides three types of offerings exempt from § 5 of the Securities Act under Rules 504, 505, and 506 of the Securities Act. The SEC promulgated Rules 504 and 505 using its authority in § 3(b) of the Securities Act, which gives the SEC blanket authority to exempt offerings, but only up to $5 million. The SEC promulgated Rule 506 under § 4(2) of the Securities Act, so it is an interpretation of the private offering exemption. The Regulation D exemptions are not exclusive. Issuers attempting to sell securities under one type of Regulation D offering are always free to argue after the fact that another exemption from § 5 (such as § 4(2)) exempts the offering.[4]

---

4. Not all three Regulation D offerings are available to all type of issuers. Rule 504 excludes investment companies, "blank check" companies, and Exchange Act reporting issuers. Rule 505 excludes investment companies and certain disqualified issuers as provided under Rule 262 of Regulation A (discussed below). Rule 506 is open to all issuers.

Regulation D imposes a variety of requirements to qualify for its safe harbors. These requirements include (1) the aggregate offering price ceiling; (2) the limitation on the number of purchasers and purchaser sophistication; (3) disclosure; (4) the limitation on general solicitation and advertising; (5) the restriction on resales; (6) the integration safe harbor; and (7) notice filing. We also discuss (8) the forgiveness provision for innocent and insignificant mistakes provided in Rule 508 and (9) the SEC's proposed but as yet not enacted reforms to Regulation D, including, most notably, a new category of private offering exempt transaction in new Rule 507.

2.1 Aggregate Offering Price Ceiling

As a policy matter, it is easier to justify imposing the fixed cost of the registered public offering process for an offering of $100 million than it is for an offering of $2 million. Regulation D embodies this policy consideration, capping Rule 504 and 505 offerings to a maximum dollar amount, the aggregate offering price ceiling. Rule 504 limits the aggregate offering price to $1 million (Rule 504(b)(2)). Rule 505 limits the aggregate offering price to $5 million (Rule 505(b)(2)(i)). Rule 506, promulgated under § 4(2), does not limit the aggregate offering amount.

What prevents an issuer from selling securities through a series of Rule 504 or 505 offerings, each individually smaller than the aggregate offering price ceiling but collectively far in excess? Suppose Ionix sells $1 million of stock through a Rule 504 offering on January 1. One week later, Ionix sells another $1 million of stock through another Rule 504 offering. Absent some restriction on multiple offerings, Ionix could easily evade the limitation on the aggregate offering price. To combat this sort of opportunism, Rules 504 and 505 both reduce the aggregate offering price ceiling by the amount of securities sold within the past year pursuant to an offering exempt under § 3(b) of the Securities Act (such as Rule 504 or 505 offerings) or in violation of § 5 (Rules 504(b)(2) and 505(b)(2)(i)). Offerings under § 4(2) or Rule 506 do not count against the limit.

Revisit Ionix's series of offerings. After the January 1 offering for $1 million under Rule 504, the aggregate offering price ceiling for a subsequent Rule 504 offering is $0 (the $1 million initial aggregate offering price ceiling minus the $1 million in securities sold within the prior year). Thus, Ionix cannot sell any more securities under Rule 504 until January 1 of the next year. This prevents it from splitting an offering into a series of transactions to get around the $1 million limitation in Rule 504. What if Ionix instead chooses to sell securities through a Rule 505 offering? The ceiling for a Rule 505 offering until January 1 of the next year is equal to $4 million: the $5 million initial aggregate offering price ceiling minus the previous $1 million in securities sold under a § 3(b) offering.

Offerings of securities may not occur in a single day; they may take weeks or months. Suppose Ionix sold $1 million of securities spread pro rata over the month of January through a Rule 504 offering. What is the Rule 505 aggregate offering price ceiling going forward into time? Until January 1 of the next year, the aggregate offering price ceiling under Rule 505 is $4 million, just as above. After January 1 of the next year, the Rule 505 offering price ceiling will rise linearly through the month of January, reaching $5 million at the end of the month.

Suppose instead that Ionix sells $10 million in securities on January 1 in an attempted Rule 506 offering. Unfortunately for Ionix, it failed to satisfy Rule 506 because it sold to unsophisticated purchasers. Absent some other exemption, Ionix's attempted Rule 506 offering will violate § 5. For the subsequent one-year period, the aggregate offering price ceiling for both Rules 504 and 505 will then equal zero, because the aggregate limit must be reduced by the $10 million sold in violation of § 5.

Why do securities previously sold in violation of § 5 count against the aggregate offering price ceiling? Unlike for prior § 3(b) offerings, there is no fear of issuers stringing together a series of offerings to avoid the aggregate offering price limitation. Instead, the reduction in the aggregate offering price ceiling punishes issuers that violated § 5 in the past by preventing them from selling more securities through a unregistered offering. But why should the punishment vary with the size of the prior offering? If Ionix had sold $1 million in securities on January 1 in a failed Rule 506 offering that violated § 5, Ionix could still sell up to $4 million through a Rule 505 offering during the subsequent one-year period. Note also that *offers* made in violation of § 5 do not reduce the aggregate offering price ceiling at all. One possible explanation is that not all violations of § 5 are willful; it is a strict liability provision. Because of the technical nature of the gun-jumping rules and the exemptions from § 5, issuers can inadvertently violate § 5. Thus, the reduction in the aggregate offering price ceiling may strike an ad hoc compromise, sanctioning issuers by reducing their ability to sell securities through Rules 504 or 505 but not completely cutting off their ability to sell in an exempt offering.

2.2 Number of Purchasers and Sophistication

Rules 505 and 506 restrict the number of purchasers to 35. In addition, Rule 506 requires that purchasers, either individually or together with a purchaser representative, have the "knowledge and experience" to judge the "merits and risks" of an investment (that is, they must be sophisticated). Although Rule 504 imposes the most stringent limit on the aggregate offering price ceiling (at $1 million), it does not restrict the number of purchasers. The $1 million limit, however, does indirectly restrict the scope of the offering and, consequently, the number of purchasers.

At first glance, Rule 506 strikes the opposite balance as in Rule 504. Although Rule 506 does not impose an aggregate offering price ceiling, the limitation to only 35 sophisticated purchasers may limit the size of a Rule 506 offering, albeit indirectly. This limit, however, is largely illusory. Rule 501(e) provides a series of exclusions from the count of purchasers toward the 35 investor limit. Critically, Rule 501(e)(1)(iv) excludes "accredited investors" from the purchaser count used to determine the 35 investor limit. Rule 501(a) defines *accredited investors* to include various entities and institutions, including corporations, trusts, and partnerships with a minimum of $5 million in total assets. In addition, three categories of individuals may qualify as accredited investors: (1) directors, executive officers, or general partners of the issuer of the securities (Rule 501(a)(4)); (2) natural persons with an individual net worth, or joint net worth with a spouse, of $1 million (Rule 501(a)(5)); and (3) natural persons with an individual income of over $200,000 in each of the two most recent years or, jointly with a spouse, of over $300,000 in each of those years (as well as a reasonable expectation of reaching the same income level in the current year) (Rule 501(a)(6)).

One can wonder whether the net worth and income tests of Rules 501(a)(5) and (6) continue to make sense today. The SEC has not revised the dollar amounts in Rules 501(a)(5) and (6) since 1982, when it implemented the individual net worth and income definitions of accredited investors.[5] Taking into account inflation, $1 million in 1982 is equal to a little over $2.1 million in 2007. Similarly, $200,000 in 1982 is equal to almost $426,000 in 2007. Unless the dollar cutoffs are revised, inflation expands the scope of individual accredited investors yearly. At the time of this book's publication, the SEC had recently announced that it would reconsider these limits.[6]

---

5. See Securities Act Release No. 6389 (March 8, 1982).
6. The SEC proposed revisions to Regulation D that included the creation of a new "large accredited investor" class of investors. For individuals to qualify as a "large accredited investor," for example, the SEC proposed an annual income requirement of more than $400,000 (or $600,000 jointly with one's spouse)

Issuers may sell to an unlimited number of accredited investors despite the limit on the number of purchasers in Rules 505 and 506. Rule 506 purchasers who are not accredited must meet the sophistication requirement of Rule 506(b)(2)(ii). As with the concept of sophistication under *Ralston Purina* and *Doran*, issuers face uncertainty in determining sophistication for purposes of Rule 506. How is an issuer supposed to know whether a particular investor is able to assess the merits or risks of an investment? Particularly for nonaccredited individual investors with a relatively low net worth and income, what factors demonstrate sophistication? No sophistication requirement applies to accredited investors, so they are the preferred targets for Rule 506 offerings.

A purchaser may demonstrate sophistication through the assistance of a purchaser representative. Rule 501(h) lists the requirements for a purchaser representative. The purchaser representative must be sophisticated, and the purchaser must acknowledge the purchaser representative's role in writing. Rule 501(h) excludes certain parties from acting as a purchaser representative, including affiliates, directors, officers, and beneficial owners of 10 percent or more of any class of the issuer's equity securities. This exclusion is removed if the potential purchaser representative is also, among other considerations, a relative of the purchaser "not more remote than a first cousin." Rule 501(h) also requires that the purchaser representative disclose any material relationship with the issuer or its affiliates as well as any compensation received from the relationship.

Many accredited investors with a net worth over $1 million or an annual income of $200,000 may hire financial advisors qualified to act as purchaser representatives. But is it common

---

among other possible qualifications. The SEC also proposed adjusting for inflation the income and net worth requirements for accredited investors in Rules 501(a)(5) and (6). See Securities Act Release No. 8828 (August 3, 2007).

for nonaccredited investors with lower net worth and income levels to hire financial advisors? If you were interested in investing only $5,000, for example, would you be willing to pay for an investment advisor?

Rather than face the legal uncertainties that surround investor sophistication under Rule 506, issuers typically prefer to sell only to accredited investors. Determining whether an investor is accredited is far simpler and more objective than determining sophistication. Moreover, accredited investors have greater investment resources than do the nonaccredited: that is where the money is. Limiting a Rule 506 offering to only accredited investors provides certainty without sacrificing much of the overall pool of investment dollars.

If most issuers prefer to sell solely to accredited investors, what kind of issuers will structure an offering to include non-accredited purchasers? Perhaps those issuers unable to find sufficient interest from accredited investors. These issuers may either be less well-known or pose a risk-return ratio greater than most accredited investors find acceptable. Nonaccredited purchasers may therefore face a "winner's curse." They are able to purchase investments that better-heeled investors choose to avoid.

2.3 Disclosure

A key factor in whether an offering qualifies for a § 4(2) exemption is the availability of information similar to that in a registration statement. That information can be made available through either access or disclosure (see *Doran*). Regulation D requires issuers to provide purchasers with information under Rule 502(b). Although issuers selling securities under Rule 505 or 506 must comply with Rule 502(b), Rule 504 does not directly require disclosure. Most Rule 504 offerings, nonetheless, are registered for sale under a state securities regime. Doing so allows the issuer of a Rule 504 offering to avoid other aspects of the Regulation D regime, including the prohibition on general solicitation (Rule 502(c)) and the resale limitations (Rule 502(d)) discussed below. Such state-based Rule 504 offerings need not comply with Rule 502(b), but instead must follow the disclosure requirements of the particular states in which the issuer has registered. The North American Securities Administrators Association (located at *www.nasaa.org*) provides information on the registration forms used in the various states, including the Small Company Offering Registration Form (otherwise known as the SCOR Form).

Rule 502(b) provides hierarchical levels of required disclosure. Rule 502(b)(1) does not include mandatory disclosure to accredited investors. Despite the lack of any legal mandate for disclosure, most issuers will give accredited investors an offering circular containing information similar to that found in a registration statement, including a description of the business, properties, management, principal shareholders, capital stock, and audited financials. Without this voluntary disclosure, issuers will find that few (if any) accredited investors will purchase. Because most issuers voluntarily provide information, issuers that fail to distribute an offering circular send a negative signal to investors. Such an issuer must be hiding something. If you have nothing to hide, why not disclose as other issuers do?

Given the incentive to disclose voluntarily, the disclosure mandated by Rule 502(b)(2) for nonaccredited investors is a less substantial consideration. Rule 502(b)(2) varies the level of mandatory disclosure based on (1) whether the issuer is an Exchange Act reporting issuer, and (2) the dollar amount of the offering.

Rule 502(b) provides that all Exchange Act reporting issuers face the same disclosure requirement. Exchange Act reporting issuers must give nonaccredited purchasers a package of company-specific information, including the annual report, the most recent Form 10-K, the definitive proxy statement, and any more recent Exchange Act filings. Company-specific information includes a description of the business, properties, material legal proceedings, executive officers, board of directors, principal shareholders, audited financials, and so on. In addition, Exchange Act reporting issuers must give nonaccredited purchasers transaction-specific information relating to the offering, including "a brief description of the securities being offered, the use of the proceeds from the offering, and any material changes in the issuer's affairs that are not disclosed in the documents furnished" (Rule 502(b)(2)(ii)(C)).

Non–Exchange Act reporting issuers face less demanding disclosure requirements, particularly with respect to financial information. The requirements vary with the size of the offering amount. Those interested in the precise requirements may look at Rule 502(b)(2)(i) and (ii).

In addition to the mandatory disclosure requirements imposed on issuers selling to nonaccredited purchasers, we note two additional disclosure requirements under Rule 502(b). First, Rule 502(b)(2)(iv) requires that issuers must give nonaccredited purchasers a brief written description of "any material written information concerning the offering that has been provided by the issuer to any accredited investor" not already given to the nonaccredited purchasers. If nonaccredited purchasers request this information in writing, the issuer must give them the information within a reasonable time prior to purchase.

Second, Rule 502(b)(2)(v) requires that the issuer allow each purchaser the "opportunity to ask questions and receive answers" concerning the offering. Under Rule 502(b)(2)(v), the issuer must upon request give purchasers any additional information necessary to verify the accuracy of the mandatory disclosure items as specified in Rules 502(b)(2)(i) and (ii), provided the "issuer possesses [the information] or can acquire [it] without unreasonable effort or expense." Although Rule 502(b)(2)(v) does not specify that only nonaccredited purchasers are owed the right to ask questions and receive answers, Rule 502(b)(1) tells us that Rule 502(b)(2) generally only applies for nonaccredited purchasers. In any case, issuers will voluntarily provide accredited investors the right to ask questions and receive answers. Issuers that refuse to answer investor's questions will likely find few investors will buy their securities.

2.4 Limitation on General Solicitation

The requirements for the three types of Regulation D offerings discussed above focus exclusively on purchasers. Nonaccredited purchasers must receive information under Rule 502(b) for Rule 505 and 506 offerings. Both Rule 505 and 506 offerings limit the number of nonaccredited purchasers. Rule 506 also imposes a sophistication requirement on nonaccredited purchasers. In contrast, § 4(2) limits offerees as well as purchasers. Section 4(2) doctrine focuses on the number of offerees, their relationship with the issuer, and the investment sophistication of the offerees.

Should we focus on purchasers or offerees? If an investment goes bad, only purchasers are harmed. Only purchasers have standing to sue for rescission in cases of a § 5 violation under the liability provision in § 12(a)(1). If offerees are not harmed, why focus on their investment sophistication? Perhaps we are concerned with conditioning the market. Investors are not islands; they may make decisions based on the actions of other investors. Investors as a group may go into frenzies, feeding off the excitement of other investors and making poor investment decisions. Broad-based advertisements for an offering, even if the offering is ultimately restricted to certain sophisticated purchasers or accredited investors, may lead to an overall market frenzy that can affect even the more sophisticated investors. Recall the hot market for Internet stocks in the late 1990s.

Speculative frenzies aside, the ability to make an unlimited number of offers may allow issuers to cherry-pick the market for investors. These investors may seem objectively sophisticated or accredited, but they may not necessarily be making good investment decisions in a specific instance. Suppose that any particular sophisticated or accredited investor makes a good investment decision 99 percent of the time. Through a broad-based advertisement, an issuer offering a poor investment may reach many sophisticated or accredited investors. Even if the issuer convinces only one in a hundred to invest, the large net cast through a broad-based advertising campaign may allow the issuer to sell a large amount of securities. Particularly because the definition of an accredited investor is not particularly stringent, issuers with an ability to contact an unlimited number of such investors may eventually find their targets.

To maintain restrictions on offerees, Regulation D limits general solicitations and advertising in Rule 502(c). As with the information requirement of Rule 502(b), the Rule 502(c) limitations typically apply only to Rule 505 and 506 offerings. Rule 504 offerings structured to comply with the registration requirements under a particular state's securities regime are exempt from Rule 502(c).[7] Issuers of such Rule 504 offerings may make broad-based solicitations and advertisements without interference from the federal securities regime. Nonetheless, state law requirements may limit such solicitations. Moreover, the small size of such offerings, $1 million or less, limits the incentive of issuers to advertise the offering broadly, which can be quite expensive.

---

7. Although we do not expand on the registration under state law component of Rule 504, note that one avenue for complying with the state law component is to register securities under the laws of a state that also "require[s] the public filing and delivery to investors or a substantive disclosure document before sale," among other things. Rule 504(b)(1)(i).

What counts as general solicitation? Placing an advertisement in the *Wall Street Journal* announcing an offering would certainly violate the prohibition on general solicitation. But what about more restricted offers? The SEC faced this issue in *In the Matter of Kenman Corp.*[8] Issuers sold limited partnership interest securities to investors to finance various apartment building complexes and Dairy Queen restaurants. Although the securities were not registered, the issuers attempted to comply with the Rule 506 exemption. Kenman, the agent for the issuers, sent materials on the offerings to several different lists of potential investors (constituting thousands of individuals), including executive officers of Fortune 500 companies, physicians in California, managerial engineers employed by Hughes Aircraft Company, and presidents of certain listed companies as listed in the Morris County, New Jersey, Industrial Directory. The SEC held that because the issuer and offerees had no "pre-existing relationship," this offer was a general solicitation.

The SEC in the *Mineral Lands Research & Marketing Corporation,*[9] provided additional guidance on the importance of "pre-existing relationships" for purposes of applying the Rule 502(c) general solicitation prohibition. The SEC made two points in the No-Action Letter. First, the SEC stated that only preexisting relationships between offerees and the issuer (or someone working on behalf of the issuer) that allow the issuer to determine the "financial circumstances or sophistication" of the offerees or are otherwise of "some substance and duration" will meet the prohibition on general solicitations. Mere prior social relationships, for example, are unlikely to count as preexisting relationships for purposes of Rule 502(c). Second, the presence of a

---

8. S.E.C., [1984/1985 Transfer Binder] Fed. Sec. L. Rep. (CCH) & 83,767 (April 19, 1985).
9. No-Action Letter (Publicly Available December 4, 1985).

preexisting relationship is an "important factor" in determining whether general solicitation has taken place, but the SEC did not say that a preexisting relationship is the exclusive means of demonstrating the absence of a general solicitation. Presumably, an issuer may make offers to investors they know to be sophisticated based on publicly available information without running afoul of Rule 502(c), even without a preexisting relationship. For example, offers and sales to institutional investors may be consistent with the limitation on general solicitation.

How are issuers (or those working on their behalf) supposed to develop preexisting relationships with investors? For well-known seasoned issuers, the task is not difficult. Most WKSIs will already enjoy a number of contacts with large institutional investors. Representatives of some institutional investors may even sit on the WKSI's board of directors. For pre-IPO issuers, however, preexisting relationships with investors may be hard to come by. Such issuers may have no significant contacts with large investors.

Fortunately for such issuers, the preexisting relationship requirement with offerees may be met by someone working on behalf of the issuer. Smaller, pre-IPO issuers are channeled toward hiring placement agents with a pool of investors with whom they have previously developed financial and investment information. Placement agents, typically smaller investment banks and brokerage firms, will maintain databases of investors, collected through prior distributions of suitability questionnaires. The Rule 502(c) prohibition on general solicitation therefore works indirectly to place a gatekeeper — the placement agent — between less well-known issuers and investors. Presumably the placement agent will only bring issuers to market that meet certain minimum requirements set by the placement agent because its own reputation will be at stake with the offering. The placement agent may also screen for accuracy in the offering documents.

2.5 Resale Restrictions

Rule 502(d) restricts investors who purchase securities through a Regulation D exempt offering from freely reselling their securities. Resale requires either another exemption from § 5 or a registered offering. As we will see in Chapter 10, the restrictions on resales do not continue indefinitely. Instead, the SEC has provided resale safe harbors under Rule 144 and 144A.

The resale limitation generally applies only to offerings under Rules 505 or 506. Rule 504 offerings that comply with the registration requirements under a particular state's securities regime are not restricted. Securities sold under such a Rule 504 offering can be freely resold, leading many to deem Rule 504 offerings to be *mini-public offerings*. State law requirements, however, may limit resales for Rule 504 offerings. In addition, the small size of such offerings, $1 million and under, makes it unlikely that a liquid secondary resale market will arise for such securities.

To understand the importance of the resale restrictions under Regulation D, consider what would happen if Regulation D permitted free resale after a Rule 505 or 506 offering. Suppose Ionix were to sell securities in a Rule 506 offering to one accredited investor, Goldman Sachs, a large investment bank. Because Goldman is an accredited investor and obviously sophisticated, there is no general solicitation problem; Ionix may sell an unlimited amount of securities to Goldman. Unless resales are prohibited, however, Goldman could turn around and resell to an unlimited number of unsophisticated investors through broadly disseminated solicitations. Accordingly, Rule 502(d) restricts resales to prevent their use to skirt the various requirements relating to general solicitations, number of purchasers, and sophistication of purchasers.[10]

---

10. We note that even without any explicit exemption on resales, investors that purchase from an issuer and immediately resell those securities are likely to

Rule 502(d) requires that issuers take reasonable care to discourage investors from making resales, but it does not specify the means required to do so. Rule 502(d) provides a non-exhaustive list of possible measures issuers may take to block resales, such as disclosing in writing to the investors the restricted status of the securities or placing a legend on the securities indicating their restricted status.

The restriction on resales places a large economic burden on investors in a Rule 505 or 506 private placement. The return from an investment in stock can come in the form of dividends or through capital appreciation. The inability to resell severely limits the ability to benefit from potential capital appreciation. Investors wanting to rebalance their portfolio will find it difficult to adjust their holdings of restricted securities if resales are prohibited forever. Not surprisingly, to entice investors to purchase the restricted securities, private placements of equity securities typically require a large discount relative to public offerings. To reduce this discount, when a public company issues private equity (often referred to as a private investment in public equity or PIPE transaction), the public company often agrees to give the purchasers registration rights or otherwise to allow them to register the securities at a later date. When the securities are later registered, the purchasers may then resell broadly into the public capital markets. Giving registration rights to purchasers in a PIPE transaction reduces the discount purchasers will demand from the price of the publicly traded equity.

---

be treated as purchasing with a view to the distribution of the securities. Such investors would therefore qualify as underwriters under § 2(a)(11) of the Securities Act. As we discuss in Chapter 10, the presence of an underwriter removes the § 4(1) exemption from § 5 for such resale transactions. Absent some other exemption, § 5 applies to the resale, regardless of whether Rule 502(d) applies.

2.6 Integration Safe Harbor

The SEC does not develop rules in vacuum; it considers the reaction of issuers and other securities market participants to the rules it promulgates. In the context of Regulation D, issuers may act opportunistically, creating a series of transactions to avoid the various requirements imposed by the SEC. In the preliminary notes to Regulation D, the SEC states that "Regulation D is not available to any issuer for any transaction or chain of transactions that, although in technical compliance with these rules, is part of a plan or scheme to evade the registration provisions of the Act." In addition to the broad prohibition on sham transactions, we have seen that the aggregate price ceiling under Rules 504 and 505 is reduced by the amount of securities sold in the prior one-year period under a § 3(b) exemption (such as Rules 504 or 505) or in violation of § 5. The reduction of the aggregate offering price ceiling prevents issuers from using a series of offerings to get around the aggregate offering price limitation.

The SEC applies an alternative doctrine—integration—to stop issuers from using a series of transactions to get around the requirements of exempt transactions. The SEC takes the position that two transactions will be integrated into one transaction depending on the balance of certain factors.[11] These factors include whether (1) the sales are part of a single plan of financing; (2) the sales involve issuance of the same class of securities; (3) the sales have been made at or about the same time; (4) the same type of consideration is received; and (5) the sales are made for the same general purpose.

What consequence does integration have for Regulation D? Unlike aggregation, which focuses only on one dimension of the Regulation D requirements—the aggregate offering price ceiling—integration affects all Regulation D requirements.

---

11. Securities Act Release No. 4552 (November 6, 1962).

By treating two offerings as one, integration requires that the *combined* offering amount, number of purchasers, manner of solicitation, implementation of resale restrictions, and information disclosure all meet the requirements of a Regulation D exemption.

As with many of the other multifactor balancing tests under the securities laws, the application of the integration factors is uncertain. Suppose Ionix sells securities in two Regulation D exempt offerings spaced only one week apart, but the offerings are ostensibly for different purposes: one to expand marketing and the other to fund research and development. Should the two offerings be integrated and therefore treated as one transaction for purposes of the Regulation D exemption?

To address this uncertainty, the SEC provides issuers with a safe harbor from integration under Rule 502(a). Imagine that an issuer sells securities through a series of Regulation D offerings. To understand the application of Rule 502(a), we need to begin by anchoring ourselves to one of the offerings (call this the *anchor offering*). We then ask whether the safe harbor protects that particular offering from integration with any of the other offerings. Rule 502(a) answers this question by specifying a safe harbor window that starts at the date six months prior to the start of the anchor offering and ends six months after the end of the anchor offering. Note that an offering may take weeks or months to complete. Thus, the safe harbor window may stretch longer than twelve months. If Rule 502(a) applies, offerings outside the safe harbor window are deemed not integrated into the anchor offering.

Rule 502(a) then specifies that the safe harbor protection against integration applies only if during either the six month period prior to the start of the anchor offering or the six month period after the end of the anchor offering the issuer does not offer or sell securities that "are of the same or similar class as those offered or sold under Regulation D." To see how this works, consider the following two hypotheticals:

1. Ionix sells common stock through offerings on January 1, March 1, and October 1. Let's treat the October 1 offering as the anchor offering; will either the January 1 or the March 1 offering be integrated into the October 1 offering?

Answer: Because the October 1 offering starts more than six months after the March 1 offering (with no other offerings), the Rule 502(a) safe harbor will apply to protect the October 1 offering from integration with both the January 1 and March 1 offerings.

2. Ionix sells common stock through offerings on January 1, May 1, and October 1. Let's continue to treat the October 1 offering as the anchor offering; will either the January 1 or the May 1 offering be integrated into the October 1 offering?

Answer: Because the October 1 offering starts less than six months after the May 1 offering and the two offerings are both for common stock, the Rule 502(a) safe harbor will not protect the October 1 offering from integration. Now the issuer must consider whether the integration factors will require integration with both the January 1 and May 1 offerings.

We note one last, somewhat technical, point on integration under Regulation D. Looking at the first integration example above, consider what happens if we make the March 1 offering the anchor offering. In this case, because of the presence of the January 1 offering, the March 1 offering does not enjoy the Rule 502(a) integration safe harbor. Therefore, in assessing whether the March 1 offering fits into one of the Regulation D offerings, we must take into account the possibility that the January 1 and the October 1 offerings may be integrated into the March 1 offering. But how can it be that the October 1 offering may be integrated into the March 1 offering but the March 1 offering would not be integrated into the October 1 offering (as we determined in the first example above)? The answer is that integration under Regulation D is one-sided.

For any given anchor offering, integration occurs *only* for purposes of determining whether the anchor offering satisfies a Regulation D exemption. If the combined offering fails to meet one of the Regulation D safe harbors then *only* the anchor offering securities fall out of Regulation D. To determine whether the other offering satisfies Regulation D, we must repeat our analysis, treating the other offering as the anchor offering.

So suppose we integrate the October 1 offering securities with the March 1 securities, with the March 1 offering as our anchor offering. We then determine that the combined offering fails to meet a Regulation D safe harbor. This conclusion would cause only the March 1 offering to drop out of the Regulation D safe harbor. To determine the fate of the October 1 offering, we must treat it as the anchor offering and repeat our analysis assessing (1) whether the Rule 502(a) safe harbor protects the October 1 securities offering from integration; and (2) if Rule 502(a) does not apply, determining whether other offerings integrate into the October 1 offering solely for the purpose of assessing whether the October 1 offering drops out of Regulation D. Because we need to repeat the analysis for each of the offerings, Rule 502(a) is sometimes referred to as a one-sided integration safe harbor.

2.7 Form D Notice

Rule 503 requires that issuers file a Form D notice with the SEC no later than fifteen days after the first sale of securities under Regulation D. Rule 507, in turn, provides that Regulation D is not available for issuers "subject to any order, judgment, or decree of any court of competent jurisdiction temporarily, preliminary or permanently enjoining such person for failure to comply with Rule 503."

2.8 Innocent and Insignificant Mistakes

Recall the purpose of Regulation D: to provide needed certainty for issuers seeking to sell securities through a private placement exempt from § 5. Despite the goal of providing certainty, two types of uncertainty remain under Regulation D. First, not all Regulation D requirements rely on bright-line rule assessments. For example, the requirement that nonaccredited purchasers in a Rule 506 offering are sophisticated either individually or together with a purchaser representative adds considerable uncertainty for issuers seeking to sell to nonaccredited purchasers. Issuers can avoid this uncertainty by structuring their offering to avoid the more uncertain portions of Regulation D, such as by selling securities only to accredited investors under Rule 506.

Second, issuers face uncertainty in implementing Regulation D requirements. The information that must be disclosed to nonaccredited purchasers under Rule 502(b) for Rule 505 and 506 offerings is well specified. Nonetheless, despite its best intentions, an issuer may fail to send the necessary information to each nonaccredited purchaser. The issuer's agents may fail to send a particular purchaser the required information or the information package may get lost in the mail. Similarly, an issuer may intend to sell only to accredited investors. But despite the issuer's good faith efforts, an error may occur and a nonaccredited investor may become classified as an accredited investor. More perniciously, nonaccredited investors may misrepresent themselves as accredited, leading the issuer to sell securities erroneously to these investors in a Regulation D offering.

Harsh consequences follow from failing to satisfy Regulation D. Because the entire offering is treated as a single transaction (see the discussion in the *Doran* case above), a failure to find some other exemption from § 5 will mean that all purchasers in an offering will be able to sue the issuer and those soliciting on behalf of the issuer under § 12(a)(1) for violating § 5. Suppose the issuer makes a mistake and forgets to send the required information package to a single nonaccredited investor. Without some protection, this minor failure could cause the offering to fall out of Regulation D, potentially resulting in a § 5 violation. Even accredited investors (who were not owed an information package at all) will then be able to sue for rescission under § 12(a)(1).

Rule 508 limits the negative consequences of certain failures by issuers to meet the Regulation D requirements. Rule 508 applies only to those situations where "failure to comply did not pertain to a term, condition or requirement directly intended to protect that particular individual or entity" (Rule 508(a)(1)). If an issuer forgets to send the required information package to a nonaccredited purchaser, that specific purchaser will still be able to sue for rescission under § 12(a)(1). Rule 508 blocks other investors, however, from bringing suit under § 12(a)(1) for this particular failure. Rule 508 does not afford forgiveness across the board. Rule 508 only limits private causes of action. The SEC may still bring an enforcement action against those who fail to meet the requirements of Regulation D. Nonetheless, given the harsh application of § 12(a)(1) private liability, Rule 508 provides welcome relief for issuers.

Rule 508 only applies to those situations where the failure to comply was "insignificant with respect to the offering as a whole" (Rule 508(a)(2)). The SEC defined certain types of failures to comply as automatically significant, thereby making Rule 508 unavailable. These failures are listed in Rule 508(a)(2) as follows:

1. the general solicitation prohibition (Rule 502(c));
2. the aggregate offering price ceiling (Rules 504(b)(2), 505(b)(2)(i));
3. the number of purchasers (Rules 505(b)(2)(ii) and 506(b)(2)(i)).

Rule 508 lastly requires that "[a] good faith and reasonable attempt was made to comply with all applicable terms, conditions, and requirements of Rule 504, 505 or 506" (Rule 508(a)(3)).

Although Rule 508 explicitly excludes the determination of the number of purchasers from the list of insignificant mistakes, issuers nonetheless may find forgiveness from another source. Several of the Regulation D requirements and terms include the qualifier that the issuer only "reasonably believes" that the requirement or term is met. The requirements that include a "reasonably believes" qualifier are as follows:

1. the accredited investor definition (Rule 501(a));
2. the nature of purchasers (Rule 506(b)(2)(ii));
3. the purchaser representative definition (Rule 501(h));
4. the resale limitation ("reasonable care"; Rule 502(d));
5. the number of purchasers (Rules 505(b)(2)(ii), 506(b)(2)(i)).

Both Rules 505(b)(2)(ii) and 506(b)(2)(i) require that the issuer reasonably believes that the number of purchasers is 35 or less. Rule 501(a) requires only that an issuer reasonably believes that investors arc accredited to justify giving the investors accredited investor status. Rule 506(b)(2)(ii) requires that the issuer reasonably believes that nonaccredited purchasers are sophisticated; likewise, Rule 501(h) requires only that the issuer reasonably believes that the purchaser representative meets all the requirements of Rule 501(h). These "reasonably believes" qualifiers forgive issuers for mistakes as long as the mistakes are objectively reasonable.

In three ways, the "reasonably believes" qualifiers built directly into the Regulation D requirements provide a broader excuse provision for the issuer than does Rule 508. First, the "reasonably believes" qualifier protects the issuer against liability from all purchasers in the offering. Rule 508, in contrast, does not provide an excuse with respect to those investors intended to be protected by the excused provision in question.

Second, Rule 508 does not protect against SEC enforcement. In comparison, if the issuer meets the "reasonably believes" qualifier, there is no Regulation D violation and thus no SEC enforcement action. Third, Rule 508 requires that the violation be insignificant and that it occurred in good faith after a reasonable attempt to comply. Arguably, the requirement of a "reasonable attempt" in Rule 508 encompasses more effort on the part of the issuer compared with merely having a "reasonable belief."

Despite the potential for forgiveness, two provisions in Regulation D lack the "reasonably believes" qualifiers: general solicitation and the aggregate offering price ceiling. Why is the SEC less forgiving here? One possible explanation is that the determination of the aggregate offering price ceiling is more within the issuer's control. Although one can imagine that the issuer may err in determining the number of purchasers or the accredited investor status of particular investors, especially if the issuer must rely on information supplied by investors, it is more difficult to imagine an innocent mistake in determining the aggregate offering price. A similar argument may be made for the prohibition against general solicitation. Solicitation activities are largely under the control of the issuer, making innocent mistakes less likely. Nonetheless, one can imagine a loose cannon agent of the issuer making a general solicitation without the knowledge or approval of the issuer. The SEC has taken a sympathetic stance toward the exposure of issuers to loose cannon agents, requiring only that the issuer structure selling efforts to avoid general solicitation. If so structured, "the fact that one potential investor with whom there is no such prior relationship is called may not necessarily result in a general solicitation."[12]

---

12. Securities Act Release No. 6825 (March 14, 1989).

2.9 Reform to Regulation D

As of the writing of this book, the SEC has proposed but not yet acted on a series of reforms for Regulation D. The SEC's first proposal would modify the accredited investor definition under Rule 501(a). The proposal adds alternative standards for individuals and entities to become accredited investors that focus on the amount of investments owned, rather than on income or net worth. For individuals, the SEC proposed that an individual owning $750,000 in investments would also be considered an accredited investor. Personal residences and places of business would not count toward this figure. The SEC further proposed to provide for inflation adjustments for the dollar thresholds provided for in Rule 501 starting in the year 2012.

The SEC proposals also included a new category of exempt transaction to join those found in Rules 504, 505, and 506. The proposed reform would create a new Rule 507 allowing private placement sales to a new class of "large accredited investors." The SEC proposed that the definition of large accredited investors would include the following:

> Legal entities that are considered accredited investors if their assets exceed $5 million would be required to have $10 million in investments to qualify as large accredited investors. Individuals generally would be required to own $2.5 million in investments or have annual income of $400,000 (or $600,000 with one's spouse) to qualify as large accredited investors, as compared to the current accredited investor standard of $1 million in net worth or annual income of $200,000 (or $300,000 with one's spouse).

Securities Act Release No. 8828 (August 3, 2007).

In many ways, proposed Rule 507 would function similarly to the current private placement exemption in Rule 506. Under proposed Rule 507, an issuer could sell an unlimited amount of securities to an unlimited number of large accredited investors (paralleling the Rule 506 provision for sales to accredited investors). Rule 507, however, will not allow issuers to sell to anyone who is not a large accredited investor, unlike the provision under Rule 506, which allows sales to up to 35 sophisticated, nonaccredited purchasers. As in Rule 506, offerings under Rule 507 would result in "restricted securities" subject to the limitations on resales under Rule 502(d). Issuers would be required to exercise reasonable care that the investors in a Rule 507 offering are not underwriters. Issuers would also be required to file a Form D notice under Rule 503.

Although the limits on general solicitation and advertising in Rule 502(c) would continue to apply, the proposed Rule 507 would nonetheless allow issuers to make a limited written advertising of the offering (including in newspapers and on the Internet, but not in a radio or television broadcast). The advertisement must state prominently that the offering is available only for large accredited investors and that the securities are not registered or approved by the SEC. The advertisement could also, at the issuer's discretion, include short, descriptive information on the issuer's identity (name and address) and its business, the securities being offered, any suitability standards and minimum investment requirements, and a contact person from whom additional information could be obtained.

3 OTHER EXEMPTIONS FROM SECTION 5

Regulation D and § 4(2) are not the only exemptions from § 5, but they are the most important economically, particularly the exemption under Rule 506. Brief discussions of a few other exemptions follow for readers interested in comparing them with the Regulation D and § 4(2) exemptions.

3.1 Regulation A

Small business issuers typically seek to raise only a limited amount of capital. For issuers raising small amounts of money, a registered offering may not make economic sense. The high fixed cost of an offering will not be justified for small amounts of capital. For such issuers, the Regulation D exemptions are an imperfect substitute. Securities sold through Rules 505 and 506 are, among other things, restricted from subsequent resales. Issuers must also comply with stringent restrictions on their solicitation of investors. Although Rule 504 offerings are exempt from these restrictions if they qualify under a particular state law regime, issuers may raise no more than $1 million.

In response to the needs of small business issuers, the SEC responded with Regulation A of the Securities Act. Regulation A provides a § 3(b) exemption from § 5. In keeping with the focus on small business issuers, only U.S. domestic and Canadian, non–Exchange Act reporting issuers may utilize Regulation A. Other issuers are excluded from Regulation A, including development stage issuers with no specific business plan or purpose. Regulation A further disqualifies certain so-called bad actor issuers from the use of its exemption under Rule 262.

Regulation A allows issuers to offer and sell securities in a mini-public offering. One benefit of public offering status is that securities sold through Regulation A can be freely resold. Regulation A limits an issuer to an aggregate offering price of $5 million, reduced by the amount of securities sold in reliance on Regulation A in the prior twelve months. Selling security holders may also take advantage of Regulation A, but they are limited to an aggregate offering price of $1.5 million. (This must be subtracted from the overall $5 million aggregate offering price ceiling.)

The Regulation A offering process tracks that of a registered public offering. Instead of a registration statement, the

Regulation A offering process requires an offering statement. A subset of the information in the offering statement, termed the offering circular (similar to the statutory prospectus), is distributed to investors. Two key events occur in the offering process: (1) the filing of the offering statement with the SEC; and (2) the SEC's determination that the offering statement is *qualified* (similar to effectiveness for a registration statement). Sales may commence only after an offering statement has been qualified.

Despite these similarities with a registered public offering, Regulation A mini-public offerings differ from registered offerings in a number of respects. First, the disclosure requirements of the offering statement and offering circular are less demanding. Form 1-A specifies the information in the offering statement. Although Form 1-A requires nonfinancial disclosure similar to that in the registration statement, it requires less financial disclosure. Form 1-A requires that issuers file a current balance sheet dated within 90 days prior to the filing of the offering statement. The issuer must also file an income statement and statement of cash flows and other stockholder equity "for each of the 2 fiscal years preceding the date of the most recent balance sheet being filed, and for any interim period between the end of the most recent of such fiscal years and the date of the most recent balance sheet being filed, or for the period of the issuer's existence if less than the period above." Issuers must prepare financial statements according to U.S. GAAP accounting rules; Form 1-A does not require, however, that the issuer have the financial statements audited.

Second, in the period prior to the filing of the offering statement (comparable to the pre-filing period in a registered public offering), Regulation A gives issuers greater leeway to solicit feedback from investors. Rule 254 allows issuers to provide prospective investors with "a written document or make scripted radio or television broadcasts to determine whether there is any interest in a contemplated securities offering." Issuers must submit the documents or broadcast script to the SEC pursuant to Rule 254(b), after which the issuer may begin oral communications and other broadcasts prior to filing the offering statement, even if such communications might condition the market (see Rule 254(a)). As we saw in Chapter 7, non-WKSI issuers cannot mention the offering before filing the registration statement. Under Regulation A, small business issuers can "test the waters," gauging investors' reaction. The ability to gauge interest in an offering allows small business issuers to terminate the offering quickly if demand is inadequate.

Many of the 2005 Public Offering Reforms that loosened the requirements in a registered public offering do not apply to Regulation A mini-public offerings. Issuers must send purchasers a preliminary or final offering circular 48 hours before the mailing of the confirmation of sales (Rule 251(d)(2)(i)(B)). The final offering circular must be delivered with the confirmation of sales, if not delivered sooner (Rule 251(d)(2)(i)(C)).

Regulation A affords considerable flexibility to small business issuers, but the restriction on the aggregate offering price of $5 million limits its usefulness. Back in the mid-1990s, some issuers started to use Regulation A to sell securities to investors over the Internet. Most notably, Spring Street Brewing Company raised $1.6 million through an online offering using Regulation A without the assistance of underwriters or the payment of brokerage commissions. With the collapse of Internet stocks in the early 2000s, the market for Regulation A offerings also largely dried up.

3.2 Regulation S

Issuers that offer and sell securities outside the United States may use the exemption in Regulation S. Regulation S exempts transactions that occur "outside the United States." Much of the complexity in the operation of Regulation S arises from its effort to distinguish offers and sales made outside the United States from those made within the country. For example, suppose an issuer places an advertisement in the *Wall Street Journal* for an offering to take place in France. Despite the locus of the transaction in France, the directed advertisement into the United States through the *Wall Street Journal* ad will disqualify the transaction from the Regulation S exemption from § 5.

The other difficult issue with Regulation S lies with resales back into the United States (termed *flowback*). Suppose an issuer sells securities to investors in France but the investors turn around and resell the securities the next day back into the United States. If flowback is not checked, any issuer could use Regulation S and a foreign intermediary investor to make a backdoor public offering in the United States. Regulation S therefore prohibits resales of securities back into the United States; securities sold pursuant to Regulation S are deemed restricted securities pursuant to Rule 144. As with other Rule 144 restricted securities, resales into the United States must await the passage of the Rule 144 holding period (see the discussion in Chapter 10).

Regulation S also imposes certain offering and transactional restrictions. These restrictions vary based on the type of issuer (U.S. or foreign), the type of security (debt or equity), and whether the issuer is an Exchange Act reporting issuer. The SEC deems U.S. issuers selling equity securities abroad as posing the greatest risk of flowback and imposes the most stringent offering and transactional restrictions on such offerings. Among the offering restrictions, distributors of the Regulation S securities must agree in writing that offers and sales during a defined "distribution compliance period" occur only through transactions exempt under Regulation S, some other exemptive provision, or through a registered offering under § 5. Among the transactional restrictions, the issuer must include a legend on each security indicating its

Regulation S restricted status. Each purchaser must certify that they are not a U.S. person and that they are not acquiring for the account of a U.S. person.

3.3 Intrastate Offerings

Issuers offering and selling securities solely within a single state may use the exemption in § 3(a)(11) for intrastate offerings. Section 3(a)(11) exempts from § 5 "[a]ny security which is a part of an issue offered and sold only to persons resident within a single State or Territory, where the issuer of such security is a person resident and doing business within or, if a corporation, incorporated by and doing business within, such State or Territory." To provide clarity in the application of § 3(a)(11), particularly with respect to what it means to be "doing business" in a single state, the SEC promulgated Rule 147.

Why exempt single-state offerings? Offerings that take place within a single state pose less danger to investor confidence in the national marketplace. Single-state offerings are also typically smaller than national ones, which may make the high fixed cost of the registered public offering process under the federal securities law prohibitive. In addition, state securities regulators may provide a degree of regulatory protection for investors. Finally, if offerings take place in a single state, investors may know more about the operation and business of the issuer.

3.4 Exempt Securities

The securities laws also exempt certain types of securities from the operation of § 5 and other aspects of the securities regime. As provided in § 3(a) of the Securities Act and §§ 3(a)(10) and (12) of the Exchange Act, exempt securities include government and municipal bonds and commercial paper (notes with a maturity of less than nine months typically used to finance working capital, accounts receivables, and other short-term liabilities of a corporation). Government and municipal bonds typically pose a lower risk of default, thus making the protection of the securities laws less essential. Similarly, the short-term maturity of commercial paper makes such investments low risk for investors.

～ 10 ～

Resale Transactions

Holo, Inc., a designer of 3-D graphic images for display over the Internet, is a non-Exchange Act reporting company. Holo recently sold $10 million of its common stock through a private placement under Rule 506 of Regulation D to 100 accredited investors. Una, one of the accredited investors, now owns $200,000 of Holo common stock. Now, six months after the offering, Una would like to diversify her portfolio and sell her Holo shares to some of her college friends who are interested in getting in at the ground floor on a pre-IPO Internet company.

Investors have many reasons for wanting to resell securities. Some reasons arise from the investor's personal situation. An investor may need cash to pay off debts or to pay tuition or unexpected medical bills. Alternatively, an investor may want to rebalance her portfolio, shifting money from one investment to others. The investment itself may offer reasons to resell securities. Investors may realize, after some painful reverses, that a particular investment does not suit their risk preferences, leading them to sell it to cut their losses. At the other extreme, a company may have performed extremely well, causing investors to want to sell to lock in investment profits.

Investors value the ability to resell securities and will discount the securities of companies that restrict resales. Companies may restrict resales directly in their corporate charters. They may, for example, attempt to control the shareholder base by requiring that shareholders only resell their shares back to the company itself (or offer a right of first refusal).

If resale is valuable, why do the federal securities laws restrict it? Consider the various requirements of the Regulation D exemptions we discussed in Chapter 9, including the limits on the number of purchasers, information requirements, and prohibition on general solicitation among others. Without a restriction on resale, an issuer could construct a sham public offering. The issuer could first sell to a single accredited investor who would then turn around and resell to the general public, thus undermining the Regulation D restrictions. Are there other reasons to block resales?

The federal securities laws restrict resales through the operation of § 5 of the Securities Act. Recall that § 5, as we discussed in Chapter 7, provides the regulatory requirements for the public offering process, including mandatory disclosure documents (the registration statement and statutory prospectus) and the gun-jumping rules. The § 5 regime is backed up by the enhanced civil liability provisions of §§ 11 and 12. Despite our focus on § 5 in the context of registered public offerings, the scope of § 5 is far broader. Its requirements apply whenever any person uses an instrumentality of interstate commerce in the offer or sale of a security.

The broad scope of § 5 means that even an ordinary secondary market transaction between two outside investors, whether a public corporation, such as Microsoft, or relatively closely-held one, such as Holo, must meet the requirements of § 5. Few outside investors, however, can sell their shares through the public offering process of § 5. If you were an outside shareholder of Microsoft with 100 shares to sell, how would you get Microsoft to file a registration statement for those shares?

Key to understanding resales is the § 5 starting point. Absent an exemption, § 5 effectively blocks most investors from all resales unless they comply with the public offering requirements. From this starting point, our analysis under the securities laws focuses on one question: Does any § 5 exemption permit resales?

In this chapter, we discuss the various § 5 exemptions allowing resales under the Securities Act. We start with a discussion of the underlying statutory exemptions provided by the Securities Act and the case law interpreting those exemptions. We then discuss two important SEC rule-based safe harbors for resale: Rule 144 and Rule 144A.

1 SECTION 4(1) AND UNDERWRITERS

Section 4(1) of the Securities Act exempts "transactions by any person other than an issuer, underwriter, or dealer" from § 5. Consider a typical secondary market transaction involving Microsoft shares. Sarah wants to sell 1,000 shares of Microsoft. She places a market order with her broker to sell the shares at the best available price. Her broker may match the sell order with another customer's corresponding buy order for Microsoft shares or may sell the shares to a market maker specializing in Microsoft shares. In either case, the transaction involves no issuer or underwriter.

One difficulty exists for the application of § 4(1), however. Section 2(a)(12) of the Securities Act defines *dealer* to include not only those engaged in the business of buying and selling securities (traditional dealers) but also those assisting others in securities transactions for a commission (traditional brokers). Courts, nonetheless, routinely ignore this difficulty. Despite the presence of a traditional broker in most secondary market transactions, the mere presence of a broker will not disqualify the outside investors from using § 4(1).[1] Following the same

---

1. See e.g., *Ackerberg v. Johnson, Jr.*, 892 F.2d 1328 (8th Cir. 1989). ("Were [the brokers] involvement enough to deny the § 4(1) exemption to persons not issuers, underwriters or dealers, few secondary transactions involving the resale of restricted securities would be exempt under § 4(1).")

logic, for purposes of applying § 4(1) to exempt an ordinary secondary market transaction, courts would presumably also ignore the presence of a market maker acting to buy and sell securities for its own account and thereby providing liquidity to the marketplace.

The Second Circuit in *S.E.C. v. Chinese Consolidated Benevolent Ass'n, Inc.*[2] made it clear that § 4(1) is a *transaction* exemption. In the case, the Second Circuit wrote:

> Even if the defendant is not itself "an issuer, underwriter, or dealer" it was participating in a transaction with an issuer. . . . The argument on behalf of the defendant incorrectly assumes that Section 4(1) applies to the component parts of the entire transaction we have mentioned and thus exempts defendant unless it is an underwriter. . . . Section 5(a)(1), however, broadly prohibits sales of securities irrespective of the character of the person making them. The exemption is limited to "transactions" by persons other than "issuers, underwriters or dealers." It does not in terms or by fair implication protect those who are engaged in steps necessary to the distribution of security issues.

What is the significance of treating § 4(1) as a transaction exemption? If any participant in an offering is classified as an issuer, underwriter, or dealer, no participant can rely on § 4(1).

In the absence of an issuer or dealer (other than a broker acting on commission or a dealer acting as a market maker), as is the case for most resale transactions, the key issue for the application of § 4(1) is whether the transaction involves an underwriter. The definition of underwriter is broad. Section 2(a)(11) defines underwriter to include any person who

1. purchases from an issuer with a view to, or offers or sells for an issuer in connection with, the distribution of any security;

---

2. 120 F.2d 738 (1941).

2. participates or has a direct or indirect participation in any such undertaking; or
3. participates or has a participation in the direct or indirect underwriting of any such undertaking.

Most secondary market transactions are exempt under § 4(1) from the requirements of § 5. Such a secondary market transaction may take the following form:

Investor   ⟶   Investor
X   Y

But what if an issuer sold the securities to Investor X initially? Then we would have the following:

Issuer ⟶ Investor ⟶ Investor
          X   Y

As discussed above, any broker or market maker assisting X in its resale to Y will not be deemed an underwriter if the resale takes place in an ordinary secondary market transaction. However, another underwriter may be present: Investor X may act as an underwriter for the issuer when it purchases and then resells the securities. If X is an underwriter for the issuer, X is, in reality, acting as a conduit for the issuer's sale to Investor Y. Once X is viewed as an underwriter, X's resale to Y no longer comes within the § 4(1) exemption. X's resale must, absent some other exemption, comply with the registration requirements of § 5.

Who counts as an underwriter? As you might expect, the purchase from an issuer of an allocation of shares by Wall Street investment banks for resale in a firm commitment public offering counts. The scope of § 2(a)(11), however, extends beyond traditional Wall Street underwriters to encompass a variety of entities and even individuals.

Gilligan, Will & Co. v. SEC[3] demonstrates the breadth of the underwriter definition. Crowell-Collier Publishing Company (Crowell) sold $100,000 of convertible debentures to Gilligan without registering them with the SEC. Gilligan represented to Crowell that it was purchasing "for investment" and had "no present intention of distributing" the securities. Despite these representations, less than a year after purchasing the Crowell securities, Gilligan noticed that Crowell's magazine advertising was not increasing. Concerned, Gilligan converted the debentures into common stock and sold the stock on the American Stock Exchange. The court held that Gilligan was an underwriter under § 2(a)(11) and therefore could not rely on the § 4(1) exemption.

The *Gilligan* court equated the concept of *distribution*, in the § 2(a)(11) definition of an underwriter, with *public offering*. Citing the *Ralston Purina* decision for what constitutes a public offering, the court noted that the investors who purchased from Gilligan did not have access to information similar to that in a registration statement. Accordingly, the court held that Gilligan, with the resale of the Crowell common stock, engaged in a distribution.

The court also concluded that Gilligan purchased with a "view to" this distribution, thus fitting within the "view to" language in the § 2(a)(11) definition of underwriter. Although Gilligan's conversion and sale of stock occurred more than ten months after his purchase from the issuer Crowell, the court held that Gilligan's holding period was not long enough to demonstrate that he had originally purchased with investment intent. The court rejected the notion that a change in the

---

3. 267 F.2d 461 (2d Cir. 1959).

issuer's circumstances (such as Gilligan's observation that Crowell's advertising revenues were not growing) could be relied upon to prove original investment intent.

1.1 The Consequences of Underwriter Status

What is the consequence of determining that an initial purchaser in a private placement is acting as an underwriter when she resells the securities? Consider the following chain of transactions:

> Holo, Inc., sells 100,000 shares of common stock to Una, an accredited investor, pursuant to Rule 506 of the Securities Act. One month later, Una, who needs money to buy some birthday presents, decides to sell the 100,000 shares to her friend Lauren, a non-accredited investor.

If Una is an underwriter, she acts as a conduit for the ultimate purchaser, Lauren. The presence of an underwriter renders the § 4(1) exemption unavailable for the transaction. Una's resale, absent another exemption, must satisfy the requirements of § 5.

What is the consequence of Una's resale for Holo, the issuer? When an underwriter buys and then resells securities, we look at the purchaser from the underwriter (*the ultimate purchaser*) to assess the issuer's offering exemption from § 5. Even if Lauren is the ultimate purchaser, it is possible that the transaction may still qualify under the issuer's original offering exemption. If Lauren can step into Una's shoes for purposes of the Rule 506 exemption, the issuer's offering exemption remains valid. Moreover, Una would not violate § 5: The entire transaction from Holo through Una and ultimately to Lauren would fall under Rule 506.

In this specific fact pattern, can Lauren step into Una's shoes? To reach this conclusion, a number of obstacles must be overcome. Without a preexisting relationship between

Lauren and Holo or Holo's placement agent, Holo will have made a general solicitation (prohibited under Rule 502(c)). In addition, Lauren may not have received the information package required to be sent to non-accredited investors under Rule 502(b). Lauren's presence as a purchaser may mean that Holo has exceeded the 35 purchaser limitation. Even if the numerical limit is not exceeded, Lauren may not qualify as sophisticated.

Lauren's unexpected presence may therefore cause Holo to lose its Rule 506 offering exemption and, except for those instances forgiven under Rule 508, expose Holo to § 12(a)(1) rescission liability. One final twist though. Recall from *Pinter*, discussed in Chapter 8, that § 12(a)(1) allows only purchasers in direct privity with a seller to sue. Lauren is in privity only with Una and thus may use § 12(a)(1) only to sue Una. If a § 5 violation occurred in Una's resale to Lauren, Holo faces a § 12(a)(1) claim from Una, but not from Lauren. Of more substantial concern to Holo is that all other direct purchasers in Holo's failed Rule 506 offering will also have § 12(a)(1) claims.

1.2 Change in Circumstances

The *Gilligan* court rejected changes in the issuer's circumstances as evidence of investment intent. Rather than looking at a change in the issuer's circumstances, courts have instead focused on a change in the investor's personal circumstances. For example, if an investor suddenly needs money to pay for an unexpected operation, the sale of securities to raise this money will be deemed to occur out of a changed circumstance. Courts generally have rejected changes in circumstances that are foreseeable. Thus, if an investor sells securities because she has recently retired, this will not be deemed a change in circumstance.

The passage of time alone may distinguish those that purchase with a view to reselling securities and those with true investment intent. Courts have developed rules of thumb to assess how much of a holding period is required to impute investment intent. Typically, after two years courts will apply a rebuttable presumption that the investor had investment intent when initially purchasing securities. After three years the presumption becomes irrebuttable. The two/three-year presumptive rule of thumb allows initial purchasers from a private placement to avoid underwriter status and therefore to take advantage of the § 4(1) exemption from § 5.

The logic behind this holding period presumption is that those who purchase only to act as conduits for an issuer typically will not want to bear any investment risk; if they do, they will demand a large premium from the issuer. Requiring that initial purchasers wait a certain amount of time before reselling helps distinguish conduit purchasers from those who purchase with investment intent. But how much time? If you agreed to act as a conduit for an issuer, how long would you be willing to bear the risk that the issuer's securities may fall in value? Would you really choose to hold onto a significant and undiversified pool of the issuer's securities for ten months? Six months? Even three months?

The passage of time is relevant to investment intent for another reason: information advantages. Investors purchasing directly from an issuer in a private placement often obtain material nonpublic information from the issuer. Although Regulation FD prohibits selective disclosure of information during private placements (absent a confidentiality agreement), Regulation FD only applies to Exchange Act reporting issuers. Private issuers, without any Exchange Act reporting requirements, are allowed to make selective disclosures. Moreover, it is these private issuers for which publicly available information is lacking. Consequently, investors in private placements by non-reporting issuers may obtain a considerable information advantage over other outside investors. One consequence of the focus on investment intent and the two/three-year presumptive rules of thumb is that any informational advantage an initial purchaser may enjoy over other secondary market investors is likely to have dissipated during that time.

Does it make sense to allow resales from one uninformed investor to another? Uninformed sellers should enjoy no systematic advantage over uninformed buyers, but not all investors will stay uninformed. Some investors may expend considerable resources researching securities in the absence of publicly available information. This may result, as we discussed in Chapter 2, in duplicative and wasteful research expenditures. Moreover, an information vacuum may encourage some investors to lie, misrepresenting what they know about the issuer. Such fraud is more common in a trading environment lacking information because information to counter the lie is not available.

A final note on the change in circumstances test for underwriter status: The SEC rejects the test. The SEC wrote in its preliminary notes to the Rule 144 safe harbor for resales, "Experience has shown . . . that reliance upon such factors . . . has led to uncertainty in the application of the registration provisions of the Act." Courts could ignore the SEC's position and apply the change in circumstances test developed in the case law, but it is questionable whether today — given the presence of Rule 144 — they would do so.

1.3 Distribution

The *Gilligan* court indicated that a person must not only purchase securities from an issuer with a "view to" but also intend a "distribution" of the securities for underwriter status to attach. *Gilligan* defines the word *distribution* in § 2(a)(11) by reference to the concept of *public offering* embodied in the § 4(2) exemption from § 5 (discussed in Chapter 9). Under this view, an initial purchaser reselling, even immediately, to investors who can "fend for themselves" under *Ralston Purina* would not be an underwriter. Without an issuer, underwriter, or dealer in the transaction, § 4(1) would exempt the initial purchaser's resale from § 5.

The use of the § 4(2) private offering factors to define underwriter for purposes § 2(a)(11) and § 4(1) has most often occurred in the context of control person resales. These sales are often termed § 4(1½) transactions, as discussed below. In theory, the resale exemption applies even for non-control person resales, sometimes referred to as a secondary private placement.

A difficulty exists with secondary private placements. Consider the following chain of transactions:

> Holo, Inc. sells 100,000 shares of common stock to Una in a § 4(2) private placement. Assume that Una is sophisticated and can fend for herself per *Ralston Purina*. Una turns around the next day and resells the 100,000 shares to Timothy and Ella. Both Timothy and Ella are sophisticated and can fend for themselves. Assume that Una gave Timothy and Ella the same information package she obtained from Holo the day before.

In this chain of transactions, Holo could have sold directly to Timothy and Ella under § 4(2). Una is removed from the definition of an underwriter because her sales are not a distribution, because Timothy and Ella can fend for themselves. Treating Una as a non-underwriter does not allow Holo to sell indirectly (through Una) to investors that Holo could not sell to directly in the first place.

Consider this alternate transaction:

> Holo, Inc. sells 100,000 shares of common stock to Una in a Rule 506 private placement. Assume that Una is accredited

and has a preexisting relationship with Holo. Una turns around the next day and resells the 100,000 shares to Katrina and Kevin. Although both Katrina and Kevin are sophisticated and can fend for themselves, neither has a preexisting relationship with Holo.

Note that Holo could not sell directly to Katrina or Kevin under Rule 506 due to the lack of a preexisting relationship. Offers to them would be a general solicitation prohibited under Rule 502(c). Nonetheless, Una's sales to Katrina and Kevin would not count as a distribution under *Gilligan*. Thus Una is not an underwriter and the sale from Una to Katrina and Kevin is a separate transaction from Holo's sale to Una. Because Una's resale is a separate transaction, Una can use the § 4(1) exemption from § 5. Holo now has accomplished indirectly, through Una, what it could not do directly under 506: It sold securities to Katrina and Kevin. Presumably even if Una purchased with a "view to" reselling to Katrina and Kevin, because the resales were not a distribution, she is not an underwriter. Perhaps one could argue that although in technical compliance with the securities laws, this chain of transactions should be collapsed (for example, it's a sham), thereby eliminating the Rule 506 exemption. But remember that the § 4(2) exemption might still be available for the issuer.

2 CONTROL PERSON RESALES

There are several types of control relationships. The most obvious occurs when one company controls another company, for example through stock ownership, as with a parent corporation and its subsidiary. In this situation, both the parent and subsidiary corporation are considered to be control persons or affiliates. Control may also arise out of situations of common control. A parent corporation may control two subsidiaries. Each subsidiary would then be considered a control person or affiliate of the other subsidiary (and of the parent corporation). Whether controlling or controlled, entities in such a control relationship often have access to nonpublic material information that gives them an advantage over outside investors. Moreover, this advantage, unlike the information accorded an outside purchaser in a private placement, is enduring.

If a control person is present in a resale, two things should be remembered. First, the control person is generally *not* considered an issuer. Absent an underwriter or dealer in the transaction, the control person may rely on the § 4(1) exemption from § 5 in reselling securities. Second, those offering and selling for the control person in the resale may be considered underwriters for the control person. Although the control person is not generally treated as an issuer, the control person is deemed an issuer for the purposes of the definition of an underwriter under § 2(a)(11). If the control person has an underwriter, the control person cannot rely on the § 4(1) transaction exemption.

The following diagram depicts a typical control person resale transaction:

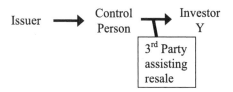

Whenever faced with a control person resale transaction, we must answer two questions to determine whether § 4(1) exempts the resale from § 5: (1) Is the control person an underwriter for the issuer? (2) Is there a third-party acting as an underwriter by facilitating the control person's resales? For the first inquiry, the investor's status as a control person is irrelevant. Instead, what matters is the control person's own holding period and intention in purchasing the securities from the issuer, just as with any other initial purchaser from the issuer. For the second inquiry, two possible underwriters exist for the control person. First, a third-party may assist the control person in the resale, for example, a broker soliciting offers to buy. Second, any investors purchasing from the control person (such as Investor Y) may be deemed underwriters if they resell with a "view to" the "distribution" of the securities.

In applying this two-part inquiry, courts have used the so-called § 4(1½) exemption to allow control person resales. Of course, there is no § 4(1½) in the Securities Act. Where does this exemption come from?

The Eighth Circuit in *Ackerberg v. Johnson, Jr.*[4] dealt with the issue of control person resales and the application of the § 4(1½) exemption. Johnson, the chairman of Vertimag Systems Corporation and its controlling shareholder, sold unregistered shares of Vertimag to Ackerberg, a sophisticated investor, with the assistance of the brokerage firm Piper, Jaffray & Hopwood (PJH). In the subscription agreement for the sale, Ackerberg represented that he was an accredited investor with liquid assets of over $500,000. Ackerberg was given "full and complete" information regarding Vertimag; he also affirmed that the sale was unregistered and that the shares were not freely transferable. The Eighth Circuit addressed whether § 4(1) exempted Johnson's sale of securities to Ackerberg.

In assessing whether an underwriter was present in the transaction, the *Ackerberg* court undertook two inquiries. First, the court assessed whether Johnson was acting as an underwriter for the issuer, Vertimag. Johnson had purchased his shares from Vertimag at least four years earlier. The court applied the two/three-year rule of thumb, holding that Johnson was not an underwriter for Vertimag.

---

4. 892 F.2d 1328 (8th Cir. 1989).

The court's second inquiry was necessitated by the presence of PJH. Because Johnson is a control person of Vertimag, any person who offers or sells securities on behalf of Johnson may be an underwriter, including PJH. *U.S. v. Wolfson* teaches that if an underwriter is present, even if the underwriter is for a control person and not the issuer, § 4(1) is no longer available.[5] In making its second inquiry, the court applied the so-called § 4(1½) exemption from § 5. As the court noted, there is no § 4(1½) exemption; the term refers, rather, to an interpretation of § 4(1) using § 4(2) doctrine as reflected in *Ralston Purina* and other cases. Given the importance of controlling public sales of securities, the court equated *distribution,* in the definition of underwriters under § 2(a)(11), with *public offering*, as reflected in § 4(2). The court found Ackerberg was able to fend for himself. Consequently, the court held that PJH, in assisting Johnson in the sale to Ackerberg, was not an underwriter. Without an underwriter — whether Johnson for the issuer or PJH for Johnson — Johnson's resale to Ackerberg was exempt from § 5 under § 4(1).

If parties who assist a control person in reselling securities are underwriters, the limitation on resales for control persons persists indefinitely. Moreover, the limitation applies regardless of whether a control person is reselling restricted or nonrestricted securities. A control person of Microsoft may purchase unrestricted shares of Microsoft on the Nasdaq. Because § 5 applies to any person and any transaction, the control person cannot freely resell the Microsoft shares, even though the shares were sold initially in a registered public offering.

Why limit a control person's resales this way? Control persons may enjoy an enduring informational advantage relative to outside investors. Even with the passage of time, Donna, the CEO and founder of Holo, will continue to know more about

---

5. 405 F.2d 779 (2d Cir. 1968).

Holo's prospects than would the ordinary outside investor. Resale restrictions channel Donna toward selling securities in a registered offering. Registration will reduce Donna's information advantage over outside investors.

Channeling control persons toward registration does not impose an unreasonable burden. Control persons are, by definition, in a position of control and thus presumably have the power to force a corporation to register the control persons' shares for sale. Thus, requiring registration is not overly onerous for the control person. This rationale, however, can be questioned. The definition of control is somewhat ambiguous. What if those considered to be in control, such as a director of a corporation, do not individually have the power to force registration? Even for those with the power to force registration, the public offering process is costly and time consuming. Such costs, even for a control person, may limit the ability to resell shares, thereby reducing the incentive of control persons to hold large blocks of shares.

If we believe that control person resales should be limited, why should this limitation turn on having a third party assist the control person in the sale? The control person is not an issuer for purposes of § 4(1), only for the § 2(a)(11) definition of underwriter. Thus, if no underwriter or dealer participates in the transaction, the control person may rely on § 4(1). If Donna were to sell Holo securities directly in a negotiated transaction with another investor without the assistance of a third party, the sale would be exempt under § 4(1). Perhaps the presence of a third party, assisting in the sale, acts as a rough proxy for a particular type of transaction. Brokers are needed to assist in the sale if the control person wishes to sell to a large number of investors. In contrast, brokers are less necessary if the control person seeks to sell to a small number of buyers that he or she already knows. Who are such buyers? Typically other insiders or large block shareholders of the corporation who do not need the protections of the § 5 registration process.

3 RULE 144

To address the uncertainties facing private placement investors and control persons seeking to resell their shares, the SEC promulgated Securities Act Rule 144. Along with reducing uncertainty, the SEC also sought to reconcile the regulation of resales with the need for investor protection. In adopting Rule 144, the SEC emphasized three important factors: (1) the presence of "adequate current public information" about the issuer; (2) the presence of a holding period to ensure that the investor is not acting as a conduit for the public sale of unregistered securities; and (3) the impact of the resale transaction on the trading markets. (A large volume of resales could disrupt the trading markets.)

Two definitional provisions are important in understanding Rule 144. First, an *affiliate* of an issuer is defined as "a person that directly, or indirectly through one or more intermediaries, controls, or is controlled by, or is under common control with, such issuer" (Rule 144(a)(1)). *Affiliate* corresponds with the control person concept discussed above. Second, a *restricted security* is defined to include, among others, securities subject to the resale limitations of Rule 502(d) of Regulation D (for example, securities sold pursuant to a Rule 505 or 506 offering). Restricted securities also include securities "acquired directly or indirectly from the issuer, or from an affiliate of the issuer, in a transaction or chain of transactions not involving any public offering" (Rule 144(a)(3)).

Rule 144(b) provides the operative exemption from § 5 for the resale safe harbor. Two distinct types of resale transactions are covered in Rule 144(b): (1) non-affiliate resales of restricted securities[6] and (2) affiliate resales of restricted and unrestricted securities (including those selling on behalf of affiliates). If applicable, Rule 144 provides an exemption from underwriter

---

6. Non-affiliates may not have been affiliates during the preceding three months prior to the resale.

status (as defined under § 2(a)(11)). If there is no underwriter, assuming no issuer or dealer is present in the transaction, the reselling investor may then rely on § 4(1). Rule 144 provides an exemption only from § 5; antifraud provisions continue to apply.

Why are unrestricted securities included for affiliate-related resales? Recall that § 2(a)(11) may treat any third party assisting an affiliate in a resale as an underwriter, thereby destroying the § 4(1) exemption. Rule 144 allows affiliates and those selling on their behalf to rely on § 4(1) to resell both restricted and unrestricted securities.

Rule 144 sets forth two basic requirements to qualify for its exemption from § 5: current public information (144(c)) and a minimum holding period for restricted securities (144(d)). Rule 144 is not an exclusive rule for those seeking to resell securities. Investors are always free to argue that under § 4(1) and the case law we discussed earlier in this chapter that a change in circumstance has taken place or the investor otherwise has investment intent. The SEC has also provided an alternate safe harbor rule for resales under Rule 144A, discussed at the end of this chapter.

3.1 Information Requirement

To understand the information requirement, we first discuss when the requirement applies (Rule 144(b)) and second what is encompassed under the requirement (as provided in Rule 144(c)). The applicability of the information requirement turns on the type of issuer, the type of security, and the holding period for the securities. Non-affiliates selling restricted securities of non-Exchange Act reporting issuers do not have an explicit information requirement (Rule 144(b)(1)(ii)). On the other hand, affiliates (or those selling on behalf of affiliates) reselling either restricted or unrestricted securities always face the information requirement (Rule 144(b)(2), (3)). The story is more complicated for non-affiliates selling restricted securities of reporting issuers, who face the information requirements up until a one-year holding period. Once one year has passed from the later of the purchase from the issuer or from an affiliate, the information requirement no longer applies (Rule 144(b)(1)(i)).

The information requirement is found in Rule 144(c). Rule 144(c) specifies that adequate current public information must be available for the issuer of the securities resold under Rule 144. For Exchange Act reporting issuers, information is deemed publicly available if two conditions are met: (1) The issuer met the qualifications of an Exchange Act reporting company for at least 90 days immediately preceding the sale of the securities; and (2) for the past 12 months, the issuer has filed all required Exchange Act periodic disclosure filings (that is, Form 10-K and 10-Q filings).

For non-reporting issuers, Rule 144(c) specifies that certain information provided in Rule 15c2-11 is publicly available. Rule 15c2-11 lists the information that broker-dealers must keep reasonably current on non-Exchange Act reporting companies if the broker-dealers "publish[es] any quotation for a security or . . . submit[s] any such quotation for publication, in any quotation medium." A broker-dealer must make the Rule 15c2-11 information reasonably available upon request to any person expressing interest in the securities. The Rule 15c2-11 information items include, among others, the name of the issuer, the state of incorporation, the nature of the issuer's business and products or services offered, the name of the chief executive officer and members of the board of directors, and summary financial statements. See Rule 15c2-11(a)(5)(i) to (xiv).

3.2 Holding Period

Rule 144(d) imposes a holding period on restricted securities. The length of the holding period turns on the type of issuer. For securities of Exchange Act reporting issuers, Rule 144(d) imposes a six-month holding period from "the later of the date of the acquisition of the securities from the issuer or from an affiliate of the issuer." For securities of non-reporting issuers, Rule 144(d) requires a one-year holding period. Acquisition may take place through purchase or other means, such as acquiring the securities as a gift. Rule 144(d) does not focus on when a specific investor acquired the securities but instead when the securities were acquired from the issuer or an affiliate. Why? Consider the following chain of transactions:

> A reporting issuer sells restricted securities (in a private placement) to Alice on January 1. On April 1, Alice sells the securities (through a non-Rule 144 exemption from § 5) to Baker. On August 1, Baker sells the securities to Charles, hoping to rely on Rule 144.

What is the holding period for Charles? Because Rule 144(d) focuses on when the securities were originally purchased from the issuer (or affiliate), Charles has a holding period of seven months on the date he purchases. Put another way, Charles is allowed to tack onto his own holding period the holding periods of Alice and Baker. As a result, Charles meets the Rule 144(d) holding period requirement.

Let's focus a bit more on the case of affiliates. Consider the following chain of transactions:

> A reporting issuer sells restricted securities (in a private placement) to Alfred, an affiliate, on January 1. On April 1, Alfred sells the securities (through a non-Rule 144 exemption from § 5) to Betty. On August 1, Betty sells the securities to Clarise, hoping to make use of Rule 144.

Betty's holding period is only four months because her purchase from an affiliate occurs on April 1. Why do we measure the holding period from the later of the acquisition date from the issuer or an affiliate? The purpose of the holding period requirement is to discourage purchasing investors from acting as mere conduits for a sham public offering by an issuer. Perhaps this rationale also applies to secondary sales from an affiliate, although the quantity of shares sold will usually be smaller. An alternate rationale is that the holding period helps reduce any informational advantage a purchaser obtains when purchasing directly from an issuer. If purchasing from an affiliate produces a similar informational advantage, the one-year holding period should start from the date of the purchase from the affiliate.

How do the information and holding period requirements interact? The following diagram depicts the interaction of the two requirements:

	0 to <6 mos	6 mos to <1 year	1 year or more
Non-Affiliate and Reporting Issuer	No Resales (144(d)(1)(i))	Resales allowed but 144(c) information applies (144(d)(1)(i))	No restrictions on resales
Non-Affiliate and Non-Reporting Issuer	No Resales (144(d)(1)(ii))	No Resales (144(d)(1)(ii))	No restrictions on resales
Affiliate (or on behalf of an Affiliate) and Reporting Issuer	No Resales of restricted securities (144(d)(1)(i)) Resales of unrestricted securities allowed but must comply with all 144 requirements	Resales allowed but must comply with all 144 requirements	Resales allowed but must comply with all 144 requirements
Affiliate (or on behalf of an Affiliate) and Non-Reporting Issuer	No Resales of restricted securities (144(d)(1)(i)) Resales of unrestricted securities allowed but must comply with all 144 requirements	No Resales of restricted securities (144(d)(1)(i)) Resales of unrestricted securities allowed but must comply with all 144 requirements	Resales allowed but must comply with all 144 requirements

From the diagram, observe that while non-affiliates resell-ing the restricted securities of non-reporting issuers do not have an information requirement (Rule 144(b)(1)(ii)), the non-affiliates are not able to resell the securities until after a one-year holding period (Rule 144(d)). While 144(b)(1)(i) imposes an information requirement on non-affiliate resales of the restricted securities of reporting issuers, this require-ment applies only during the six-month to one-year holding period — a time period during which a non-affiliate would be blocked from reselling at all under Rule 144 for the restricted securities of a non-reporting issuer.

Also note from the diagram that there is no holding period for resales of unrestricted securities by affiliates and those selling on behalf of affiliates (although affiliates must comply with all the other provisions of Rule 144 including the Rule 144(c) information requirement). Suppose Donna, the CEO and largest shareholder of Holo, Inc., purchases 10,000 shares of Holo through Nasdaq. One week later, Donna has her broker resell the shares, again through Nasdaq. Although Donna may use Rule 144 to exempt her resale, she will not need to comply with any holding period requirement because Rule 144(d) does not apply to unrestricted securities. Nor need anyone who purchases the securities from Donna worry about a holding period for subsequent resales.

If we are worried about either large sales on the part of affiliates (akin to public offerings) or informational advantages learned from an affiliate, why are resales of unrestricted secu-rities permitted without any holding period? Affiliates typically will purchase unrestricted shares only for Exchange Act report-ing issuers. Indeed, finding unrestricted shares for non-Exchange Act reporting issuers is extremely difficult. For Exchange Act reporting issuers, sufficient public information already exists in the form of the periodic disclosure filings, greatly reducing the informational advantage of affiliates, meaning that investors purchasing from affiliates are unlikely to obtain much advantage. Indeed in most cases the purchaser will be unaware they have purchased from an affiliate because they will buy in an anonymous exchange transaction. There is little chance that any nonpublic material information will be transmitted to the purchasing investors in such a transaction.

The Rule 144(d) holding period was originally two years before it was reduced to the current six months for reporting issuers. Private placements provide issuers who wish to avoid the public offering process a substitute means of raising capital through the sales of securities. Private placements are not a perfect substitute. Although selling through a private placement allows an issuer to avoid the gun-jumping rules and heightened civil liability that attaches to a registered public offering, private placements also result in restricted securities. Because of resale restrictions, investors who purchase restricted securities will typically demand a large discount. As the holding period before resales are allowed under Rule 144 shrinks, the discount investors will demand for purchasing restricted securities will similarly decline — increasing the attractiveness of private placements relative to public offering.

For those who wish to channel issuers toward registered public offerings and away from private placements, Rule 144 poses yet another problem: hedging transactions. In its 2007 proposing release for reforms to Rule 144, the SEC provided the following example of hedging transactions:

> [P]rior to the expiration of the required holding period, a security holder may enter into an equity swap agreement with a third party, under which the security holder exchanges the dividends received on the restricted securities for the dividends on, for example, a securities index. In addition, that shareholder may agree to exchange, at a set date, any price change in the security since the date of the agreement for any price change in the securities index. The effect of such a transaction would be the economic equivalent of selling the

restricted securities before the holding period has expired and purchasing the securities index.[7]

Hedging transactions allow issuers to sell securities in a private placement to an initial investor who turns around and resells the economic risk associated with these securities through hedging transactions immediately into the broad public capital markets. Hedging transactions transform the private placement into a transaction that has a similar distribution of the economic risks of ownership as a public offering. Despite the possibility of hedging transactions, the SEC chose to ignore such transactions in computing the holding period under Rule 144(d) because of administrative difficulties in limiting the practice.

3.3 Affiliate-Specific Rule 144 Requirements

Rule 144 imposes a number of additional requirements for sales by or for affiliates. These requirements include volume limits, manner of resale restrictions, and a notice requirement.

Rule 144(e) limits the amount of securities that can be sold through Rule 144 for affiliate transactions. For sales by an affiliate (and on behalf of an affiliate), Rule 144(e) limits the amount of restricted and unrestricted securities that may be sold. To simplify somewhat, the limit is the greater of (1) one percent of the outstanding shares the investor is attempting to resell or (2) the average weekly trading volume of the shares over the four weeks prior to the filing of the notice of sale. Rule 144(e) provides a separate volume limit for affiliate-related resales of debt securities equal to 10% of outstanding debt securities.

Suppose Holo has an outstanding market capitalization of $200 million for its common stock. Because Holo is not

---

7. Securities Act Release No. 8813 (June 22, 2007).

actively traded, its average weekly trading volume is negligible. In this situation, the Rule 144(e) ceiling is set at $2 million.

The volume limitation under Rule 144(e) arises from the SEC's concern that large amounts of Rule 144 resales within too short a time period may disrupt secondary market trading for an issuer's securities. Large amounts of resales may also require the use of solicitation and other sales activities forbidden by Rule 144. Although Rule 144(f) (discussed below) prohibits solicited transactions, limiting the size of the resale amount reinforces that restriction on sales tactics.

If we assume that the sale of a large quantity of shares into the marketplace will disrupt the market, presumably sales of all securities of a given type, whether restricted or not, will affect the market. Why then does Rule 144(e) only apply to resales by or for an affiliate? One response is that non-affiliates generally do not accumulate large blocks of shares, so the possibility of market disruption from the sale of unrestricted shares may be remote. Non-affiliates also lack the same enduring informational advantage of an affiliate, and thus the danger to uninformed investors from non-affiliate resales is less compared with affiliate resales.

3.4 Manner of Sale

Concern over the possibility of market disruption led the SEC also to limit the manner of sale used in a Rule 144 resale transaction. Rule 144(f) requires that affiliates (and those selling on their behalf) resell securities through either brokers' transactions (as defined by § 4(4) of the Securities Act), through a direct transaction with a market maker or through a riskless principal transaction. Moreover, the selling investor may not solicit or arrange for solicitation of orders to buy the securities or make payments related to the resales "to any person other than the broker who executes the order to sell the securities."

Rule 144(g) interprets the § 4(4) exemption for "unsolicited broker's transaction[s]." According to Rule 144(g)(1) and (2), in an unsolicited transaction the broker must do "no more than execute the order or orders to sell the securities as agent for the person for whose account the securities are sold; and receives no more than the usual and customary broker's commission." In addition, Rule 144(g)(3) includes a number of exceptions from the definition of solicitation. Among others, Rule 144(g)(3) allows "inquiries by the broker of his customers who have indicated an unsolicited bona fide interest in the securities within the preceding 10 business days." Note that customers that make an inquiry of the broker concerning a similar security or class of securities that includes the resale security are not included in this exception. The exception is thus less useful for the resale of non-Exchange Act reporting issuer securities; few outside investors will make inquiries of such small, unknown issuers.

Finally, Rule 144(g)(4) requires that the broker make "reasonable inquiry" to determine whether the investor reselling securities is an underwriter or otherwise reselling as part of a distribution of securities for the issuer. Rule 144(g)(4) provides a laundry list of possible inquiries, including the length of time the investor has held the securities, the nature of the transaction in which the investor originally acquired the securities, and so on.

3.5 Form 144 Notice

If an affiliate (or a person selling on behalf of an affiliate) seeks to resell more than 5,000 shares or other units of a security or securities with an aggregate sales price of more than $50,000 in any three month period, the investor must file a Form 144 notice with the SEC (Rule 144(h)). If the sale involves securities trading on any national securities exchange, the investor must also file the Form 144 with the principal securities exchange where the securities are listed.

3.6 Rule 144 Hypothetical

Assume that Holo, a non-reporting issuer, sold 500,000 shares of common stock through a Regulation D, Rule 506 private placement to ten accredited investors. Consider the application of Rule 144 in the following questions.

1. Jason, an accredited investor, purchased 10,000 shares from Holo's private placement. Ten months after his purchase, he makes a gift of the securities to his cousin Fran. Three months later, Fran uses a broker to solicit potential purchasers and resells the securities to ten investors, none of whom qualify as accredited. Assume that neither Jason nor Fran is in a control relationship with Holo.

Answer: Rule 144 applies to the resale. As a result, Fran is not an underwriter and is able to use the § 4(1) exemption from § 5 of the Securities Act. Two things to note: First, Fran is able to tack Jason's holding period onto her own holding period (Rule 144(d)(3)(v)). Fran is thus able to meet the one-year holding period requirement for the resale of restricted securities of non-reporting issuers given under Rule 144(d). Second, Fran does not need to comply with the manner of resale limitation in Rule 144(f) (requiring, among others, an unsolicited broker's transaction) because Fran is not an affiliate (nor is she selling on behalf of an affiliate). Fran does not face an information requirement (Rule 144(b)(1)(ii)).

2. Donna, the CEO, founder, and largest shareholder of Holo, also purchased from Holo's private placement. She seeks to resell the 100,000 shares she purchased 30 months after the private placement closed. Donna used a broker to solicit several wealthy investors for her sale, eventually selling the 100,000 shares to a hedge fund manager.

Answer: Rule 144 does not apply to the resale. Donna is an affiliate of Holo. Because she is an affiliate, even after 30 months she must comply with the various volume limitation, information, manner of sale, and notice requirements of Rule 144 to qualify for its safe harbor (Rules 144(b)(2),(3)). The use of solicited broker's transactions dooms the resale for Rule 144 purposes. Note that Donna may still try to argue that the hedge fund manager is able to fend for herself and thus the resale qualifies for the § 4(1½) exemption discussed above. To qualify, however, not only the hedge fund manager but all the other "wealthy investor" offerees would need to be able to fend for themselves.

3. Thirty months after the private placement closed, Donna resells the 100,000 shares she purchased to Frank, a wealthy, sophisticated investor. Frank waits two months before reselling the shares through solicited broker transactions to retirees in New York City.

Answer: Rule 144 does not apply to the resale, and Frank's resale likely violates § 5. Let's assume that Donna's resale to Frank, standing alone, would be covered under § 4(1½), due to Frank's sophistication and access to information from Donna. Frank's resale to the retirees in New York City, however, is problematic. In reselling only two months after purchasing from an affiliate (Donna), Frank is potentially an underwriter for Donna, removing § 4(1) as a possible exemption. Rule 144(d), moreover, requires a one-year holding period, since the private placement securities are restricted and the issuer is non-reporting (Rule 144(d)). The holding period starts from the "later of the date of the acquisition of the securities from the issuer or from an affiliate of the issuer" (Rule 144(d)). Thus, Frank's two month holding period does not meet the requirement of Rule 144(d).

4. Now assume that Holo is a reporting issuer. Donna, the CEO of Holo, purchased 10,000 shares of Holo from the Nasdaq market. Two days later, Donna decides to resell the 10,000 shares, again through Nasdaq, using a broker to assist in unsolicited resales. Twenty investors buy from Donna.

Answer: This likely qualifies under Rule 144. If Rule 144 applies, the broker assisting Donna is not an underwriter, and Donna can use the § 4(1) exemption from § 5. To see if Rule 144 applies, we need to make sure the various requirements are met. First, Rule 144(c) requires current public information. Here we need more information on whether Holo has filed all its periodic filings in the past 12 months. Second, the Rule 144(d) holding period does not apply because the securities were not private placement securities, but instead were publicly traded securities purchased from Nasdaq. Third, we need to check whether the volume limitation of Rule 144(e) was met. Here again we need more information on the number of outstanding shares and the average weekly trading volume of Holo common stock. Fourth, the use of unsolicited broker transactions would appear to meet Rule 144(f) (although we would want to check whether the broker complied with the requirements of Rule 144(g)). Lastly, Donna would need to file the required Rule 144(h) notice with the SEC and the Nasdaq.

4 RULE 144A

The capital markets of the United States are part of a larger global marketplace for investment dollars. In this global market, the New York Stock Exchange competes with the London Stock Exchange, the Tokyo Stock Exchange, and others, for both issuers and investors. Both issuers and investors value a liquid market. The greater the investment dollars in a particular market, the lower the cost of capital for issuers. Similarly, the more investment dollars trading in a market, the more confidence investors will have that they will be able to sell or buy securities quickly, at low cost, and at the best possible price.

To help lure foreign issuers into the U.S. capital markets, the SEC promulgated Rule 144A in 1990. Rule 144A also represents the SEC's recognition that offers and sales of securities to large institutional investors require less regulatory protection.

The relevant institutional investors are defined by Rule 144A as *qualified institutional buyers* (commonly known as QIBs). Rule 144A(a)(1) defines qualified institutional buyers to include various institutions that in the aggregate own and invest on a discretionary basis at least $100 million in securities of non-affiliated issuers. These institutions include, among others, insurance companies, investment companies, investment advisors, corporations, partnerships, and business trusts. Rule 144A defines banks as QIBs if the bank in the aggregate own and invest on a discretionary basis at least $100 million in securities of non-affiliated issuers and the bank has an audited net worth of at least $25 million. Rule 144A applies a lower threshold for dealers to qualify as QIBs. They need only own (or invest on a discretionary basis) $10 million in securities (Rule 144A(a)(1)(ii)). Certain dealers acting "in a riskless principal transaction on behalf of a qualified institutional buyer" are also treated as QIBs (Rule 144A(a)(1)(iii)). In a riskless principal transaction, the dealer acts as intermediary, typically between a customer of the dealer and another dealer or market maker.

Rule 144A(b) and (c) set forth the operative exemption from § 5 for transactions meeting the requirements of Rule 144A. Rule 144A(b) provides that any person, other than an issuer or dealer, is deemed not to be engaged in a "distribution" of the securities and thus not to be an underwriter pursuant to the definition § 2(a)(11). This allows the seller to rely on the § 4(1) exemption. Dealers, however, may not take advantage of § 4(1) even if they are not deemed underwriters; they must use § 4(3). Accordingly, Rule 144(c) provides that a dealer meeting the Rule 144A requirements is deemed not to be a "participant in a distribution" of the securities within the meaning of § 4(3)(C) and therefore not to be an underwriter for purposes of § 4(3)(A). As a result, dealers may rely on the § 4(3) exemption. Rule 144A only provides exemption from § 5; antifraud provisions continue to apply.

Rule 144A imposes a number of requirements on those seeking its exemption from § 5. Offers and sales may only be made to qualified institutional buyers (144A(d)(1)), and the seller and those working on behalf of the sellers must take "reasonable steps" to advise the purchasers that the sale is being made pursuant to an exemption from § 5 (144(d)(2)). Securities sold through Rule 144A may not be fungible with a class of securities, such as common stock, already trading on a U.S. national securities exchange (144(d)(3)). Thus, Rule 144A is more commonly used for the sale of debt instruments, which are generally not fungible because they have different terms and interest rates.

Why does Rule 144A impose a fungibility requirement? The rationale arises with the initial impetus behind Rule 144A. The SEC promulgated Rule 144A primarily to meet competitive pressures from other securities markets and to attract foreign issuers into the U.S. marketplace. Restricting Rule 144A only to nonfungible securities fosters this goal, although it does not exclude U.S. domestic issuers selling nonfungible securities.

Even domestic issuers may avoid the nonfungibility requirement to an extent. Domestic issuers will commonly sell convertible debt securities through Rule 144A. The debt securities are not fungible with the issuer's common stock trading in the secondary markets. Investors may, however, later convert the debt securities into common stock. Through convertible debt securities, the issuer is therefore able to make use of Rule 144A to sell investors a partial equity exposure. The SEC limits this stratagem by requiring that convertible securities have a conversion premium of 10 percent or more to be treated as nonfungible with the security into which they convert (Rule 144(d)(3)(i)). Suppose Holo has a class of common stock trading on Nasdaq that trades at $100 per share. Holo sells debt securities convertible into its common stock at a conversion price of $120 per share. Because the conversion premium is 20 percent more than the trading price at the time of the 144A issuance, the convertible securities are treated as nonfungible.

Finally, Rule 144A requires that the holder and prospective purchasers must have the right to receive from certain issuers (including certain non–Exchange Act reporting issuers) the following information:

> A very brief statement of the nature of the business of the issuer and the products and services it offers; and the issuer's most recent balance sheet and profit and loss and retained earnings statements, and similar financial statements for such part of the two preceding fiscal years as the issuer has been in operation (the financial statements should be audited to the extent reasonably available). (144A(d)(4).)[8]

Why would an issuer voluntarily agree to continue providing updated information under Rule 144A(d)(4), not only to the initial holder but to all subsequent purchasers? Without such information, those purchasing securities from the issuer will have a difficult time subsequently reselling. As a result, these purchasers will demand a discount when purchasing their shares. Ultimately, the issuer will bear this discount and may choose, to avoid the discount, to provide ongoing disclosure so that purchasers can resell under Rule 144A.

Rule 144A is a resale provision. Nonetheless, in terms of economic importance, the greatest use made of Rule 144A is to facilitate exempt offerings by issuers. How does Rule 144A facilitate exempt offerings? Rule 144A, unlike Rule 144,

---

8. The holder and prospective purchasers must also have received the information if requested. Rule 144A(d)(4).

does not require a holding period. Thus, an initial purchaser from the issuer may turn around and immediately resell through Rule 144A. Rule 144A also does not limit the amount of securities, number of QIBs, or selling method employed to reach QIBs (so long as no offers take place to non-QIBs). Finally, Rule 144A(e) protects from the consequences of a Rule 144A sale any previous and subsequent offer or sales of the securities relying on another exemption or safe harbor from § 5.

Suppose Holo — not yet listed on an exchange — structures the following transaction. Holo sells $200 million of common stock in a Rule 506 offering to Morgan, Inc., a Wall Street brokerage firm and investment bank. As an investment bank, Morgan is clearly accredited. Moreover, despite Holo's lack of any preexisting relationship with Morgan, Morgan's obvious investment sophistication, combined with the small number of offerees (one), eliminates general solicitation concerns. Suppose Morgan purchases the $200 million of common stock at a 5 percent discount and then turns around immediately and resells the common stock at full value to a large number of institutional investors (all QIBs). The resale by Morgan, assuming the other requirements of Rule 144A are met, will qualify for the Rule 144A exemption from § 5. Moreover, despite the close proximity in time between the Rule 506 offering and the Rule 144A resale, the two are not integrated (Rule 144A(e)).

What sort of transaction have Holo and Morgan constructed? Economically, the sale at a discount to Morgan followed by a quick resale at full price to a large number of investors looks a lot like a firm commitment offering. Through a combination of Rules 506 and 144A (often simply referred to as a *144A offering*), issuers may sell unlimited numbers of securities to QIBs without registration. The only important difference from a public offering is that only QIBs may participate.

Foreign issuers frequently use Rule 144A to raise capital in the United States, avoiding the public offering requirements of § 5. U.S. issuers, because of the fungibility requirement, typically will not sell equity through a 144A offering, but instead sell investment grade debt. Annually, hundreds of billions of dollars are raised through 144A offerings.

Interestingly, Rule 144A has had less of an impact as a resale provision for secondary market resales among QIBs. One reason is securities sold through Rule 144A are deemed "restricted" securities. QIBs therefore may not immediately resell the 144A securities absent an exemption from § 5. After the requisite six-month holding period (one-year for non-reporting issuers), QIBs may resell their 144A shares to any investor using Rule 144.

What happens if a QIB resells to a non-QIB prior to the availability of Rule 144? Consider the following series of transactions:

> Holo sells securities to Goldman Sachs, which in turn resells immediately to Calipers, a pension fund QIB, in a Rule 144A offering. After one month, Calipers turns around and resells the securities to James, an accredited individual investor but not a QIB. (Only institutions can qualify as QIBs.)

Absent some other exemption from § 5, Calipers must register the resale to James under § 5. But why does § 4(1) not directly apply to the resale by Calipers? After all, Calipers is not an issuer, nor is Calipers a securities dealer. Calipers, however, may be an underwriter for the issuer if Calipers sells as part of a chain of unregistered transactions starting from the issuer. (Calipers could argue, however, that under the § 4(1½) exemption, James can fend for himself, and thus Calipers is not engaged in a distribution.)

If Calipers violates § 5 in its resale to James because it is an underwriter for the issuer, what does this mean for the issuer and other purchasers in the chain of transactions leading up to the Calipers resale to James? On the one hand, the lesson of *Chinese Consolidated* discussed above is that § 4(1) is a transaction exemption. If the § 4(1) exemption is lost for Calipers, it is lost for all participants in the overall transaction. On the other hand, the issuer initially relies on Rule 506 and § 4(2) for its exemption. Moreover, Rule 144A(e) specifies that 144A offers and sales shall not affect the availability of any exemption or safe harbor for any previous transaction. Perhaps the issuer's initial sale to Goldman can be characterized as a previous and therefore separate transaction? If so, perhaps Calipers isn't an underwriter for the issuer after all? But under this approach, what stops the issuer from structuring a sale to Goldman and then to Calipers, expecting that Calipers will turn around and resell to individual investors? The preliminary notes to Rule 144A explicitly treat a series of transactions in technical compliance with Rule 144A as not qualifying for 144A if "part of a plan or scheme to evade the registration provisions of the Act."

To review Rule 144A, consider the following hypothetical. Assume that Holo — its common shares listed on Nasdaq — sold five million shares of preferred stock through a Regulation D private placement to one accredited investor, Morgan, Inc. The investment bank turned around and immediately resold the shares to dozens of large, institutional investors. Assume that all purchasers are QIBs. Consider the application of Rule 144A in the following questions.

1. What if Morgan, Inc. also sold a portion of the Holo preferred stock to the fabulously successful individual investor Warren Jackson? Assume that Warren Jackson has over $2 billion of his own money invested in U.S. securities. **Answer:** Rule 144A does not apply. Warren Jackson is an individual, and individuals cannot be QIBs (Rule 144A(d)(1)).

2. To find sufficient numbers of qualified institutional buyers to purchase Holo's preferred stock, Morgan, Inc., cold calls numerous institutional investors. At the end of Morgan's sales

pitch on Holo's offering, the investment bank informs each institutional investor that only institutions that qualify for QIB status would be allowed to purchase.

Answer: Rule 144A likely does not apply. Simply putting a disclaimer that the recipient of an offer is not allowed to participate unless meeting certain qualifications does not exclude the communication from the definition of an offer. Instead, as we saw in Chapter 7, any communication that conditions the market may qualify as an offer. Morgan, Inc., is therefore likely making offers to non-QIBs when it undertakes broad-based solicitation of numerous institutional investors. Not all institutional investors are QIBs.

3. Suppose that instead of preferred stock Holo sold 5 million shares of common stock through Morgan, Inc., to dozens of qualified institutional buyers.

Answer: Rule 144A does not apply. Holo's common stock trades on Nasdaq, a national securities exchange. Rule 144A(d)(3) imposes a nonfungibility requirement, excluding securities of the same class as securities listed on a national securities exchange. Although Holo may sell preferred stock through a Rule 144A offering, it may not sell common stock fungible with that already trading on Nasdaq.

Index